CHRISTIAN CHAOS

Revolutionizing the Congregation

THOMAS G. BANDY

ABINGDON PRESS
Nashville

CHRISTIAN CHAOS: REVOLUTIONIZING THE CONGREGATION

Copyright © 1999 by Abingdon Press

This book is printed on acid-free paper.

Library of Congress Cataloging-in-Publication Data

Bandy, Thomas G., 1950–
    Christian chaos : revolutionizing the congregation / Thomas G. Bandy.
        p.   cm.
    Includes bibliographical references.
    ISBN 0-687-02550-8 (alk. paper)
    1. Church renewal.   I. Title.
BV600.2.B325   1999
250—dc21   99-35511
                                                                            CIP

Scripture quotations, except for brief paraphrases or unless otherwise noted, are from the New Revised Standard Version Bible, copyright © 1989, by the Division of Christian Education of the National Council of the Churches of Christ in the United States of America. Used by permission.

That noted NKJV is from The New King James Version. Copyright © 1979, 1980, 1982, Thomas Nelson Inc., Publishers.

00 01 02 03 04 05 06 07 08—10 9 8 7 6 5 4 3 2

MANUFACTURED IN THE UNITED STATES OF AMERICA

In Appreciation

This book is dedicated to my father,
Joseph G. Bandy,
a musician in the midst
of the corporate business world.

I also thank the many congregational partners,
church leaders, and consultants,
whose prayers, advice, and support
have helped me focus my energies for change.
In particular, I thank Bill Easum
for many instructive conversations.

The love, patience, support, and intelligent advice
of my wife and family as I pursue my peculiar calling
is a source of constant celebration for me.

CONTENTS

WELCOME TO THE REAL WORLD

The real world is a world of chaos. Culture is changing so quickly, with such diversity, in so many simultaneous directions, and using so many learning methods, that church groups organized around traditional principles can't keep up. They find themselves spending more and more energy lamenting change, resisting change, struggling with change, expressing anger about change, desperately trying to "manage" change, or just plain "surviving" change. Change, however, will not go away. It is relentless—and accelerating.

There is a logic about chaos that frightens traditional church organizations. Change *will find its own way*. Life will go on. Culture will multiply. However we try to shape it, manipulate it, direct it, or control it, change will burst all barriers and overwhelm all structures. This has always been true, of course, but the creativity made possible by immediate communication networks, mass ethnic migrations, increasing population density, and technological innovations has allowed change to do what it has always done—*only faster.*

Spiritual change is like a river. In the Christendom period, it was a slow river, a meandering river, a silted river laden with the accumulated flotsam and jetsam of centuries of ecclesiastical experiments. Like rivers anyone can see from an airplane, the rivers of spiritual change have wandered at will through the cultural countryside, cutting new channels, eroding old riverbanks, and undermining institutional retaining walls. Yet they did all this *slowly.* The ecclesiastical machines of Christendom could keep up with the change. Today spiritual change is like a raging river. It is rushing, splashing, spraying, roaring, foaming, and careering on its course. It erodes traditional channels in seconds, undermines ecclesiastical "dikes" in weeks, and overwhelms institutional structures with shocking regularity. Like a river, *it will find its way!* It will follow the channel that works, or create a channel that works, to flow around any boundary and flood the surrounding culture—and it will do this relentlessly, constantly, and speedily.

Leadership in the twenty-first century is not about *controlling* the river of change. It is about *chaos surfing*. Such leadership requires a different kind of organization. These are not organizations that try to control the flow of spiritual change. These are organizations that equip leaders to surf the turgid waters to an unknown destination. In a sense, they are always building a better surfboard—not a better dike. They are unafraid of chaos. They seize chaos like a surfer grabbing the largest wave, and they ride that chaos as far as they can go.

My Tortoise Has Wandered from Home!

I read a newspaper article recently about a man who was advertising in the community about a lost tortoise. It seems that he had

had a pet tortoise for many years, which lived in an enclosure of water and sand in his backyard. He loved that tortoise. The tortoise had never shown any signs of dissatisfaction with its surroundings. One day a gate was left open, and the tortoise wandered away. The man was in a panic to find it. The situation leads me to ask an *organizational* question. How can a tortoise just "wander away"—and nobody notice? After all, how fast can a tortoise wander?

The case of the "wandering tortoise" illustrates the peculiar situation of traditional ecclesiastical organizations.

First, traditional church organizations are in the business of *raising tortoises!* They assume that personal transformation and spiritual formation will be at the very least evolutionary, and certainly slow. Tortoises can be easily guided, managed, and controlled. Whenever a tortoise is elected to the Official Board, one can be assured that the nominations process will take time. Whenever decisions of the board need to be made, one can be assured that several redundant levels of management will revisit that decision several times. Whenever board members feel restless or spiritually hungry, one can be assured that a few shreds of generic denominational "lettuce" will feed them—and then they will pull in their heads and sleep. Tortoises are not known for their imagination. They are methodical, dutiful, and persistent, but they will never go faster than the oldest members of the church. If any tortoise should ever get away (and can anyone seriously imagine that?), the church organization will have plenty of time to retrieve her or him.

Second, traditional church organizations build enclosures *designed to contain tortoises!* The organization has solid walls (mandates), and clearly defined sandy areas (committees) where tortoise eggs (creative ideas) can be hatched. They provide opportunities for sunlight and shade to be available in predictable regularity through the Christian Year so that the tortoises can exercise or sleep. Enclosures for tortoises need not be particularly elaborate, and they will likely all look alike. Perhaps the most important function of a tortoise enclosure is not to keep tortoises in (how difficult can that be?), but rather to keep other cultural "predators" out. The organization is as much designed to *keep out* encroachments from culture beyond the church, as it is to keep the tortoises content on the inside.

Third, *even tortoises eventually get bored!* Given the experience of the man whose tortoise wandered away, apparently even tortoises get bored. All the other creatures of the cultural forest are more imaginative, more fleet-footed, and have already wandered away from the traditional church organization. Ethnic minorities, people with nontraditional lifestyles, men under fifty, men and women under forty, youth, singles, dual-career couples, and many others have left the enclosure already. Today, however, even the tortoises are restless. The veteran church leaders who have given the institution years of faithful service are moving to the margins of the organization. They decline nominations, refuse to attend annual meetings, and appear sporadically in worship. They may not know what kind of organization would be more exciting (how enthusiastic can a tortoise get?), but they do know that organizational life as it is is fruitless.

Fourth, *life will find a way out*—even a tortoise life! Even these veterans are now finding ways to grow spiritually and fulfill themselves outside the traditional church organization. They are escaping the enclosure and wandering away into the cultural wilderness. It is not so much a quest for adventure (how adventurous can a tortoise be?), as simply a yearning for a different way. This is the chaos principle at its most profound. Even the slowest, least imaginative creatures of the forest *will find a way to grow!* Survival is never, ever enough. Ultimately, even the tortoise will take a risk.

Fifth, traditional church organizations *habitually fail to notice the exodus!* There is one species of animal that is even slower than a tortoise, and that is church management. Traditional church managers are so preoccupied with maintaining the enclosure, that they fail to see that the intended inhabitants are disappearing. Indeed, they *habitually* fail to see this disappearance. I suspect that the man who lost his pet tortoise had actually been visiting the enclosure regularly. He probably threw in lettuce for the tortoise to eat every day. If the tortoise was invisible, the owner assumed it was under water, or resting behind a lily pad. If the congregation was absent from worship or an annual meeting, the church managers assumed they were temporarily at the cottage, ill, or away on business. But they would be back. They were really still there. They were still surviving inside the enclosure. Improbable as it may seem, only such habitual inattention can explain how a tortoise can have the time to wander away. Preoccupation with survival leads to inattention about persons.

Chaos and the Christian Church

Historically, the Christian church has never dealt with chaos very well. The Gentile mission of Paul (and his company of entrepreneurs including Silas, Priscilla, Lydia, Onesimus, and others) was an exercise in instant adaptability and flexibility. It pushed the limits of creativity, and it spread very rapidly across the known world. When Paul wrote in his first letter to the Corinthians, "I have become all things to all people, that I might by all means save some" (9:22), the traditional religious organization back home in Jerusalem became truly alarmed. Paul and his company meant exactly what he said.

Nothing was sacred to them, certainly not any particular organizational structure.

Forced to return home for some "heavy accountability," Paul was forced to defend the Gentile mission against those traditionalists who wanted Gentile converts to obey traditional Jewish rules and lifestyles. Scripture mentions their concern about dietary restrictions, observances of the Sabbath, and the "customs of Moses" (Acts 15). Presumably, behind this were deeper concerns about the leadership roles of women, the authority of rabbinical teaching, and the importance of Jewish tradition. Behind this were even deeper concerns about organizational principles related to the accountability of evangelists, the authority of the "central office," the celebration of the sacraments, and the governance of the church.

Fortunately, "the apostles and the elders, with the consent of the whole church" (15:22) had enough sense to create the first "permission-giving" church organization. Surrendering the *prescriptive* organization with its long lists of what participants could or should do, they embraced a *proscriptive* organization which simply defined the boundaries beyond which participants could not go, but within which participants were free to shape their lives as they pleased. The core values of organized Christian life identified essentials such as abstaining from foods offered in sacrifice to other gods and from sexual promiscuity—but within such boundaries allowed Christians to shape their lifestyles as they pleased.

The Corinthian church was perhaps the most chaotic Christian community in the whole, chaotic Gentile mission—and it is instructive to see how Paul brings order into the chaos. What he does *not* do is impose a hierarchy of authority, a bureaucracy of management, or prescriptive mandates and job descriptions that precisely define what everyone can or should do. What does he do?

1) Paul declares the organization to be clay (2 Cor. 4:7). The organization is merely a vessel that contains the extraordinary power of God. The vessel can be shaped in many ways. It may even be shattered and reshaped in ways yet unimagined. Most important, the vessel is not designed to *hold* the gospel, but rather to *transport* the gospel to the place and people with greatest need.

2) Paul articulates core values and beliefs. The basic boundaries of congregational life reported in Acts reappear. Paul warns against sexual promiscuity (1 Corinthians 5, 6, 7) and idolatry (1 Corinthians 8). He emphasizes the importance of the sacrament (1 Cor. 11:17-34). Most important, he identifies the core values of congregational harmony (2 Cor. 5:11–7:1) and the health of the whole body of Christ (1 Cor. 10:23-24).

3) Paul articulates the core message and vision. Paul articulates the core message of Christ the power and wisdom of God (1 Corinthians 18–31). Note that focus is not broadly theological, but christological. The congregation may explore many beliefs, but the essence of the organization is faith in Christ crucified (1 Corinthians 2) and Christ resurrected (1 Corinthians 15).

4) Paul builds a continuity of teams. Paul appeals to the congregation to have clarity and consensus about its values, beliefs, vision, and mission: "that you be perfectly joined together" (1 Cor. 1:10). He blocks any codependent relationship on leaders like himself or Apollos, and fixes unity in the continuing experience of God's grace as shared by a continuity of leaders with diverse functions each serving in their appointed time (1 Cor. 3:5-15). He emphasizes servant leadership (1 Cor. 4:1). He rhapsodizes over each part of the body having their place in the whole, and the least deserving part the greater honor (1 Corinthians 12).

5) Paul empowers the individual. Paul describes the individual as the "temple of God" (1 Cor. 3:16). He links the intrinsic value of the individual with the God-given spiritual gifts with which every individual is created (1 Cor. 12:27-30). He declares that every Christian is the "fragrance of Christ" proclaiming good news (2 Cor. 2:15), embodies the story of salvation (2 Cor. 3:1), and possesses a destiny of transformation into the image of the Lord (2 Cor. 3:18).

6) Paul motivates self-starting volunteer leadership. He links motivation to calling (2 Cor. 4:1). He reassures Christian believers that they can be victorious even over pressure, perplexity, and persecution (2 Cor. 4:8-11). He encourages the believer to live by *faith*, rather than by *sight* (2 Cor. 5:7).

7) Paul orients the organization beyond itself. He states that ultimate joy lies in "the riches of liberality" and exhorts the organization to fulfill itself through generosity to those in need *beyond* the organization (2 Corinthians 8). Life is complete only as it is given away, because "God loves a cheerful giver" (2 Cor. 9:7).

8) Paul limits his role to midwifery. He speaks as a mother, alternately scolding or encouraging her little children in order that they might fulfill the potential with which they were born (2 Corinthians 10). He speaks of strength in the depths of weakness, of spiritual parenthood, and of sacrificing self that the child might thrive (2 Cor. 12:10, 14, and 19).

Paul will say more about issues of accountability. Specifically, he will comment about the discernment of false prophets (2 Corinthians 11), the importance of forgiveness (2 Cor. 2:5-11), and the basics of orderly worship (1 Cor. 14:26-36). He says little about what we might describe as Board policy formation and activity, but he will suggest ways to measure the success of the organization (1 Cor. 1:4-7 and 2 Cor. 1:1-11). The issue for Paul is never what is "lawful" (*prescriptive* thinking), but rather what is "beneficial" (*proscriptive* thinking). It is this attitude toward congregational organization that is so alarming to the "central office" in Jerusalem, and so liberating to the mission units in the field.

The Corinthian church cannot be treated as a case study for congregational organization in the Gentile mission, since it is not intended as an illustration of healthy institutional life. Indeed, the Gentile mission is so diverse, that no "blueprint" for congregational organization can be described. After all, congregational organization in Athens, Ephesus, and Rome may look very different. The point is simply that, when it comes to congregational organization,

Christians in the chaos of the twenty-first century have more to learn from Christians in the chaos of the first century, than we do from the orderly structures of intervening Christendom. The apostolic churches were founded on permission-giving principles that defined basic boundaries, and then empowered individuals to explore life and faith as they desired within those boundaries.

The organizational strategy of the Gentile mission was appropriate to the diversity of the cultural forest in the first century. The prescriptive organizational strategy of the early Jerusalem church simply would not work in the tumultuous world of spiritual seekers. The church could not control the Gentile seekers, nor could it merely assimilate them into the ecclesiastical institution. Instead, it had to embark on a radical and risky strategy of lay leadership empowerment. There was no strategic plan to the Gentile mission. There was only disciplined adult faith formation, openness to creative experimentation, and trust that the mysterious future was in God's hands.

Radical Organizational Change

In my earlier book *Kicking Habits: Welcome Relief for Addicted Churches*, I explained that systemic change precedes organizational change. First, the *system* of congregational life changes. The purpose, process, movement, or flow of congregational life shifts from a declining system in which people were initiated, enrolled, informed, supervised, and kept—to a thriving church system in which people are changed, gifted, called, equipped, and sent. The meandering river enters a new and different topography in which it no longer wanders slowly across a civilized floodplain, but now plunges and rushes amid the cliffs and gorges of the ever-changing cultural wilderness.

Someone once asked me if the contrast between the declining church system and the thriving church system must be an either-or choice. The answer is that, although the thriving church system embraces multiple choices to an extreme that the declining church system could never accept, it nevertheless must be a distinct choice. The meandering, nearly stagnant stream *cannot coexist* with the rushing river without ceasing to be stagnant. You cannot have it both ways. You cannot have a stagnant pond *and* a rushing river. As soon as the system of congregational life becomes a river, the pond disappears. That may well imply that there will be fewer turtles and more trout, and that the relaxing hum of busy insects will be replaced by the roar of moving water that is intent upon going somewhere.

Organizational change will not achieve systemic change, and this is why restructuring the board never really changes the church. Systemic change, however, eventually demands organizational change, and there are only three alternatives. First, the rushing river of systemic change may simply burst the riverbanks and control mechanisms of offices, committees, parliamentary procedures, and bureaucracy. This will flood congregational life with both positive and negative stress, and though the rushing waters will eventually create a new organizational path a good many leaders will have perished along the way. Second, wise leaders may recognize and welcome the transformation of a stagnant pool into a rushing river, and create new organizational models to harness its energy and channel its mission. Third, addicted leaders will call in the denominational "Corps of Engineers" to build new dikes, shore up the old channels, slow down the rush of water, and tame the rushing river to become a stagnant pool once again.

The point is that organizational change is demanded by systemic change. The creation of the new organization will be stressful. It will require risk-taking and experimentation, which in turn will require strong leadership development. And if organizational change *does not* happen, then whatever positive systemic change has occurred will rapidly dissipate and things will return to "normal."

In *Kicking Habits*, I tried to place organizational change in the larger context of systemic change, and described in broad terms the permission-giving organization that prioritized spiritual growth and leadership development within an "energy field" of values, beliefs, and vision. In *Growing Spiritual Redwoods,* Bill Easum and I tried to identify the *organic* nature of this organization in contrast to the ecclesiastical machines that dominated the age of Christendom. In *Moving Off the Map: A Field Guide to Changing the Congregation,* I described processes for leadership development, discernment of congregational identity (core values, bedrock beliefs, motivating vision, and key mission), and "ministry mapping" as methods to prepare the congregation for organizational change. In this book, I hope to describe in detail and in practice what that emerging organization will look like.

The first section, entitled "Spiritually Contained Anarchy," will be more theoretical. I want to acknowledge my appreciation in advance to the management model described by John and Miriam Mayhew Carver, which has been so successful in transforming nonprofit, municipal, and corporate organizations. The concepts of policy governance and executive limitation described in John's best-seller *Boards That Make a Difference* and the "policy circle" pictured in four quadrants in John and Miriam's *Reinventing Your Board* have been both inspiring and instructive.[1] From time to time, I will make specific connections between the organizational model I describe for the transformed congregation and the organizational model the Carvers describe for secular clients.

The congregational model I describe, however, is unique to the "Spiritual Redwood." In the end, it is quite distinct from the Carver model. It cannot simply be adapted to secular organizations, nor is it intended to critique those organizations. Similarly, the Carver model designed for secular organizations cannot simply be implemented in a Christian congregation. Generally speaking, this is because the organizational model I describe is rooted in the *thriving church system,* and not in other business, government, or social service systems. Specifically, the organizational model I describe diverges from the Carver model in at least five ways.

1) It embraces the apocalyptic character of biblical visioning. The vision of a church organization is not created by its participants, nor does it

———— 21 ————

emerge from their fertile imaginations or personal dreams. It is revealed only through a spirituality of waiting for God. When God reveals vision, it not only changes the direction of organizational life. It radically changes the corporate identity of the organization. To speak in biblical metaphors, it not only carries the organization out of Egypt and into the promised land, but, by the time the organization gets there, it is an entirely different people. This apocalyptic inbreaking of the Holy simultaneously shatters and creates new forms. Unlike secular organizations, the church organization of the pre-Christian era is in a constant state of divine peril.

2) *It is designed to facilitate personal and social transformation.* The reason for being of a church organization is not simply the delivery of a beneficial service or the manufacture and distribution of a valuable product. It is personal and social transformation. Among the anticipated *results* of organizational life, the most fundamental goal is a revolution of spirit within the human heart and a shift in attitude or spiritual perspective in society. Religious organizations are uniquely different from charitable, political, or business organizations. It forces religious leaders like Paul to use unusual metaphors to describe the church. What secular organization would ever describe itself as a smell? The church, Paul says, is the "aroma of Christ."

3) *It recognizes the simplicity and spirituality of the "Body of Christ."* The link between the organization and the divine makes church organization both simpler and more complex than secular organizations. It is simpler in that the organization may not need much, if any, of the bureaucracy, technology, or infrastructure of a contemporary incorporated body. A church is simply a community in which two or three persons are gathered together, and Christ is in their midst. On the other hand, the link with the divine makes church organizations more complicated than secular organizations. There are nuances in the life of church organizations that cannot be easily managed, supervised, strategized, and evaluated—and yet these

nuances are more decisive to the work of the organization than anything else. While a service club or incorporated body may pray prior to a meeting, the church organization actually waits for an answer before moving on to the agenda. That agenda may dramatically change by way of the smallest circumstance.

4) It extends ownership for identity and policy direction to the whole congregation. The shaping of the identity and purpose of the organization is not done by a board with reference to a constituency or a market. Identity and purpose are defined, refined, and celebrated by the congregation itself. This responsibility cannot be delegated in the church, as it might be in service clubs and charitable organizations, because the identity and purpose of the congregation flows out of the experience of the Holy Spirit moving among the interactive people and inspiring "even the least of Christ's brothers and sisters." While the Carver model maximizes creativity in productivity, the Christian congregation is even more extreme in maximizing creativity in identity formation and organizational purpose.

5) It incorporates the unique leadership of the Christian "pastor." While the church has generally been more clear about what a "pastor" *is not*, than what a pastor *is*, the church has recognized that the spiritual leader of a congregation plays a decisive role in the organization. The spiritual leader is *not a* "Chief Executive Officer," and congregations that treat the spiritual leader as such do not thrive in the pre-Christian world of the twenty-first century. Bill Easum and I introduced the metaphor of "Spiritual Midwife" to identify the heart of spiritual leadership to help others give birth to their full personal and spiritual potential. The very fact that spiritual leadership no longer requires entitlements or certifications bears witness to the fact that this person must be understood differently in the thriving church. They decisively influence what happens in the organization, but cannot be said to *control* it. Their spirit pervades every mission of the organization, but they cannot be said to *manage* it. The inspirational, shepherding, coaching, synthesizing, and motivating roles of the spiritual leader are unique.

Having identified these contrasts, however, I strongly recommend that readers become familiar with the model and methods described by John and Miriam Mayhew Carver. We are all adjusting organizational models to address the ferment of changing culture. The church has far more to learn from business, nonprofit, and government sectors today than it cares to admit—and business, nonprofit, and government sectors have far more to learn about spiritual formation and identity than they care to admit. The revolutionary changes of the postmodern and the post-Christendom worlds are interconnected. The boundary between the secular and sacred is less distinct every day.

The second section, entitled "Turning the Laity Loose," will be more practical. It is intended to describe how the new organization develops and works in the regular activity of congregational life. There are many excellent small group, cell group, or spiritual growth resources available today. Most of them can easily be adapted to my experience with disciplined partnerships for discovery, discernment, and mission. Once again, however, the cell model I describe is unique to the "Spiritual Redwood," and to the thriving church system. It diverges from most manuals on cell group ministry in at least four ways.

1) *It links growth with calling and mission.* Most cell group manuals help people grow personally, relationally, and spiritually, but they do not move people forward toward discernment of personal destiny or calling. The organization of a "Spiritual Redwood" is a dynamic movement among distinct spiritual disciplines related to discovery, destiny, and mission.

2) *It identifies the risks and opportunities for organizational change.* Most cell group manuals understand small group life to be a *program* of the traditional church organization. The "Spiritual Redwood" demonstrates that cell group growth *is* the church organization. Therefore, the multiplication of cells inevitably forces traditional church bureaucracies or hierarchies to collapse.

3) It recognizes the deeper, hidden stresses of volunteer leadership empowerment. Most cell group manuals do not prepare traditional church organizations for the stress of organizational change. Volunteers not only must commit themselves to spiritual disciplines, but they must be sensitized to identify inevitable corporate addictions to control.

4) It orients salaried staff to an entirely different leadership role. Most cell group manuals place the salaried staff in the role of small group leaders or small group managers. The "Spiritual Redwood" requires salaried leaders not only to train and coach volunteer cell leaders, but also to "surf the chaos" that is the ferment of congregational life.

Readers will certainly benefit by using many of the small group development manuals available today. The key is to remember that cell group ministry is an aspect of a larger thriving church system. Groups are not replicated as if in a machine; they are the growth units of the organism known as the "Spiritual Redwood."

In the beginning, we are told in Genesis, "the earth was without form, and void; and darkness was on the face of the deep, and the Spirit of God was hovering over the face of the waters" (NKJV). Even so, God is hovering over the stagnant pools and meandering streams that characterize ecclesiastical organizations in the post-Christendom era. Systemic change is transforming the cultural topography, and organizational change is revolutionizing congregational leadership.

Christendom people always assumed that the divine creative moment brought *structure* and *control* to creation. And Christendom churches also assumed that God would only bless *structure* and *control* in the church organization. The six days of organizational creation, therefore, were as follows:

"In the beginning, earth was without form and void, and the Spirit brooded upon the waters of the deep. And God said:
'Let there be a long prescriptive mission statement.

Let there be a clear ecclesiology to separate the church from the world.
Let there be committees that yield fruits of every kind.
Let there be programming by day and by night.
Let there be parliamentary procedure and interoffice memos, creeping or flying between administrative units.
Let there be elected officers of every kind, and let the pastor be the CEO.'
And on the seventh day God rested from labor and saw that Christendom was very good."

And church people have been exhausted ever since.

Faithful people of the emerging pre-Christian era no longer assume that divine creativity brings structure and control. They recognize that divine creativity creates chaos. God says:

"Let there be light," to illumine the panorama of diverse creation.
"Let there be a separation between water and dry land," to multiply the ecosystems for abundant life.
"Let there be plants and trees," in millions of species, ever changing, multiplying in every direction, by every method, and beating all odds to flourish.
"Let there be day, night, and seasons," to create environments for dynamic and unexpected growth.
"Let there be creatures," of every size, shape, and description, multiplying and evolving into countless different species.
"Let there be human beings," every one with a unique personality and spiritual gift, equipped to try anything, go anywhere, and build anything—and each one so precious that he or she has a distinct destiny in God's unfolding plan for the universe.

This is chaos, not structure. This is freedom, not control. It is a riot of diversity that cannot even be contained in the human imagination.

Similarly, thriving churches in the pre-Christian era no longer assume that God blesses structure and control above all else in church organization. Instead, God blesses growth in a riot of diversity, risk in multiple experiments, and the single-minded mission to help every human being experience the transforming power of God and walk daily with Jesus. Life is not about survival, but about growth. Church organizations are not about maintaining a heritage or a corporate ideology, but about birthing the potentialities of God.

"And God saw that it was very good." God rested *only one day*—and then threw herself into the joyous chaos that had been created.

I. Spiritually
Contained Anarchy

— 1 —

THE PERMISSION-GIVING CHART FOR THE THRIVING CHURCH SYSTEM

Congregational organization is as much a philosophy as it is a practice. Most congregations approach organization with assumptions that they never raise to conscious scrutiny. These assumptions are carried into the church from their changing workplace, their imperfect experience with government or volunteer charities, or their unique experience with family dynamics. These assumptions shape—and are shaped by—the denominational polities and congregational traditions of their church. The potential to entrench corporate addictions in organizational life is high. Dysfunctional family habits, individual frustrations with other social institutions, and conflicts from the workplace easily warp the effective organization of the congregation. Congregations continually restructure without ever examining their "philosophy" of organization. As a result, most organizational restructuring simply rearranges the furniture without ever renovating the house.

The *system* of congregational life will dictate the *organization* of congregational life. If the system of congregational life is to enable people to be *enrolled, informed, nominated, supervised, and kept* (as I described the declining church system in *Kicking Habits*), then the *organization* of congregational life will tend to be hierarchical, large, and controlling. There may be many practical variations of the organization, but the philosophy of organization remains the same. The organization is designed to achieve the desired system. On the other hand, if the *system* of congregational life is to empower people to become leaders through the experience of being *changed* by God, the disciplines of discerning *gifts* and *callings,* the opportunities for becoming *equipped* for quality ministry, and the intention of being *sent* for simultaneous faith witness and social action (as I described the thriving church system in *Kicking Habits*), then the *organization* of congregational life will tend to be team-based, streamlined, and permissive. Again, there may be many practical variations, but the philosophy remains the same. The organization is designed to achieve the desired system.

In my earlier book *Moving Off the Map,* I described "Ministry Mapping" as *the art of finding your way in a chaos of cultures.* Organizations must achieve the systems for which they were designed in this increasingly chaotic clash of cultures. Therefore, *church organization is the methodology with which congregations find their way in a chaos of cultures.* Organizations that seek to fulfill the declining church system will tend to do strategic planning. Organizations that seek to fulfill the thriving church system will tend to do ministry mapping. A thriving church *organization* cannot survive long in a *declining church system,* precisely because the methodology for future planning does not truly fit the expectations of the congregational participants. Declining church systems do not require, and do not want, a *ministry map* that relies on disciplined adult spiritual formation, clear consensus about values, beliefs, vision, and mission, and risk-taking. If that is what the organization delivers, then the system will cast it out. On the other hand, thriving church systems do not require, and do not want, a *strategic plan* that relies on managing a five-year plan, clear lines of authority, and guaranteed success. Again, if that is what the organization delivers, then the system will cast it out. There is a direct link between the system, the organization, and the method of future planning within congregational life. Much of the stress of church transformation has to do with misunderstanding that link.

The congregational organization for the thriving church system is described by the chart pictured on the next page.

Congregational Organization
for the Thriving Church System

Prescriptive

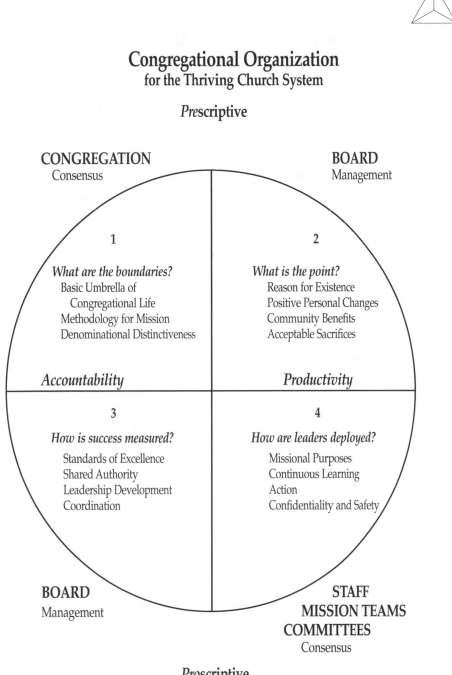

CONGREGATION
Consensus

BOARD
Management

1

What are the boundaries?
Basic Umbrella of
Congregational Life
Methodology for Mission
Denominational Distinctiveness

2

What is the point?
Reason for Existence
Positive Personal Changes
Community Benefits
Acceptable Sacrifices

Accountability

Productivity

3

How is success measured?
Standards of Excellence
Shared Authority
Leadership Development
Coordination

4

How are leaders deployed?
Missional Purposes
Continuous Learning
Action
Confidentiality and Safety

BOARD
Management

STAFF
MISSION TEAMS
COMMITTEES
Consensus

Proscriptive

In this section, I will explain in detail each quadrant of the chart. However, first note that the chart looks remarkably like the cross-hairs in the scope of a target rifle. The philosophy that lies behind the organization of the thriving church system functions as a targeting device. It *aims* the organization at the systemic change that is desired. It allows the organization to accurately *target* the goal of enabling Christian people to be changed, gifted, called, equipped, and sent.

The intersecting lines of the "crosshairs" represent the two key tensions within the thriving church organization. The first tension is between *"prescriptive"* and *"proscriptive"* organizational life. This is as much a way of thinking as it is a method of structuring the organization. Prescriptive thinking lists everything that a committee, program, or church office *can or should do*. It prescribes activity in the same way that a doctor prescribes medicine for a patient. Proscriptive thinking defines the boundaries beyond which a ministry team, program, or church leader *cannot go, but within which they are free to take initiative*. In a sense, *pro*scriptive organizations simply define *what one cannot do*.

Declining church systems that are preoccupied with belonging and institutional membership think almost entirely *pre*scriptively. They produce detailed church constitutions, long committee mandates, and complex job descriptions that essentially list everything they expect to be done, exactly how these tasks should be done, and in what partnerships these tasks must be done. Their concern with procedure indicates their conviction that the central organizational board must involve itself in the management of the institution down to the last detail. Church committees, officers, and groups do what they are told—and little else. The metaphor of the doctor prescribing medicine communicates the not-so-hidden condescension in such organizations. It is as if committees and officers are *assumed* to be generally incompetent or too ill to understand their own responsibilities. *Pre*scriptive organizations will inevitably import denominational "experts" to solve systemic or organizational problems in the same way that medical specialists will be invited to consult in a particularly baffling diagnosis.

Thriving church systems that are preoccupied with changing people and the world tend to be *proscriptive*, and at first glance are noteworthy for the extensive freedom they offer teams, programs, and leaders. On closer examination, however, these organizations achieve a clearly defined *balance* between *prescriptive* and *proscriptive* thinking. The details of this balance will be explained as we examine each quadrant of the chart. Here it is simply important to see the mode of thinking that is part of the organizational philosophy of a permission-giving church. These organizations think *proscriptively*. Their concern for clarity of congregational identity indicates their conviction that the central organizational board should *distance itself as far as possible* from the management of the ministries of the church. If systemic or organizational problems emerge, they will more likely concentrate on resolving ambiguities regarding the core values, beliefs, vision, and mission of the congregation, or on reshaping general policy for congregational life, or on improving quality in leadership. The organization celebrates an implicit *trust* and *mutual respect* among congregational participants.

The contrast between these two modes of thinking is dramatic. Prescriptive thinking drives declining church organizations to gain clarity about procedure and the institutional role played by every officer or committee of the church. *Proscriptive* thinking drives thriving church organizations to gain clarity about congregational identity and the missional purpose of every officer or ministry team in the church. This is why declining church organizations tend to live in a fog about core values, beliefs, vision, and mission, but often run meetings like well-oiled machines. It is also why they tend to multiply middle management and supervisory positions, which have little biblical warrant and no clearly Christian purpose.

On the other hand, this same contrast explains why thriving church organizations tend to live in a ferment of redundant activity, but run fewer and faster meetings. It is also why they tend to deploy leaders with a clear sense of spiritual calling and a readiness to take risks. *Prescriptive* thinking drives the organization to err on the side of control. *Proscriptive* thinking drives the organization to err on the side of freedom. As we shall see, however, it is the *clarity* and *balance* between *pre*scriptive and *pro*scriptive thinking that lies at the heart of the thriving church organization.

The second tension represented in the "crosshairs" of the chart is between "accountability" and "productivity" in organizational life. Accountability is the process through which the organization evaluates the performance of church leadership with reference to congregational identity, congregational policies, and congregational expectations for quality leadership. Productivity is the process through which the organization maximizes positive ministry benefits to the community and the world. Both mechanisms should be processes for empowerment of congregational leadership. The first grounds and orients leaders for ministry, while the second multiplies possibilities for ministry.

Declining church organizations that think *pre*scriptively tend to be overwhelmingly concerned with accountability. Note that accountability tends to be conceived in the atmosphere of condescension I have described. It is not really a process of empowerment, but a process of protection. It is the vehicle through which the congregation defends itself from litigation brought about by the potential stupidity of its committees and leaders. It is the vehicle through which the heritage of the institution is preserved and biblical visions are rationalized. Accountability means constant monitoring of committees, programs, and leaders to confirm they are indeed doing everything that is "prescribed" for them to do. A very distant second concern is that they are doing these things well. And a very, very distant third concern is that these activities are actually effecting positive, significant change in the public. It is not that declining church organizations ignore productivity completely. They simply limit productivity dramatically. The actual mission opportunities seized by the organization are few, but the supervision and management of those few mission opportunities involve the intensive labor of many, many congregational participants.

Thriving church organizations that think *pro*scriptively tend to carefully balance accountability and productivity. Accountability tends to be team-based, peer supervision that unfolds in an atmosphere of mutual trust. It is truly a vehicle for empowerment. The primary concern of the organization is not "Have you done everything we told you to do?" but rather "Have you gone beyond any boundaries, or contradicted any policies, in whatever experiments in ministry you are currently pursuing?" Accountability helps ground leaders more deeply in congregational identity and focuses their efforts more clearly on the missional purpose of their team or office. It does not limit possibilities for ministry, but only stresses that *quality* is crucial no matter what ministry might emerge. The primary purpose for accountability is to better focus and equip leaders for ministry beyond the church. These organizations are primarily concerned with *outcomes*. Their goal is not to protect a heritage or maintain an institution, but to generate the greatest positive change possible in the world—in the spirit of Christ.

Once again, the contrast between these two processes is dramatic. Accountability in the declining church organization orients the congregation toward institutional survival; accountability in the thriving church organization orients the congregation toward mission. Productivity in the declining church organization tends to be measured by maintenance of property and pastoral care for church insiders. Productivity in the thriving church organization tends to be measured by multiplication of mission and ministries of simultaneous faith sharing and social action among church outsiders. In the declining church organization, accountability without productivity equals *mere control*. The less productive the church becomes, the more preoccupied they are with accountability. In the thriving church organization, productivity nurtured by accountability creates a permission-giving environment. The more preoccupied the church becomes with reasonable trust, the more productive the church becomes.

Again, these two tensions in the chart resemble crosshairs in the scope of a target rifle. As they are adjusted and balanced, the congregational organization can accurately target the creation of a thriving church system in which church participants are changed, gifted, called, equipped, and sent. Note that the four quadrants formed by the crosshairs indicate clearly where consensus is crucial in the organization—and where it is not crucial. They indicate where board management is crucial in the organization—and where it is not crucial. In the thriving church organization, the location of consensus and management in the organization is different from that in declining church organizations.

In thriving church organizations, there are only two places where consensus is crucial—and neither of them is management. This is the reverse of what is true for the declining church organization. First, consensus (defined here as at least near unanimous agreement) is crucial in the definition of the core values, beliefs, vision, and mission which together form the congregational identity. It is also crucial to the formation of the general policies which govern organizational life. This consensus will be defined, refined, and celebrated by the congregation as a whole. Second, consensus (defined here as united vision or effort on the part of a staff, team, or committee) is crucial to the ministries that emerge from the interaction of the church and culture. This consensus will be developed by the cell or unit within the congregation that shares a common missional purpose.

Notice that consensus is *not* sought in the management of the church and its unfolding ministry work. Leaders, teams, and committees are free to discern opportunities, design ministries, and implement ministries through their own internal agreement, and within the broad boundaries of congregational identity. What exactly they do, what exact methods they use, and what partnerships they share to do it, are decisions left entirely to the cells or units of mission. The church board deliberately *distances itself* from this kind of church management. The decisions and work plans of each cell or unit do not need to be approved by the board, are not discussed by the board, and will not be changed by the board. Even the budget is not reviewed by the board, since this task is delegated to an administration team of the church.

In the thriving church organization, board management is concentrated in two directions. First, the board concentrates on maximizing the productivity of church leadership. They research the mission field and sharpen the point of mission outcomes. They define the degrees of risk the congregation is willing to accept, and keep the work of the church oriented to "that which is to die for" in the mission of Christ in their world today. Second, the board concentrates on the concrete measurements of success for productivity that will be communicated clearly to congregational members and the general public. In small part, this involves performance reviews for leaders (salaried and volunteer). In large part, this involves regular performance reviews of the *congregation as a whole* in the eyes of the world. In answering the questions "What is the point?" and "How is success measured?" board management is not just about holding others accountable to the church, but holding the entire congregation accountable to the mission field and to God.

Notice that the board does not create, imagine, or define congregational identity. They articulate congregational identity, and make sure that this identity is immediately transparent to every single person in the congregation and every visitor to the congregation. The personal tastes, perspectives, or lifestyles represented among the individuals of the board are entirely irrelevant for the definition of congregational identity, and hence for the mission productivity of the church. At the same time, the board takes interest not in the tactics of mission and ministry, but only in the degree to which any mission or ministry fulfills the congregational vision and addresses the point of their Christian existence.

Keep in mind that the chart as I have generally described it is similar to, and yet distinct from, parallel charitable or nonprofit organizations. The permission-giving organizations of the church *are* different in significant ways from other charitable institutions.

1) The congregational consensus is not simply around governance policies, but around congregational identity. Moreover, this identity arises not only from rigorous self-examination, but from spiritual discipline that waits for the inbreaking of God's vision for the

church. In other words, congregational identity is as much *received* as it is *created*.

2) Discernment of the point of congregational mission is tied to both social change and personal transformation. The organization not only seeks to provide beneficial services, but opportunities to experience spiritual transformation in relationship to Jesus. Therefore, the risk to be considered by the organization is not merely financial, but literally existential.

3) Success is measured not only through the link between the board and the cells or units of mission, but through the link between the congregation as a whole and the world mission field where God's call is most clearly revealed. In this organization, accountability to God is not theoretical, but practical. Reference to the world beyond the parent corporation or charity is not optional, but essential.

4) Staff, teams, and committees must be called, not merely appointed. This spiritual component implies that leadership will be committed to a degree of risk-taking unknown in most charitable organizations. It also implies that the heart of leadership will not be program implementation of an institutional agenda, but spiritual midwifery to give birth to the potentialities of God.

Generally speaking, in church organizations the twin tensions between *pre*scriptive and *pro*scriptive thinking, and processes of accountability and productivity, tend to be open to the unexpected influences of God. The chaos of culture is a significant enough challenge for most nonprofit and charitable organizations. However, the Christian chaos caused by the interaction of Christ and culture is even more unpredictable. It is far safer to be a participant in the United Way than in a thriving Christian church!

— 2 —

PRESCRIPTIVE THINKING

Introduction

The object of prescriptive thinking is to identify clearly the standards, principles, or policies which fix the identity of the congregation and focus the congregation's purpose and Christian calling. Yet prescriptive thinking is often misunderstood by congregations and their official boards. Traditional congregations often make long lists of what can or should be done, but fail to identify governance policies. They make lists of activities and programs that they feel obliged to implement, but fail to set clear boundaries for experimentation based on the shared identity of the participants. They describe in detail the denominational or local heritage that the congregation wishes to protect, but fail to articulate the shared calling that is the passion of the participants. As a result, congregations are often very busy, and official boards have many long management meetings, but all the dust and fury of congregational activity becomes remarkably passionless and pointless. Why should congregations do prescriptive thinking differently?

1) Spirituality: When congregations simply list what can or should be done, they limit the power of the Holy Spirit to interrupt the strategic plan and carry congregational energy in new directions. However, when congregations concentrate on broad policies which shape the congregational way of life, activities can flow in unexpected directions from the spiritual formation discipline of the participants.

2) *Integrity:* When congregations simply make lists of activities or programs that they feel obliged to implement, they limit the imaginations of the participants and distance members from their own sense of personal destiny. However, when congregations concentrate on setting clear boundaries for values, beliefs, vision, and mission, they anchor participants in the meaning of their personal and shared daily relationships with God, and motivate any corporate activity by a quest for personal fulfillment.

3) *Purposefulness:* When congregations simply describe a denominational or local heritage that they wish to protect, they limit the potential for good that lies within the corporate body for God's world. However, when congregations concentrate on clarifying the unique calling and passion shared by participants, they focus enormous and constant energy for positive change to the neighborhood and the world.

Authentic prescriptive thinking is not easy for traditional congregations and official boards. It requires the matriarchs and patriarchs, the clergy and the denominational judicatory *to let go of control* over the identity and purpose of the local congregation. The congregation must take primary responsibility for its discipline of adult spiritual formation, and the official board must focus *on outcomes rather than processes.*

What Are the Boundaries?

Quadrant 1

The first quadrant on the chart addresses *congregational identity,* or the boundaries and standards of individual and group behavior for which all congregational leaders and participants are held accountable. Notice that this is a matter of *consensus.* The congregational identity and related policies are revisited every year in the congregational annual meeting where they are regularly defined, refined, and celebrated. This identity is transparent to every participant, and immediately clear to every newcomer. No expert or manual is needed to interpret this identity, because it is immediately apparent in the worship of the congregation and the planned and spontaneous behavior of the participants. It is clear, it is visible, and it is the primary reference point for all congregational activity.

Charities, service clubs, and nonprofit organizations gain their sense of identity primarily from the *outcomes* that result from their work. In other words, identity emerges for them in quadrant 2 as the organization sharpens the point of their existence. Identity is shaped primarily by the clarity and imagination of the board of directors. Christian congregations, however, are unique in that identity is as much a gift of the Spirit as it is a creation of the participants. Vision is apocalyptic. The calling is received, not created, and the identity of the congregation is stamped by that calling. The calling is more than a *task to do*; it is a *way of life*. Charities, service clubs, and nonprofit organizations do not seek to be a *way of life*, but this is an imperative for the Christian church. Therefore, in this organizational model, identity is located in quadrant 1, and it emerges from the entire congregation.

The congregation is responsible for the creation of this identity and related policies; the official board is responsible for the regular and clear articulation of this identity. The board intentionally refers to this identity in regard to any initiative, program, or activity. They ask, "Does this idea, initiative, or activity go beyond the boundaries?" If it does, then they have no choice but to withhold permission. If it does not, they have no choice but to support it. This is the primary vehicle of accountability for the church.

The pastor (or pastoral team) has a unique role to play in the formation of the congregational identity. The pastor does *not* deliver it or create it. The pastor is not the originator of the identity. If a pastor is replaced through retirement or denominational personnel deployment, the identity of the congregation is not changed. On the other hand, the pastor influences the continuing process to define, refine, and celebrate the congregational identity in two ways. First, the pastor creates a spiritual climate in which God can make vision and mission clear, and in which marginal people in the church and community can articulate their perceptions of God's revelation in an accepting and affirming atmosphere. Second, the pastor influences the definition of congregation through her or his spiritual authenticity. This is not a body of knowledge or clearly defined heritage, but a spiritual lifestyle or experience of struggle and grace that influences the experience of God shared by the entire congregation. This authenticity will include disciplined reflection and knowledge, and may well be linked to a heritage or tradition, but it is the lifestyle that is influential. The pastor may not be the *originator* of the identity, but she or he will be the chief *articulator* of the identity.

I have already shared an explanation and discernment process for the core values, bedrock beliefs, motivating vision, and key mission which together form the identity of the congregation. I call this identity "the basic umbrella of congregational life," and the details are found in my book *Moving Off the Map: A Field Guide to Changing the Congregation.*

• Core values are the positive preferences or choices congregational participants make, both deliberately and spontaneously, in daily life. These are the values they strive to model in their lifestyles and behavior. They may fail from time to time, but such failure will always be accompanied by sincere repentance.

• Bedrock beliefs are the principles, symbols, or faith stories to which congregational participants spontaneously and habitually return for strength, in times of confusion or stress. These are the profound beliefs that are so precious that no external pressure will force participants to compromise them.

• Motivating vision is the song in the heart, the image, or spiritual metaphor that provides the rhythm for daily living. The mere presentation of this vision excites the heart, and fills participants with a sense of noble purpose. It is the compass setting to which they turn to orient themselves in the chaos of their lives.

• Key mission is the statement or graphic which in ten words or less communicates everything the public needs to understand about the church if it is to capture their imagination. It is the audacious goal the congregation seeks to achieve for the betterment of humanity and the fulfillment of God's purpose.

The official board and the pastor hold this consensus above all the ferment of congregational life. It is the chief vehicle of account-ability, replacing the personal tastes, opinions, perspectives, and lifestyles of the matriarchs and patriarchs of the church that once dictated congregational mission. The congregation cannot go beyond the boundaries, but within the boundaries participants are free to do whatever they believe God calls them to do.

Many congregations in fact prefer not to have this clarity and con-sensus. They prefer not to have the clarity, because lack of clarity allows controllers to dictate the program of the church using their own prejudices and biases (conscious and unconscious) as the crite-ria to evaluate every idea and activity. They prefer not to have con-sensus, instead immersing congregational meetings in the details of management, because lack of consensus allows controllers to limit the inbreaking of the Holy that might provoke the congregation to take risks.

On the other hand, clarity and consensus about the basic umbrel-la of congregational life liberates the congregation to rapidly deploy diverse ministries. They can seize opportunities that emerge, because the only issues the congregation needs to address are *tacti-cal*, not *foundational*. Tactics can be left to mission teams and staff. The board simply makes sure that the boundaries are not breached. The congregation can take risks, seize opportunities, and experi-ment with creative ideas, because they have unity about their identity.

In addition to clarity about congregational identity (values, beliefs, vision, and mission), this quadrant also allows the congre-gation to devise prescriptive policies that govern the behavior of leaders and participants. These policies are derived from the congregational identity, and give the board further direction to evaluate initiatives, programs, and activities of the church. Of course, the more these policies multiply, and the more detailed they become, the more restrictive the congregational organization becomes. Thriving church congregations try to limit these policies to broad principles or expectations for leaders and participants.

A first tier of prescriptive policies might define a particular style or approach to governance with the clearly understood basic umbrella of congregational life:[1]

1) The official board must do all in its power to equip any creative idea for excellence unless it falls outside the basic boundaries of congregational identity, in which case the proposal must be turned down.
2) All initiatives considered by the board must clearly arise from the spiritual growth disciplines of congregational participants.
3) The official board must give priority to equipping and releasing initiatives that maximize the potential for cultural diversity in the congregation.
4) The official board can approve only those initiatives which involve simultaneous social justice benefits and faith witness.
5) Every member of the official board must be committed to a daily spiritual discipline of prayer, scripture reading, and conversation with the unchurched public.

This tier of policy is intended not to limit mission initiative, but rather to direct or guide mission initiatives according to the identity of the congregation. Such statements define the approach of the congregation to decision making, or their general attitude toward the mission field.

The second tier of prescriptive policies may link congregational mission with distinctive practices that define a denominational tradition, characterize a denominational practice, and stamp the congregation with a particular twist of identity. Again, even more caution should be exercised here lest the congregation develop policies which lead it into a management role best left to staff and mission teams. This tier of policies captures the essence of a particular stream of the historical church which the congregation itself perceives as crucial to the basic umbrella of congregational life. These policies might include:

1) The sacraments must be offered to all people, regardless of membership, including children, persons with mental retardation, and nonmembers of the church.
2) The Sacrament of Holy Communion (or Eucharist) must be celebrated every week with an ordained priest presiding.
3) The Sacrament of Baptism may be celebrated only once in a person's lifetime (infant or adult), and must include the symbol of water, the presence of a priest, and the sponsorship of members of the church.
4) Ritual footwashing must be observed regularly in worship.
5) The Heidelberg Confession must be the foundation for all theological conversation with other religious groups.
6) All ideas and initiatives must be considered in reference to scripture, tradition, reason, and the continuing experience of the Holy Spirit.
7) The principle of the "Priesthood of All Believers" allows every individual direct access to the grace of God.
8) The directions of a bishop or judicatory must be considered by the official board, and the congregation must seek to respond positively to requests.

It should be obvious that most of what traditional congregational organizations believe to be "essential" about denominational identity is, in fact, only "habitual." The use of Latin in the mass, for example, might once have been considered a hallmark of Roman Catholic congregations, but in fact it has been revealed to be only a "habit" that could be discarded. The same might be said of much of the music, liturgy, vestments, terminology, political structures, and other accoutrements habitually associated with a denomination.

The clear articulation of distinctive practices or characteristics embraced by the congregation also forces the congregation to avoid vague reference to the "ethos" or "heritage" of their church. The truth is that the "ethos" described in one part of the world to describe a denomination is quite different from the "ethos" described elsewhere. Much of the "ethos" traditional congregational organizations want to preserve is really a collection of local or regional habits that have no particular bearing on their core values, bedrock beliefs, motivating vision, or key mission. Permission-giving congregational organizations clearly distinguish between what is essential, and what is merely habitual. They may or may not preserve the habits, but they never make the mistake of assuming that they are policy.

These policies should evolve naturally from the congregational identity, and the congregation's consensus around values, beliefs, vision, and mission. In other words, if denominational tradition is important to the congregation, it will be incorporated in the umbrella of congregational life and be reflected in the policies derived from that identity. On the other hand, if denominational tradition is not important to the congregation, then the congregation can and must resist the imposition of denominational expectations. The real link between denominational polity and the congregation lies in congregational identity—not in congregational duty. The management of congregational ministries and activities will flow from the identity of the congregation *alone,* and will not be arbitrarily dictated by requirements imposed from beyond that identity.

The policies in this quadrant are related to the general direction and purpose of ministry that fulfills the values, beliefs, vision, and mission of the congregation. They are not statements about strategy or tactics. The goal is to define the boundaries beyond which one cannot go, not dictate how one must act within the boundaries. These boundaries prescribe how the official board, staff, leaders, and participants are expected to behave as members of the congregation. Later, the board will further define the limitations on actions of staff, teams, and lay leaders.

What Is the Point?

Quadrant 2

The second quadrant of the chart addresses *congregational* and *ministry* purpose, or the beneficial outcomes for congregational participation that deserve significant sacrifices. Note that in the system of the thriving church, this is a matter of board management. Congregational consensus has clearly identified the *Key Mission* that excites congregational participants and captures the imaginations of the public. As congregational life unfolds into creative, changing ministries, the official board must regularly refine and elaborate

- the rationale for continued congregational existence;
- the positive personal changes that are anticipated in the lives of people within and beyond the church;
- the practical community benefits that will be enjoyed or received by the public;
- the acceptable sacrifices the congregation is willing to make to achieve the above.

These definitions will need to be applied to the overall mission of the congregation, and to each ministry that is sponsored by the congregation.

Earlier I noted that *congregational* identity is shaped both by the action of participants *and* by the Holy Spirit. Therefore, the "key mission" or motivated goal of congregational life grows out of the clarity and consensus of the people receiving apocalyptic vision. This is addressed in quadrant 1. This identity will evolve over time, responding to both the changing circumstances of community and culture, and to the changing direction of the Spirit. Therefore, the primary purpose of future annual congregational meetings will be to constantly define, refine, and celebrate this identity.

While the congregation as a whole gains clarity and consensus about the overall goal of congregational life, the official board must repeatedly ask in the daily life of the church, "What is the point?"

They do so recognizing that this "point" is not fixed, nor does it determine the life or death of the congregation. In other words, congregational identity is a *way of life* primarily shaped by a relationship to God, and not by the achievement of specific outcomes. If the practical "point" of mission changes, the organization does not necessarily come to an end. On the other hand, even if the practical "point" of mission changes, there must always, always be a point! This practical "point" to participation in the church must be transparent behind every church activity. If any activity is merely *habitual*, but in the eyes of the public truly *pointless*, the key mission in turn becomes vague and the congregational identity becomes obscure.

Biblical people not only have an identity through their relationship to God, but they are always *purpose-driven* people. The covenant of Abraham stamps their identity with a distinct way of life or orientation: "If we obey and live in relationship with God, and only God, then God will multiply our numbers and make us a blessing to all humankind." Beyond this, however, God drives biblical people toward distinct purposes. There is a practical point to their daily living. The Israelites left Egypt to go to the promised land, and by God! even if it took them forty years in the wilderness they were going to get there. Esther and Nehemiah led the exiles back to Jerusalem, and they were going to rebuild those walls, even if they had to fight the whole Babylonian army to do it. Paul, Silas, and Priscilla were called to preach the Good News to the Gentiles, and even if they had to endure imprisonments, beatings, and stonings, they were going to preach that gospel. They could have stayed in Egypt, lingered in Babylon, or remained in loving fellowship with Christians in Jerusalem, and never ventured forth driven by a purpose. If they had done so, however, the *pointlessness* of their living would soon have obscured the identity God had given them. Eventually, they would have lost that identity, too, and been absorbed into the surrounding culture.

Jesus spoke constantly about being a *purpose-driven disciple.* He commanded the Twelve and the Seventy to take no bag, no spare shoes, no extra coat, and no heavy cache of snacks, but just to *get out there* on the highway and heal people and proclaim salvation—and not to let anything distract them from the cause. They did exactly that. And the followers of Jesus multiplied.

Purpose-driven discipleship lay at the core of Jesus' message. That's why he told the parables of the mustard seed and the leavened bread.

Here is this little, tiny mustard seed. It's blown about by the wind, and stepped on by indifferent passersby, but by God! it *will* grow into the greatest of all bushes. It will. That is its destiny. That is its purpose. The seed knows this. And it will do it.

Here is this bread dough just sitting there. Unappetizing, useless. Along comes the chef, who has the audacity to press into the dough the smallest amount of yeast. She says, "I know it's a big lump of dough, and I know this is just a wee bit of yeast, but by heavens! yeast was created to make dough rise up, and that is exactly what it will do."

To be a *purpose-driven church* is to have clarity about what is essential for your church to fulfill its identity *today*. What is it about your church—*today and in this world situation*—that is "to die for"? People in growing churches have a deep, shared understanding that something about their church involvement is as important to them as eating, sleeping, and working. It is "to die for." It is essential. It is the reason for living. It is *the purpose of life*.

The spiritually seeking public asks the church, *"What is the point? What is your fundamental purpose as a church? Where are you going? What is 'to die for' here? What is so important about your church that nothing—not the Rotary, not the garden club, not Weight Watchers, not aerobics class, not even the 12-step program—nothing can take the place of this church in my life? What is so important about what you are about in this church that it deserves the sacrifice of all that time and money you keep asking me for?"*

The official board must ask this question in behalf of that spiritually seeking public. Let us be clear. The role of the board in this quadrant is *not* to represent the expectations of church insiders, but to represent the expectations of church outsiders. They bring together the congregational identity and the realities of community need (spiritual, physical, emotional, relational). Every ministry, and congregational life in general, must be purpose-driven. There must be a point. It must advance the vision of the congregation. It must have an outcome that allows the congregational identity to overflow with beneficial life for people beyond the church.

There is a clear link between answering the question "What is the point?" and determining the *cost of discipleship*. Pointlessness and complacency are two sides of the coin, and understanding the point of congregational life and the risk of daily congregational living are two ways of addressing the issue of purposefulness. This is why the measurement of acceptable risk, and the determination of the point in every congregational activity, are simultaneously the business of the official board.

The pastor (or pastoral team) plays a unique role in answering the question "What is the point?" Unlike the CEO of a charity, service club, or nonprofit organization, the pastor is proactively in constant conversation with the public beyond the church. She or he is constantly surveying the changing mission field in order to perceive in advance the nuances or trends, hazards or opportunities, that may redirect the energies of the congregation and redefine the point of congregational participation. More than this, the pastor continues to nurture a climate of spiritual discernment in which the Spirit can determine in the hearts of the participants the cost of discipleship.

The organization of the thriving church differs from the Carver model (mentioned in the Introduction) in that congregational identity depends upon the consensus of the congregational participants, and the role of the board is limited only to its articulation. However, in keeping with the Carver model, the board must regularly refine and elaborate what that key mission means at any given time in the life of the church. After all, culture and community are constantly changing. The Holy Spirit can and will call the congregation to new and different missions and ministries. The examples of motivating vision and key mission which I provided in *Moving Off the Map* included the vision to be *Summer in the Soul!* to seekers wanting to grow, experiment, and flower in unexpected directions (based on a metaphor from the song "As Comes the Breath of Spring"), and the mission to *Go Now in Love!* which could be printed on the side of a city bus to capture the imagination of the public. Exactly what *outcomes* such a vision and mission anticipate, however, may vary over time. The board responsibility will be to monitor these changes. They regularly define and elaborate the point of ministry, and determine the acceptable risks that the congregation will take in order to pursue their purpose.

John and Miriam Carver are quite right to caution board members to take time to focus their answers to the question "What is the point?"[2] The answers are not easy. Christian congregations in particular are apt to err in three ways.

First, congregational boards often confuse *intention* with *purpose.* They state what they intend to do, or hope to do, and so emphasize a methodology rather than an outcome. Avoid statements like:

"We seek to make worship inclusive and joyful for all people."
"We pledge to work for the equality of all races and cultures, men and women."

Intentions cannot be measured or evaluated, and no actual change in persons or communities is really anticipated. The purpose of the congregation, therefore, is simply *to be sincere.* They can be sincere without really changing anything. That may make congregational participants feel good about themselves, but it will not inspire credibility among the public or motivate voluntarism within the church.

Second, congregational boards often confuse *tactics* with *results.* They state how they plan to act, but not what the expected outcome will be. Avoid statements like:

"We will provide multiple options for worship."
"We will have a quality Sunday school for children."
"We will be a center for community activities."

Worship and Christian education programs are merely vehicles to achieve something. Community centers may provide anything from pinochle to food banks. What, exactly, will they achieve? That is the question that must be answered. Congregations may generate all kinds of programs, curricula, and ministries without every really changing people or community. Such busy-ness gives the appearance of productivity, but is soon ignored by the community as impotent.

Third, congregational boards often confuse *ideals* with *outcomes*. They state how they wish people to be, or how they dream society should become, but not what they realistically hope to achieve. Avoid statements like:

"The people in our community will be more loving."
"The realm of God will bring peace to earth."
"The world will all hear the gospel."

Such statements are unclear. *Which* people? *What behavioral changes* will reveal that they are more loving? *What* gospel? Exactly *which demographic groups* will be hearing *which* gospel? What will peace look like in the daily commerce and activities of ordinary people? Congregations may hold many fine ideals, but if they are not clearly targeted and measurable they are mere daydreams.

When congregational boards answer the question "What is the point?" they are identifying those concrete purposes the congregation is ready to make significant sacrifices to achieve. There may be several tiers of purpose-driven statements.

The first tier is the most general, and articulates the current reason for the congregation's continued existence. I say "current" with a fairly long time line in mind. In other words, the "current" reason for the existence of the congregation in its first hundred years may well not be the "current" reason for its existence in the next fifty years. The *way of life* may be continuous, but the point may change.

Clearly, this all-embracing answer to the question "What is the point?" ought to be tied to the "motivating vision" and "key mission" identified in the basic umbrella of congregational life. This is expanded and made more concrete in direct connection to the emerging mission field of the church. The best answers here will include clear reference to the changes or benefits anticipated, the people who will most be affected, and the degree of urgency, commitment, or sacrifice (cost) required. The congregation may celebrate their vision to be "Summer in the Soul," and their key mission to "Go now in love!" but the official board will focus this mission for today. Such purposes might include:

• The public will have multiple opportunities to experience the gospel as joy, find personal fulfillment through disciplined growth and motivated, hands-on ministries, and learn to shape their lifestyles solely by relationship to Jesus.

• Broken, displaced, depressed people worldwide will experience through our church the power of God that brings physical, emotional, relational, and spiritual health.

• Asian, Caribbean, and Caucasian publics in our community will share sacramental worship together, and share responsibility for social services through continuous commitment to volunteer mission teams and without paid staff.

• Adults as singles or couples, aged eighteen to forty-five, will have a chance to experience the transforming power of God that heals broken relationships, nurtures hope, and guides all people to fulfill their destiny in God's plan for the world, without the burden of owning church property, at convenient times, and through the media they prefer.

This first tier of anticipated outcomes includes every potential ministry initiative from the church, regardless of its actual content or specific activity.

The second and third tiers of statements articulate the expected positive personal changes and community benefits which will be the outcome of congregational ministries. Positive personal changes are enduring changes to an individual's lifestyle which clearly enhance quality of life. Such positive personal changes might include:

• Seekers and people with no Christian memory will experience spiritual coaching that will help them shape their personal relationships, career paths, and lifestyles around their relationship with Jesus Christ.

• Parents (couples or singles) will become disciplined in spiritual growth and be equipped to communicate basic values and beliefs to their children at home.

• Addicted people of all ages and backgrounds will awaken to their self-destructive habits, experience liberation from higher powers, and enter partnerships to recover full health.

• Homeless, friendless people will live in safety, and learn to support one another in trusting relationships.

Community benefits are lasting changes in the neighborhood, region, or world which improve the safety and harmony of society, and generally increase the ability of each person to live to their fullest potential without hurt or hindrance to anyone else. Anticipated community benefits might include:

• Multitrack worship strategy will include options to preserve the language and cultural forms of each distinct ethnic heritage in the community.

• Volunteers motivated and informed by our values, beliefs, vision, and mission will be leaders on the governing boards of charitable organizations, boards of education, hospital boards, and municipal government in our community.

• Elderly victims of Alzheimer's disease will receive day care in a safe environment, facilitated by trained Christian volunteers, in continuing mutual support partnerships with their families.

• Business and government leaders in our neighborhood and municipality will receive regularly updated information and reliable coaching about safe environmental practices and sound environmental policies free of charge.

There may be many tactics and ministries related to worship, personal growth, or outreach, and each will have additional, specific purposes designed by the team implementing the tactic. However, the board can insist that the basic umbrella of congregational life implies that general outcomes should be expected in every tactic. These outcomes will involve both personal change and community benefits, often linked to each other.

Additional tiers of statements can focus outcomes in greater and greater detail, and this may be desirable in certain areas of congregational life. The more restrained the board is, the more creativity is encouraged among mission teams, and the more mission opportunities can be seized. Official boards should remember that the basic umbrella of congregational life is the *primary* vehicle of accountability in the permission-giving organization. The task of the official board is to define the boundaries of acceptable risk.

Therefore, the last task of the board in this quadrant is to identify the acceptable sacrifices associated with the outcomes in personal change and community benefit which the board has identified. Exactly how much is the board willing to invest—or risk—in the pursuit of their mission? As the board defines the acceptable sacrifices to be expected from participants and leaders of the congregation, they will need to consider at least seven distinct "cost centers."

- *Heritage Costs:* changes to traditional self-understanding
- *Attitude Costs:* changes to perspective to the mission field
- *Lifestyle Costs:* changes to habitual behavior patterns and comfort zones
- *Leadership Costs:* changes in expectations for staff and volunteers
- *Organization Costs:* changes in structures and communications
- *Property Costs:* changes in location, technology, facility, and floor plan
- *Financial Costs:* changes in budget and stewardship.

Probably most effective is for the board to define acceptable sacrifices in the order in which they are listed. Acceptable sacrifices regarding money are easier to define if the other six areas of expectation are already clear.

The board does not want to intrude upon the management responsibilities to shape tactics and strategies that belong in the third quadrant and will be assigned to others. The board does want to define the broad expectations that any tactic should achieve. For example, in the order of these seven "cost centers," defining statements might include:

- Nothing is sacred, or in itself deserves to be preserved, except the gospel.

- No ministry can be released into the community without a long-term strategy to implement it in a diversity of styles and media suitable to all the demographic groups surrounding our congregation.

- No person can be a member of the church without a clearly articulated spiritual growth discipline customized for their daily life.

- Every member of the official board, and every cell group shepherd, must spend at least seven hours each week in hands-on mission among the general public, and they must tithe their income to the church.

• Every board member and staff person must receive biweekly updates on activities of the congregation by fax or email from the church office.

• All property and technology owned by the church must be readily accessible, upgradable, portable, and marketable.

• The congregation must always have a manageable capital debt for mission, and any loan, lease, purchase, or sale of property or technology over $5,000 must be approved by a full, informed congregational vote.

Such policies help define the lengths the congregation is prepared to go to achieve its mission outcomes. When Jesus sent the Twelve out into the world specifically to heal and proclaim the Good News, he also defined the risks the disciples must take. They must take no money, no bag, no spare clothes, no sandals, and no staff. In the same way, the official board focuses the identity of the congregation and their relationship with God, defines the practical point of ministry, and defines the risk that the congregation is ready to take.

Generally speaking, prescriptive thinking about *accountability* and prescriptive thinking about *productivity* are all about setting boundaries or identifying outcomes which balance creativity and integrity in congregational life. Nonprofit, charitable, or service organizations will tend to rely on the board of directors to define the boundaries and focus the outcomes, with special reference to the constituency of members who contribute to the charity. Christian congregations will tend to rely on congregational consensus to determine boundaries and official board action to focus outcomes, with special reference to the general public. The nonprofit organization has the relatively simple task of assessing community needs and designing flexible programs to address those needs. The Christian congregation has the relatively complex task of discerning the interaction of culture and the Holy Spirit, and releasing flexible ministries to channel that spiritual ferment toward specific purposes.

The art of governance for the Christian congregation is to develop policies for accountability and productivity which together shape an environment in which creative ministries can emerge. Two metaphors may help describe such a governance model.

First, the prescriptive thinking of the congregation creates a "birthing room" in which unexpected, creative, and even radical initiatives can be born and thrive. Prescriptive thinking does not mean that the congregation or the official board lists everything congregational leaders or participants can or should do, but rather that the congregation and official board define the basic boundaries beyond which initiatives cannot go. What is visible to the public is not an institution, complete with parliamentary procedure and integrated committees, but rather a clearly defined spiritual environment in which participants have freedom to discover and explore.

Second, when the prescriptive thinking of the congregation and official board is finally articulated, the result is not really a church "constitution" but a spiritual "climate." It is an ecosystem of air (core values), earth (bedrock beliefs), fire (motivating vision), and water (key mission), which interact to produce specific beneficial fruits. The nature of the congregational identity will determine how much detail, and in what areas of ministry, anticipated outcomes will be defined. What is clear to the public is not a building that houses various programs, but a spiritual environment in which carefully designed and motivated mission results in positive personal and social change.

The prescriptive thinking of the congregation helps the congregation and the general public answer immediately, and with extraordinary clarity, these two questions:

Who in the name of God **are** *we?*
and
What in God's name are we **doing** *here?*

"We are the people who live daily by these values, beliefs, vision, and mission, spontaneously behave in this way and with this attitude toward the world, and are willing to take these extraordinary risks, so that the following wonderful things can happen."

— 3 —

PROSCRIPTIVE THINKING

Introduction

The ability to think *pro*scriptively is often difficult for traditional church organizations to learn. Their habit is to think *pre*scriptively in the inappropriate way described earlier. That is, the habit of most congregational official boards is to mandate offices and committees by listing everything the person or persons can or should do. By doing so, the limits of creativity are determined by the creativity of the board, and not by the creativity of the people actually doing the ministry. *Pro*scriptive thinking requires the board to think *negatively* in order to empower mission *positively*. Instead of listing everything an office or committee can or should do, the board only identifies what the office or committee *cannot* do. By doing so, the board not only frees the creative energy of its mission leaders, but it makes the task of measuring success much easier. Why should the board think *pro*scriptively?

1) Speed: When official boards mandate offices and committees with *pre*scriptive lists, original and creative ideas are exceptions that require additional bureaucracy to approve. This takes time, which the rapidly changing mission field will not allow. However, when official boards mandate offices and committees with *pro*scriptive lists, mission leaders are free to experiment without waiting for bureaucrats to catch up.

2) Creativity: When official boards write *pre*scriptive mandates, creativity is really measured by the group imagination of the board.

Before anything original can be tried, the board must be persuaded that it is possible. However, when official boards use *proscriptive* mandates, mission leaders with creative ideas need only demonstrate that an experiment is *permissible* within the boundaries of congregational life. Whether or not it is possible to implement the proposal is limited only by the imagination of the mission leader.

3) Relevance: When official boards use *pre*scriptive mandates, the congregation becomes bound to a strategic plan that is not easily changed. The surrounding culture will change quickly, but the church is still committed to implementing an immutable list of activities which are rapidly becoming irrelevant. However, when official boards use *pro*scriptive mandates, the congregation is committed to a *way of life,* not to any detailed *strategic plan.* Mission leaders rapidly adjust ministries to the changing cultural environment.

*Pro*scriptive thinking is not easy for traditional church leaders, who are in the habit of controlling the actual ministries or activities of congregational life. *Pro*scriptive thinking can only be done if the official board *lets go* of much of the management associated with traditional boards. Such management will be entrusted to the gifted, called, and equipped mission leaders who are grown and deployed by the church. The courage and confidence to let go of management only comes if the congregation has been able to authentically "think *pre*scriptively" to determine the boundaries of values, beliefs, vision, and mission, and if the board has been able to focus the purposefulness of the congregation for the current mission field.

Traditional church organizations tend to blur the expectations for spiritual discipline and responsibility for ministry shared within the congregation, just as they tend to obscure the basic umbrella of congregational life. They rely on the cultural homogeneity of the congregation to preserve the unspoken assumptions or expectations of the matriarchs and patriarchs of the church. Just as their personal opinions, lifestyles, and perspectives form the unspoken boundary for experimentation in ministry, so also their patronage or assumptions about leadership roles will limit what staff or volunteers may or may not do. At times, this authority may even contradict denominational polity. So long as the principle of homogeneity is maintained in congregational life, and the homogeneous body lives harmoniously, the ambiguities regarding leadership responsibilities are not a problem. However, when the congregation begins to reflect the full and constantly changing demographic diversity of the community, or when harmony breaks down in the face of different expectations among the public, official boards and congregational meetings become competitive arenas of power struggle.

Traditional church organizations also tend to import false assumptions about board leadership from the surrounding culture.

• They borrow the assumption that board members must be *specialists* from the social service sector. Board members are nominated, and claim credibility, because they possess a certifiable expertise that is necessary to implement and manage specific volunteer tasks.

• They borrow the assumption that board members must be *representatives* from the government sector. Board members are nominated, and claim credibility, because they speak for one of the various special interest groups that form the congregation.

• They borrow the assumption that board members must be *technicians* from the business sector. Board members are nominated, and claim credibility, because they can quantify data and manipulate organizational mechanisms to run efficiently.

• They borrow the assumption that board members must be *gurus* or *saints* from cults or exaggerated histories of sectarian religious life. Board members are nominated, and claim credibility, because they can motivate blind obedience or demonstrate traditional piety.

These assumptions reinforce the motivation of traditional boards to blur the boundaries between policy governance and management, and extend their control in both directions. They tend to distrust the ability of the congregation as a whole to build consensus around the basic umbrella of congregational life, because their representative or saintly status leads them to believe that they know better what the boundaries should be. They tend to distrust the ability of volunteers to take initiative for ministries, because their specialized skill or technical ability leads them to believe they know as much as or more than any volunteer leader. This is why the traditional board spends so much time creating and reviewing a budget. The need to approve even the smallest expenditures reveals their compulsion to intervene constantly in the management of the church.

As we move from *pre*scriptive to *pro*scriptive thinking in the organizational chart of the thriving church system, it becomes clear that none of the traditional assumptions about board leadership are important anymore.

• Permission-giving board members are not specialists, but *generalists* who discipline their lifestyles around a distinct spirituality in order to actualize and release the imaginative ministries of others.

• Permission-giving board members are not representatives, but *bridge builders* who discipline their lifestyles to listen to all the nuances of culture and perceive the full diversity of needs among the publics of the community.

• Permission-giving board members are not technicians, but *ministry mappers* who are themselves bound by, and articulate clearly, the essential identity of the congregation, and who are motivated by a deep passion for the gospel to be maximized in the world.

• Permission-giving board members are not gurus or saints, but *leaders* who model disciplines for spiritual growth and use understandable tools to measure the impact of congregational ministries on the world.

These new assumptions motivate the board to clarify the boundaries between policy and management, and to limit their control on both. They have credibility within the congregation because they truly expect the Holy Spirit to guide the congregation into the future. They have credibility among the multitude of volunteer leaders, because they truly respect their integrity and skill to take initiative. This is why the board does not have to constantly review a budget. The freedom to attend to matters of policy and long-range planning reveals their trust in the competency of mission units and administration teams to do work.

The new organizational model actually makes it easier to identify and encourage new people to join the board. Board membership in the old model was a daunting task. Not only did few people meet the criteria of expertise, popularity, technical skill, and saintliness, but most people doubted that the present board members were quite as able as they claimed to be. Who would want to join an elite board feeling chronically inadequate? However, board membership in the new model is an exciting opportunity. More people are motivated to exercise such leadership when it opens possibilities for personal growth and experimentation.

Ultimately, the harmony and growth of the congregation depend not on the expertise of the board, but on the credibility and spiritual authenticity of those who claim to reasonably interpret success. Carefully defined limitations for excellence, shared authority, leadership development, and coordination will provide both the congregation and the general public with some criteria with which to understand what a "reasonable interpretation of success" might look like. So also, clearly defined expectations for missions, personal development, action, and confidentiality will build congregational and public confidence that allows leaders to fail, learn, and try again. In the end, that is all the congregation can hope to achieve— but it is far more than the traditional congregational official board (with borrowed cultural assumptions) could deliver. Leaders who are highly trusted by the congregation and the general public for their spiritual discipline and passion for mission can push to infinity the grand project that they share together.

How Is Success Measured?

The *prescriptive* role of the official board focused the mission of the church on the current cultural situation, and defined the personal changes, community benefits, and acceptable risks which are the current targets of congregational life. This *prescriptive* role was anchored in the boundaries established by the congregation as they clarified their unique identity. Now, the *proscriptive* role of the official board is about setting limitations. They need to state clearly what standards of excellence may *not* be ignored, what limitations for authority and leadership development may *not* be breached, and what coordination assumptions may *not* be forgotten. Together these limitations will determine how success is measured.

One of the most difficult challenges facing any church organization is the need to assess the real, lasting impact of the ministries of the congregation on the lives, communities, and cultures surrounding the congregation. Statistical research and market surveys will only provide a narrow insight into the overall success of the congregational mission—and this data itself will need to be interpreted by credible and spiritually disciplined people. In the end, there will always be a degree of subjectivity in the measure of success. How is it that the new official board can do this *better* than the traditional official board?

First, the congregation recognizes that this is one of the two fundamental tasks of the board. This in itself is a breakthrough insight for many congregations and traditional official boards. Most congregations believe that success can be evaluated by congregational consensus, and they become hopelessly lost in the conflicting opinions of various power groups and factions in congregational life. Minority groups easily leverage the congregation toward guilt, and matriarchs and patriarchs easily leverage the congregation toward complacency. Similarly, most official boards devote all their time to *prescriptive* management of committees and budgets, and give almost no time to clarifying the real point of mission and monitoring its impact. They rarely look up from the ledger and the committee reports to see if the world is really changing because of the presence of their church.

The new organization has an advantage when trying to measure success, because for the first time the official board has clearly understood that it is their job. Aside from focusing the point and risk of mission, this is their primary reason for being. Their whole purpose in congregational life is not to manage a budget, or to implement programs, but to clearly target mission and devote attention to its accomplishment. If the mission field were an archery range, then traditional church boards would spend all their time feathering the arrows and adjusting the bowstrings. The new official board leaves all that to others who are better gifted, called, and equipped to do it. The board's job on the archery range is to set the target in view and make sure the arrow hits it.

Second, this task is made easier if the congregation is clear about the Basic Umbrella of Congregational Life, the board is clear about the anticipated outcomes and risks, and the paid and volunteer leaders are clear about their mission. Such clarity is rarely apparent in traditional church official boards. The interpretation of boundaries for values, beliefs, vision, and mission is usually left to the interpretation of matriarchs and patriarchs, or to the direction of denominations or clergy. Boards rarely involve themselves in listening to the public and discerning cultural trends and mission opportunities, and approach risk as an issue of "survival" rather than "gospel." Paid and volunteer leaders have little clarity about their called mission, and all too much clarity about their constitutional place in the institution. As a result, their views about the relative success of the mission of the church lack credibility both to themselves and the general public.

On the other hand, when the congregational organization does have such clarity, their ability to measure success is greatly enhanced. The official board has a concrete understanding of the assumptions, goals, and capabilities of the congregation. They can tell the difference between vague "pipe dreams" that could never have been achieved by Peter himself, and ambitious mission targets that are realistically achievable by way of the hidden potential of their congregation. The more careful and focused the congregation is about their identity, mission goals, and leadership capabilities, the more precise will be the official board's measurement of success.

Third, this task is easier when the official board clearly expresses their expectations for excellence, authority, leadership development, and coordination. This is the work of Quadrant 3, which we will discuss now. Most traditional church organizations fail to identify standards for quality ministry, and blur the lines of authority between clergy, chairpersons of the official board or committees, denominational appointees, and other leaders in the church. They tend to be driven by worry about protecting sacrosanct areas of activity from redundancy. They expand middle management and exhaust lay leaders in an ultimately fruitless effort to monitor everything the board feels can or should be done.

Quadrant 3

As we shall see, the new organization concentrates the energy of the board to specify limitations for excellence, authority, leadership development, and monitoring. Standards of quality can be transparent to all, and incorporated into the training for staff and volunteers. Responsibility can be delegated and defined, so that the church worries less about sacrosanct *work* and attends to clarity of *calling*. Evaluation and grievance procedures can be straightforward and accessible. In the end, the official board can eliminate layers of middle management, and yet have greater credibility in measuring success than ever before.

The first tier of limitations for the measure of success identifies the minimum standards of excellence acceptable to the board for all salaried and volunteer leaders. This is not a "lowest common denominator" for quality, since the congregation has already declared its policy for continuous discipline in adult spiritual formation. In a sense, clarity over the minimum standards of excellence is a clear way to ascertain the spiritual discipline expected of individual leaders and the corporate body. This first tier of limitations is worded negatively, because this makes it easier for the board to measure compliance. In other words, the official board says, "The standards for excellence in our congregational way of life, necessary to achieve our congregational purpose, *are nothing less than . . .*"

This will again require very careful consideration by the official board. Minimum standards of excellence will need to be articulated for the general performance of leaders, and for what I described in *Moving Off the Map* as the "formal" subsystems of congregational life (property, funding, and communications). The official board will need to be cautious, however, *not* imposing restrictions specifically related to any tactic of ministry that might limit the power of leaders to experiment. For example, the following limitations are unhelpful:

"The choir director cannot prepare fewer than twenty formal choir anthems per year."
"The custodian cannot mow the lawn on Sundays."
"The pastor cannot visit nursing homes less than once a month."
"Ushers cannot seat people in the last ten pews of the sanctuary."

These limitations all relate to specific tactics for ministry, which may even be considered to be habits or duties of various leaders. Such limitations may or may not be designed into the job descriptions of staff and volunteer leaders in quadrant 4, but they are useless as instruments to help the official board measure the success of congregational impact on the community and the world in pursuit of their congregational mission.

The limitations for excellence required here generally apply to all ministry tactics or leadership roles that might be deployed by the congregation, and directly help the official board ascertain the impact of congregational mission on the public. Such limitations for leadership might include:

• No one can be a *member* of the church who is not committed to a weekly spiritual discipline that includes daily prayer and scripture reading, and who does not attend at least one corporate worship experience each week.

• No mature Christian can be without a hands-on ministry, and no leader doing any hands-on ministry can be deployed by the church unless he or she is committed to a discipline for personal spiritual growth.

• No evangelism ministry can be deployed unless it includes a component of social service, and no social service ministry can be deployed unless it includes a strategy for faith sharing.

• No position of leadership will be closed to gifted, called, and equipped persons over age fourteen.

• No visitor can worship more than once with the congregation without receiving a clear presentation of our basic umbrella of congregational life and mission purpose.

The congregation may wish to identify further limitations for the formal subsystems of congregational life (property, funding, communication), which clarify expectations for excellence in ministry. These might include:

• The visual and sound systems in the worship center of the church cannot comprise anything less than the best technology available in the past five years.

• No office or education room will fail to be networked into the computer system of the church building.

• No entry or meeting room will be inaccessible by wheelchair, stroller, or funeral home gurney.

• No memorial money can be accepted that is limited in use by the church.

• No fund-raising may take place unless it directly supports the stated key mission of the church.

• No member of the church by reason of poor sight or hearing will be hindered in their participation.

• No ethnic group in our community will fail to find available statements of our congregational core values, bedrock beliefs, motivating vision, and key mission in their own language.

Notice again that the negative formulation of these limitations actually enhances the ability of the official board to measure success. The board will not be sidetracked by extraneous worries over *which* computer system is best, or whether the pastor can visit the unchurched in a bar, or whether the video screen in the worship center is above the altar or off to the side, or exactly what curriculum congregational leaders are using in cell groups, or even the cost of all of the above. All these matters and more can be safely delegated to the various leaders and mission teams in the continuing development of their job descriptions. These issues may be important, but they are not the issues addressed by the board. The board concentrates on measuring the success of the overall mission of the church in achieving its fundamental purposes, and can use these limitations as concrete vehicles to accomplish this task.

The second tier of limitations for the measure of success clarifies the diffused authority within the congregation. Generally speaking, authority in the thriving church organization is delegated by the official board, within the context of a larger biblical tradition or specific denominational polity, to three basic management teams:

• the Human Resources Team, to grow and nurture gifted ministry leaders
• the Pastoral Support Team, to train leaders and equip ministries for excellence
• the Administration Team, to deploy quality ministries.

Together, these three teams function as a "stability triangle" that coordinates and guides the ferment of creative ministries which emerge from the spiritual formation disciplines of the participants.

The thriving church organization recognizes that leaders are called to *lead!* The spiritual identity of the congregation requires visionaries who can discern God's purposes in the chaos of cultures, prophets who can alert the congregation to unexpected (and occasionally unwanted) challenges for ministry, and "ministry mappers" who can develop the long-range plans and anticipate the degrees of sacrifice that will be required for the congregation to follow Jesus into the future. This *pre*scriptive thinking is the first of two key roles for the leaders who compose the board. Once the congregation as a whole has gained clarity and consensus about the basic boundaries of congregational life, the board prescribes the *point* of ministry.

The thriving church organization also requires leaders who are risk-takers to boldly seize initiative equipped with the core values and bedrock beliefs of the congregation, entrepreneurs who can experiment with creative ministries designed to boost targeted change, and "spiritual cartographers" who can explore the cultural landscape to match God's grace and emerging needs. While traditional church organizations worry about curbing their enthusiasm, the new church organization seeks to unleash their boundless creativity. The church does this by thinking *pro*scriptively. They define clearly what these leaders *may not* do, so that they are free to do anything else to fulfill the mission of the congregation.

Accountability is important to both traditional organizations and thriving church organizations, but accountability in the former quickly becomes mere control, while accountability in the latter is a matter of establishing credible *trust.* Traditional organizations ask the question, "Have you done everything we asked you to do?" Thriving church organizations ask the question, "Have you done anything that we forbade you to do?" This latter form of accountability involves far more trust, because so much is left to the imaginations of the leaders. So long as they do not go beyond specified boundaries, they are free to do things that may even jar the aesthetic sensibilities or traditional practices that are unconsciously assumed by members of the board or longtime adherents of the congregation.

The second key role of the board, therefore, follows from the first. Once the board has *prescriptively* defined the point of ministry, it can and must establish *proscriptive* methods to measure success. The point of accountability is not to manage people to work harmoniously within an institution, but to ensure that the goals of ministry are actually achieved. If they are not achieved, then no matter how harmoniously leaders have functioned within the institution of the church, the board must hold them accountable for failure. If the goals are achieved, then no matter how much change has transformed the institution of the church, the board holds them accountable for success.

Clearly, the role of the board is both *prescriptive* and *proscriptive*. It manages the congregational organization by both sharpening the point of ministry (quadrant 2) and measuring success in achieving ministry results (quadrant 3). However, it is at this point that the unique character of the congregation as a spiritual community again changes the way the organization is designed.

The thriving church organization recognizes that the relationship of the church organization to its leadership is *unique*. The spiritual identity of the congregation requires it to be open to the unexpected inbreaking of the Holy Spirit, and consequently requires its leaders to share spiritual disciplines and authority for ministry. The situation of nonprofit, charitable, and service organizations is somewhat simpler. The identity and goals of the organization can be designed by the board, and they can delegate responsibility for management. John and Miriam Carver can orient the third quadrant exclusively to what they describe as "Board-CEO Linkage Policies," and the manner in which the CEO speaks for the organization can be clearly defined.[1] The CEO works within the governance policies and executive limitations set by the board, managing volunteers dedicated to the value of a specific task. It is as "simple" as that! In the Christian congregation, however, the delegation of authority, and the accountability of leaders for the success of the mission, is not so simple.

1) The official board does not shape congregational identity. Their leadership is simultaneously more practical and more visionary. They define the interface between congregational identity and emergent personal and public need, discerning in advance the "point" of ministry. They devise the practical vehicles to measure success. Yet they do not control the ultimate destiny of congregational life.

2) The Christian pastor is not a CEO. Her or his leadership is simultaneously more pervasive and more permission-giving. The pastor is "midwife" for the divine potentialities with which God has blessed each congregational participant and the corporate body as a whole. No one can really predict what ministries will be "birthed" in the environment of congregational life.

3) The lay leaders are not merely managers. Their leadership is simultaneously more mundane and more sublime. Lay leaders are themselves "commissioned ministers" seeking self-fulfillment through the exercise of God-given gifts. They must also devise budgets, create resources, and invent processes for ministry. Ultimately, they are accountable to the Holy Spirit, not to an institutional strategic plan.

These realities distinguish the congregation as a spiritual community from nonprofit, charitable, and service organizations. One is tempted to say that in Christian congregational organizations, *ownership* of the organization is broader and *opportunities* for participation are greater. Such a conclusion, however, is too weak. It would be closer to the truth to say that in a spiritual community the *claim* of the organization on the individual is far greater, and the *expectations* of the organization on the participants far more demanding. Unlike service clubs and charities, the spiritual community wants to enlist *leaders* and not merely workers. Unlike clubs and nonprofit organizations, the spiritual community wants to create *ministers* and not merely members.

In the absence of a CEO, and in the greater complexity of links and covenants of accountability, the organization must devise another way to measure the success of organizational performance.

Before we discuss how the organization thinks proscriptively in quadrants 3 and 4, it would be helpful to introduce the concept of *The Stability Triangle.*

ADMINISTRATION
TEAM

Much of the work in quadrant 3 involves measuring the success of these three teams in implementing the policies of the congregation and achieving the goals identified by the board. Together these three teams *are* the "Chief Executive Officer" of the congregation. The link between these teams and the board, and between each team with the other two teams, will be defined *pro*scriptively in the coming chapter.

In addition, authority is delegated to assorted Mission Teams and Cell Groups (and their leaders) to discern, design, and implement ministries within the basic umbrella of congregational life that is the consensus of the church. It is the growth, training, and deployment of these many and varied ministry leaders that is the fundamental business of the stability triangle—and it is the discernment, design, and implementation of ministries that is the fundamental business of congregational participants. The complete *pro*scriptive mandates of these teams and groups will be discussed in the context of quadrant 4.

Each team of the stability triangle has a missional purpose shaped by the values, beliefs, vision, and mission that is the consensus of the congregation, and which is further sharpened and focused by the board. Note that the identity of the team is defined not by an *institutional task*, but by a *missional purpose* beyond the institution itself. This contrasts significantly with traditional congregational organizations. Traditional congregational boards usually limit delegated mandates to a specific institutional task such as property management, fund-raising, Christian education, and so on. The designated units are by nature inward-looking. Even when a designated unit such as an "outreach committee" is told to be outward-looking, their task is defined purely administratively, and hedged by so many conditions dictated by the inner needs of the congregation, that the designated unit finds itself really looking inward to assess what the congregation will permit rather than looking outward to assess what the public needs.

The three teams of the stability triangle, however, are defined by *missional purpose*. Whatever the tasks they are performing, their concentration is on fulfilling their missional purpose. Indeed, these teams are empowered to adjust their tasks in order to better fulfill their missional purpose. They can stop doing certain tasks, modify how they do tasks, and even initiate new tasks, in order to pursue their missional purpose more effectively. Such freedom is possible because these teams are given *pro*scriptive mandates, rather than *pre*scriptive mandates. Once again this contrasts sharply with traditional congregational boards. Traditional boards continually involve themselves in the actual tasks of the designated unit and insist that they must review and approve the activities of the unit. In the thriving church organization, the board *never* becomes involved in the actual tasks of the three teams of the stability triangle. They define executive limitations beyond which the teams cannot go—and then free the teams to do whatever needs to be done to achieve their missional purpose. In the end, the achievement of the missional purpose, not the accomplishment of specific tasks, becomes the primary vehicle of accountability for the board to assess the performance of the team.

Such a strategy reverses the habitual behavior patterns of congregational leaders. Traditionally, congregational leaders spent more time looking inward toward the institution, than outward toward the public. Now, congregational leaders spend more time looking outward in order to accomplish their missional purpose. Even tasks traditionally associated with the inner workings of the congregation, such as property management or visitation, are now done with reference to missional purpose. If property is not utilized to achieve personal and social transformation among the public, then no matter how much energy leaders give to quality maintenance they are failing to achieve their missional purpose. If congregational members (including shut-ins, seniors, and children, and the institutionalized) are not growing spiritually in a way that results in some form of generosity that reaches out to others, then no matter how caring the visits may be, the visitors are failing to achieve their missional purpose.

The missional purpose of the Human Resources Team is *to grow and nurture gifted ministry leaders.* The team generally finds itself doing the tasks once associated with personnel and nominations committees—personality inventories, spiritual gifts discernment, and membership recruitment. Team members may well become involved in developing individual and group opportunities for spiritual growth and discernment of call.

The missional purpose of the Staff Team is *to train and equip ministry leaders for excellence.* The team generally finds itself developing programs, designing worship, training leaders, and coaching leaders once they are associated with the salaried staff of a congregation. It is important to note, however, that the staff team does not primarily *do* specific ministries of worship, outreach, or pastoral care. They may model leadership skills, mentor others doing ministries, or coach apprentices during the practice of ministry, but the primary focus of the team is on training those who have been identified as gifted and called to do the ministries.

The missional purpose of the Administration Team is *to deploy quality ministry leaders.* The team generally finds itself doing the tasks once associated with trustees, property and finance committees, office management and communication task groups, manse or parsonage committees, and other groups related to the daily management of congregational life.

The stability triangle is designed to pursue leadership growth, training, and deployment within the broader context of congregational identity and policy, and guided by the long-range and targeted mission planning of the board. These teams may, or may not, include salaried staff. If they do include staff, it is always clear that the staff role must be oriented to leadership development and deployment. Volunteers may be nominated and elected to these teams in rotating classes in what is already an ordinary congregational process. What is *not* ordinary about the process of identifying volunteers for these teams is that every person on the team must satisfy three conditions:

• First, any person elected or appointed to a team must be known to possess spiritual gifts appropriate to the missional purpose of the team. Members of the human resources team will likely have gifts in counseling, evangelism, hospitality, prayer, and other gifts associated with personal growth, spiritual discipline, and building quality relationships. Members of the staff team will likely have gifts of teaching, mentoring, and other gifts associated with motivation and planning. Members of the administration team will likely have gifts of administration, communication, helps, or other gifts associated with management of people, property, and technology. The point is that every member of the team has participated in a gifts discernment process and the congregation is confident that they are gifted for the team.

• Second, any person elected or appointed to a team must be recognized as having an authentic call to a ministry of spiritual formation, leadership training, or mission deployment. While some evidence of this may be provided by the spiritual disciplines, lifestyles, and experiences of potential team members, there is no doubt that there is a subjective component of sincerity and trust implicit here.

The point is that every member of the team perceives her or his role as a vocation rather than an office, and enjoys the confidence of the congregation to bring the congregation closer to their mission goals.

• Third, any person elected or appointed to a team must be continuously involved in both a spiritual discipline which can be articulated and shared with others, and a practical (hands-on) ministry that is clearly beneficial to the quality of life for others. Such commitment does not need to be showy, but it does need to be constantly, clearly visible.

These three conditions may seem unusual, because most traditional organizations do not recognize them. Their concern is that nominees are willing to do the work (competence being secondary), popular with other members (credibility among the church outsiders being secondary), or supported by key constituencies within the membership (celebration of diversity being secondary). The criteria of gift, calling, and spiritual discipline offers tangible assurance that nominees or appointees to these teams will be trainable, credible, and open to the diversity of the community. More than this, it models for both congregation and community the constant dynamic of growth, excellence, and ministry that is the essence of the stability triangle. The stability triangle mirrors the self-expectation of the congregation.

The Human Resources Team generally finds itself doing the work once associated with personnel and nominations committees, task groups for personality inventories and spiritual gifts discernment, and membership recruitment. The team may or may not include staff. The team may or may not delegate certain tasks (such as discernment processes for gifts and calling). *Pro*scriptive limitations on the authority of the human resources team might include:

• The Human Resources Team cannot fail to provide multiple options for disciplined spiritual growth and discernment for the variety of lifestyles and needs among the congregation and community.

• The Human Resources Team cannot recommend any leader for ministry training or deployment who is not engaged in a continuing discipline of learning and growth.
• The Human Resources Team cannot seek any change in pastoral relations, or agree to any contract that is not time-limited, without the consent of the congregation, and consultation with the denominational judicatory.
• The Human Resources Team cannot enter any contractual agreement with a person who does not share the core values of the congregation.
• The Human Resources Team cannot hire anyone to work more than half-time and fail to offer a pension and insurance benefits program.
• The Human Resources Team cannot nominate any person to hold office who has not participated in congregational processes for discernment of call and agreed to a continuing process of training.
• The Human Resources Team cannot fail to implement regular performance reviews for both salaried and volunteer church leaders.
• The Human Resources Team cannot design and utilize a grievance procedure that is not easily accessible and safe for any person within or beyond the church.
• The Human Resources Team cannot ignore, breach, or fail to communicate to volunteer or salaried leaders their rights as articulated in state human rights codes, labor relations laws, or denominational personnel guidelines.
• The Human Resources Team cannot remove any volunteer leader without offering options for further counseling and personal support, or further education and training.

The *pro*scriptive limitations for the human resources team provides clear boundaries for spiritual growth and leadership development in the church, but frees the team to use any tactic they wish within the boundaries. For example, the team may wish to add to the salaried staff a person with specific expertise in youth or seniors ministries, initiate quarterly training events to upgrade cell group leaders, utilize a specific community counseling service, or contract with a specific consultant, without the express approval of the board. Indeed, the board will not even discuss these issues, provided that the human resources team has not contradicted these limitations.

The Staff Team generally finds itself doing the work once associated with the professional clergy in regard to pastoral care, program development, outreach, and worship. The significant difference here is that this team does not *do* these ministries, but *equips others* to do them. The team will likely include salaried pastoral and music staff, plus volunteers who are also gifted and called to develop ministries of excellence. The team may or may not delegate certain tasks (such as the design of specific worship services) to other groups. *Pro*scriptive limitations on the authority of the staff team might include:

• The Staff Team cannot fail to equip any ministry called forth from the congregation through the spiritual discernment disciplines of the participants.
• The Staff Team cannot limit available coaching for lay ministers to anything less than twenty-four-hour support.
• The Staff Team cannot release any cell group shepherd into ministry without foundational training and regular opportunities to upgrade skills.
• The Staff Team cannot negotiate any contract for consultation or training without the approval of the Human Resources Team.
• The Staff Team cannot limit the possibilities for worship style or missional purpose, or deploy any worship service without clear processes to monitor and improve quality.
• The Staff Team cannot restrict curricula or learning resource options unless such resources contradict the core values, beliefs, vision, or mission of the congregation.
• The Staff Team cannot perform any ministry themselves without simultaneously mentoring an apprentice to do that ministry.

• The Staff Team cannot work independently from denominational networks of accountability and communication.

The *pro*scriptive limitations for the staff team provide clear boundaries for spiritual discernment and leadership development within the church, but free the team to use any tactic they wish within the boundaries. For example, the team may develop several tracks of worship using various musical styles, provided that each track involves tactics to pursue excellence. The team will be free to equip study groups in the church with both denominational and nondenominational resources. Although the team cannot ignore denominational networks, they are free to participate in any other professional association. The board will not even discuss these issues, provided that the team has not exceeded the boundaries.

The Administration Team generally finds itself doing the work once associated with trustees, property and finance committees, office management and communications task groups, manse or parsonage committees, and other groups related to the daily management of congregational life. This is the team that builds and monitors the annual congregational budget. The team may or may not include staff. The team may or may not further delegate certain tasks (such as annual fund-raising campaigns) to other groups. *Pro*scriptive limitations on the authority of the administration team might include:

• The Administration Team cannot say "no" to any creative idea, unless it goes beyond the boundaries of core vision, bedrock beliefs, motivating vision, or key mission that is the consensus of the congregation.
• The Administration Team cannot deploy any leader for any ministry who is not gifted, called, and trained for that ministry.
• The Administration Team cannot deploy any ministry without a concrete strategy to learn from failure.
• The Administration Team cannot carry an operating deficit into a new fiscal year.

• The Administration Team cannot seed any new ministry with more than $1,000 without the approval of the board.

• The Administration Team cannot deny the use of church property to any community group unless the activity contradicts or inhibits the core values, bedrock beliefs, motivating vision, or key mission that is the consensus of the congregation.

• The Administration Team cannot buy, sell, or lease property, or engage major capital debt, without the approval of the denominational judicatory.

• The Administration Team cannot fail to have an annual fund-raising campaign that includes every church member and invites participation from the general public.

• The Administration Team cannot invest money in any portfolio that is linked to any corporation or institution whose products or activities contradict the core values, beliefs, vision, and mission of the congregation.

• The Administration Team cannot limit liability insurance in any way that risks the mission of the congregation.

• The Administration Team cannot provide a housing allowance for staff less than the fair rental value for a suitable home for members of the church with similar family needs.

• The Administration Team cannot deploy any salaried staff person without providing the means for Internet communication.

• The Administration Team cannot use environmentally unfriendly methods or products to maintain church property.

The *pro*scriptive nature of these limitations defines clear boundaries of the administration of the church, but frees the administration team to use any tactic they choose within these limitations. For example, the team is free to experiment with any ministry, use the church hall for overnight accommodations by street people, paint the sanctuary any color, utilize any fund-raising strategy, or insure property with any agency, without the approval of the board. On the other hand, they may not be able to invest money in any way that might indirectly support armament manufacturers, genetic research, or other activities that contradict congregational values. Indeed, the board will not even discuss these issues, provided that the administration team does not contradict these clear limitations.

The third tier of limitations for the measure of success concentrates on leadership development. These link with the previous proscriptions related to excellence and authority, and also link with the continuing leadership development roles of each team of the stability triangle. The measure of success for the permission-giving organization is much more demanding for continuous growth and learning than in most traditional organizations. It is not optional, and it is not restricted to institutionalized continuing education. *Pro*scriptive limitations for leadership development might include:

• No leader (paid or volunteer) can be deployed by the church unless he or she participates in a cell group for personal and spiritual growth.

• No unspent continuing education money for training clergy or lay leaders may be left over at the end of the budget year.

• Volunteers cannot be deployed in ministry unless they have participated in a clearly articulated discernment process to identify their gifts and calling, and are committed to continuing training.

• The pastor cannot devote less than 15 percent of his or her weekly agenda to involvement with unchurched members of the public.

• No person can serve on the board who is not engaged in a discipline of study regarding demographic trends and faith formation, and who is not also active in some charitable organization beyond the church.

• The annual budget to subsidize continuing education for lay leaders cannot be less than the same budget for clergy, nor less than X percent of the total budget for property maintenance.

Such limitations apply to any and all leaders in the church. For example, no staff assistant or maintenance worker can be hired unless they, too, are willing to participate in a cell group. No one can hold an office, serve on the board or teams of the stability triangle, without meeting expectations for growth and learning. Such clear proscriptions increase the expectations for salaried and volunteer leaders, but they also increase their opportunities for growth.

The last tier of limitations for the measure of success concentrates on coordination. Such limitations establish policies broadly related to communication and calendar management, so that the ferment of ministries unleashed by the spiritual growth of the congregational participants can leave them as free as possible to fulfill their potential.

• No cell group or ministry can block the work of any other cell group or ministry within the basic boundaries of congregational life.
• No technology can be reserved for the exclusive use of a single mission unit.
• No financial or mission information can be confidential, or inaccessible for either congregational participants or the general public.
• No one can be a member of the church without receiving regular updates regarding mission work and ministry opportunities in more than one medium.
• Web sites, voice mail, and other electronic links to the public cannot remain unposted for longer than one month.
• No person, either within or beyond the congregation, should have difficulty gaining access to, understanding, or using the congregational grievance procedure or lack confidence in its safety and confidentiality.

Such limitations define board expectations, without unduly involving the board in the detailed management of running the church. This can be left to the teams of the Stability Triangle. For example, the Administration Team can build any number of creative communication networks, but they know print, audio, video, and electronic media will all be utilized so that every person receives messages in two media. The Human Resources Team can customize the grievance process to suit their cultural context, with reference to unique denominational or civil expectations, but it must be accessible and safe. The Staff Team can train leaders and develop ministries in whatever direction the Spirit leads, but must protect the autonomy of each cell even if their activity offends the aesthetic tastes or personal perspectives of another cell. So long as a mission unit does not go beyond the boundaries of core values, beliefs, vision, and mission—and does not contradict fundamental policies or limitations of the board—then it should be permitted to *do it,* and do it *with excellence.*

In the permission-giving organization of the thriving church system, quadrant 3 involves much more than the "Board-CEO Linkages" of the nonprofit organization. It really describes the methodology with which spiritually gifted, trusted leaders seek to measure the success of the congregation in the pursuit of God's vision for their organization in the world. The essential "links" of congregational life are between God and the mission field, and between God and the spiritual development of individuals, and these links are constantly changing. How, then, is success really measured in an organization which, by its very nature, is open to so many mysteries?

Traditional church organizations of the Christendom era assumed an organizational predictability akin to secular organizations. Their methodology to measure success was based on two practices:

• a planned, proportionate balance between maintenance and mission
• management by consensus involving the whole board monitoring prescribed tasks.

Maintenance of the enduring institution (property, heritage, corporate structure) was one pole of activity, while mission (local, regional, or world) was the other. The corporate structure reflected the balance, and some denominations even separated a "Board of Stewards" and a "Session." The budget also reflected this balance, and some denominations introduced stewardship envelopes allowing members simply to divide their contributions between "Operating Budget" and "Mission."

Along with a planned balance between maintenance and mission, the traditional Christendom organization relied on consensus management to monitor prescribed tasks. The entire board (and, indeed, the congregational annual meeting itself) immersed itself in management. The congregation would be satisfied with its performance if every task in every mandate had been accomplished. These seemed reasonable in the Christendom era, because the maintenance of the institution was itself an unquestioned mission of the church.

The measure of success in the traditional organization paralleled the methodology of other cultural organizations (businesses, agencies, and governments).

- *Money:* Are the assets of the organization increasing?
- *Property development:* Is the property being improved?
- *Membership:* Are there more and more contributing members?
- *Contentment:* Is there continuing harmony among the members?

The statistical yearbooks of Christendom denominations reflected this methodology to measure success. Such statistics constituted the essential information with which one congregation could be compared with another congregation.

As Christendom has died, the methodology that once measured success works no longer. The proportionate balance between maintenance and mission has been lost. Both the corporate structure and the budget have been taken over by maintenance, and this has been acceptable to declining churches because the bottom line of mission in the Christendom era was the survival of the institution. The corporate unit of the organization associated with mission finds itself looking ever more *inward.* Mission has become a matter of taking care of the paying members, so that they will be motivated to maintain the institution. If, after that, there is energy and money left over for the rest of the world, such mission is a beneficial extra. This is why efforts to rewrite traditional budgets proportionately balanced between maintenance and mission in some descriptive way miss the point of organizational change. Although they repetitively use the word "mission" to describe "mission through property," "mission through communications," "mission through salaries," the *mission field* is not given priority by the organization. "First, we fulfill our mission to maintain our institution, and second, we fulfill our mission to do anything else God wants us to do."

Permission-giving organizations in the thriving church system assume an essential and inevitable organizational *unpredictability*. In a sense, that is also what John and Miriam Mayhew Carver assume in the design of the nonprofit secular organization. The difference is that the Christian congregation knows that this essential unpredictability is not only due to rapidly changing cultural contexts, but also due to the inbreaking of divine grace, and the surprising personal and spiritual growth of people of faith. Unlike traditional Christendom organizations, the new Christian organization measures success on the basis of two different practices:

• a planned, proportionate balance between *mission* and *growth*
• management by a trusted, gifted few monitoring proscribed boundaries of action.

Mission to accomplish God's ever-changing work in the ever-changing mission field is one pole of activity, and the personal or spiritual transformation and growth of individuals is the other. "Maintenance" is merely a tactic to achieve both. It does not have any more elevated status, because the survival of the institution itself has no longer become important. The corporate structure is oriented around missional purposes to grow, train, and deploy missions. The budget is balanced between funding strategies for personal development, and funding strategies for social change.

Along with an intentional balance between mission and growth, the new Christian organization relies on management by a trusted, gifted few to monitor proscribed boundaries for action. The teams of the stability triangle have credibility by virtue of their disciplined spirituality and acquired skills, the congregation has confidence about policy by virtue of their congregational consensus building strategy and visionary board, and the management of daily institutional life can be left to designated leaders. The board and the congregation need not immerse themselves in management, but rather they can distance themselves from management and get on with the disciplines of growth and the refinement of the point of mission.

The measure of success in the permission-giving Christian organization is distinct from that of other cultural organizations.

- *Growth:* Are individuals experiencing transformation and personal or spiritual growth?
- *Leadership:* Are individuals discerning gifts and callings, and involved in ministry?
- *Participation:* Are the publics of the community all finding ways to relate to the church?
- *Social Change:* Is the world specifically different because this church exists?

The statistical yearbooks of Christendom denominations are remarkably disinterested in these measures of success, but they are the keys to the measurement of success of the new congregational organization.

One of the marks that distinguish the new Christian organization from the traditional is their remarkable readiness to risk, fail, and even institutionally die in the pursuit of growth and mission. If the institution survives after all the growth and mission have taken place, that is a beneficial extra. The good news is that in the twenty-first century, the only organizations that do survive tend to be those that prioritize growth and mission. These new Christian organizations understand that an institution is *not* a mission. It is merely a tactic.

How does a board measure success with integrity? The traditional board relies upon elected officers to measure money, property development, membership, and harmony. However, can a Christian congregation be said to be successful simply because it has experienced increasing revenues, added seven new stained-glass windows, confirmed more teenagers than buried church veterans, and made most members happy? In the post-Christendom era, certainly not. Traditional organizations that rely on such measuring rods quickly find themselves experiencing chronic operating deficits, liability insurance nightmares, membership decline, and internal conflict. Ironically, they may feel like failures—but for the wrong reasons! The real problem is that they have not grown individuals spiritually, developed ministry leadership, involved the publics of the community, or achieved any noticeable impact on society—and they have *not* tried to measure any of this.

The permission-giving Christian organization measures success by relying on spiritually authentic leaders to measure growth, leadership development, public participation, and social change. While traditional boards sought reports from their committees, the permission-giving board monitors its cell groups and mission teams. It monitors the *pro*scriptive limitations for excellence, shared authority, leadership development, and coordination. The number of people involved in personal and spiritual growth disciplines, the number and diversity of multiplying cell groups, the number of options for leadership training, the number and quality of lay volunteers deployed in ministries within and beyond the church, the demographic diversity and numbers of people linking themselves to congregational ministries, and the feedback from the public regarding the effectiveness of congregational ministries can all involve quantifiable data to measure success.

The measurement of success, however, ultimately requires more than integrity. It requires credibility. Carefully defined limitations for excellence, shared authority, leadership development, and coordination really only provide the congregation and public with some criteria with which to understand what a reasonable interpretation of success might look like. Their trust, however, is another matter. Neither congregational participants nor the general public respects *office holders*. A board that claims success in ministry may well be correct, but may well not be believed, if their interpretation is simply based on quantifiable statistics gathered by their office. People only respect true *leaders*. Such leaders are spiritually authentic individuals, recognized as individuals, and known for their personal commitments to the very things they are measuring: personal growth, shared leadership, inclusive participation, and positive social change. Only such leaders can be trusted to look behind objective statistics, and perceive accurately the nuances, trends, and qualitative realities that are the real core of a healthy, corporate, Christian lifestyle. Ultimately, trust in leadership is the most profound measure of organizational success.

How Are Leaders Deployed?

It should be clear by this time that the permission-giving organization of the thriving church system relies on a high degree of reasonable trust. God's mission for the church is targeted through the twin polarities of *accountability-productivity* and *prescriptive-proscriptive thinking*, but the relationships between the leaders of the organization are characterized by a high degree of justifiable confidence.

• The congregation trusts the board, and is confident to do so because they have clarity about the basic umbrella of congregational life (core values, bedrock beliefs, motivating vision, and key mission);

• the board trusts detailed management of the congregation to the three teams of the Stability Triangle, and is confident to do so because board members have clearly refined and articulated the point of mission and the measurement of success;

• the three teams of the stability triangle trust an infinite variety of cell groups, teams, staff, and volunteers, and are confident to do so because they have clearly defined missional purposes and expectations;

• the infinite variety of ministry leaders and teams trust that the entire organization will support their ministries with enormous sacrifice and dedication, and are confident to take great risk because they share an identity and believe in a mission that they themselves have helped define.

What strikes the observer of the permission-giving organization at work is the strength of its mutual support and trust. This trust is not naive. It is founded on the mutual respect congregational participants have for one another and the spiritual authenticity of everyone in leadership. Everyone is engaged in disciplines that build faith. Everyone is committed to personal and spiritual growth. Everyone is dedicated to a quest for excellence. Everyone is convinced that the mission of the congregation is worth dying for.

Once again, the contrast with traditional congregational organizations is remarkable. Since traditional congregations are often consciously or unconsciously modeled after other cultural organizations, trust does not fundamentally stamp the relationships between leaders. The almost universal *pre*scriptive thinking of the organization creates a climate in which no one is really allowed to do anything unpredictable. Endless reports, reviews, and liaisons reduce the freedom of any leader to take a risk. The harmony that is created is a watchful harmony. It is a harmony built upon the confidence that every single leader knows everything that is going on and is satisfied that nothing might undermine the authority of her or his office. Such fundamental distrust erupts into conflict as the traditional congregational organization declines and experiences financial and membership crises.

• The congregation distrusts the board, because they do not have clarity about their shared core values, beliefs, vision, and mission;
• the board distrusts committees and staff, because they do not have clarity about the point of mission or the measure of success;
• the staff and volunteers distrust the entire organization, because they do not share ownership for the identity and mission of the church, and do not believe that the organization will support them in taking any significant personal risk.

What strikes the observer of the traditional organization at work is the number of meetings required in order to get anything done. This is called "consensus management," and it is really a form of control. Everyone shares responsibility for the smallest decision, and no decision can be made unless there is near unanimity of opinion. The congregation is united, not in a shared spiritual discipline, but in allegiance to a tradition and obedience to a hierarchy. The trouble is that in the twenty-first century, fewer and fewer people find tradition and office to be worth dying for.

Close examination of the organizational chart reveals that there are only two places in the organization where consensus is important—and in those two places it is absolutely crucial. Consensus is crucial in quadrant 1 to define, and regularly refine, the basic umbrella of congregational life. This consensus involves the entire congregation. Consensus is also crucial in quadrant 4 to discern, design, and implement missions. This consensus involves small groups and teams.

Management, on the other hand, is specifically associated with quadrants 2 and 3. The board does it by refining the point of mission and identifying key expectations for the congregation and all its leaders, and by defining the executive limitations which will guide the work of the Stability Triangle and any other mission teams of the church. The three teams of the stability triangle do it by growing, training, and deploying ministries. Once the ministries are deployed, however, the actual work of the ministry is really not part of the business of the board. Aside from ensuring that broad limitations are not breached, and that the overall target of mission is addressed, the board does not care *how* the ministry gets done.

Control is an issue for both traditional and permission-giving organizations, but for very different reasons. Traditional boards struggle to exercise control *over others*. Permission-giving boards struggle to exercise *self-control*. The traditional organization devises overlapping layers of supervision to ensure that the enthusiasm of staff and volunteers does not lead them to do anything crazy. Supervisors are always intruding into the detailed mission work of others. The permission-giving organization is disciplined to constantly guard itself from interferring unnecessarily, and to restrict its work to policy formation and the measurement of overall success in the mission field. The permission-giving board is trying to *let go* of as much as possible, entrusting mission to the initiative of volunteer entrepreneurs.

In the permission-giving organization of the thriving church system, leadership is more important than office. Personal integrity and credibility are more significant than nominations and appointment processes, because mission cannot succeed in the twenty-first century without transparent respect for the spiritual authenticity of individual congregational leaders. This does not mean that nominations, elections, and appointments do not occur; it does mean that there is considerably more concern that those who are nominated, elected, or appointed clearly have the integrity and credibility needed for the success of the congregational mission. Institutional experience, long-standing membership, related skills from other organizations or businesses, or mere availability and willingness are really not relevant. Clarity of mission, spiritual discipline, and commitment to growth are the real keys for successful leadership.

In the permission-giving organization of the thriving church system, freedom is more important than procedure. Each unit of mission has freedom to discern, design, and implement missions within the boundaries of the basic umbrella of congregational life, and within the executive limitations established by the board. Procedures to coordinate and evaluate work can be dramatically simplified, because performance is primarily evaluated by peer support within the team and continuing leadership development in cooperation with the stability triangle. Mission can be speedy, adaptable, relevant, and effective because each mission unit is trusted with profound autonomy.

The practicalities for *turning the laity loose* for mission are largely described in section 2. There I compare the traditional and permission-giving organizations using the contrasting images of training dogs and raising rabbits. But here, as I describe the theoretical framework of proscriptive limitations which allows the laity to be turned loose, another metaphor comes to mind. The deployment of laity for missions of the church resembles a soda bottle that is shaken and eventually erupts into the open air.

• The bubbles contained in the soda bottle represent the many, diverse ministries born from the spiritual discipline of the congregation.
• The bottle itself represents the clear boundaries of values, beliefs, vision, and mission that is the consensus of the congregation.
• The bottle cap represents the board that has the motivation and courage to let go control, provided that the mission God has entrusted to the church is accomplished.
• The shaking of the bottle occurs as three forces interact: the rapid change of culture, the disciplined spiritual growth of the people, and the intervention of divine grace.
• The eventual eruption of all those bubbles represents the multitude of missions that are released—an eruption that appears to be chaotic, but which also has a specific target.

Like all metaphors, this one does not entirely capture the performance of the permission-giving organization. The pressure released for mission is not a onetime experience, but a constant and continuing eruption of gifted, called, equipped, and sent leaders. The bubbles erupting from the organization are not random, but aimed at achieving the peculiar mission goal which is their target. Finally, unlike the discarded bottle cap, the board continues to play a key role to define mission and measure success. The soda bottle metaphor does make one important point. Turning the laity loose is a messy business. It is not a carefully regulated trickle of water; it soaks the mission field thoroughly.

Authority that is centralized in the CEO of a nonprofit, charitable, or service organization is diffused in the Christian congregation. A variety of people (salaried and volunteer) all share some form of authority. The freedom to discern, design, and implement mission, and then evaluate performance, is made possible by the proscriptive boundaries designed by the congregation. Job descriptions and mandates are usually designed in partnership between those leaders who are gifted, called and trained to do mission, and the teams of the stability triangle. Such job descriptions and mandates are shorter and more pointed than those of more traditional organizations.

• They minimize reports. Initiative is entrusted to the leader or leadership team, it is not dependent on the approval of those beyond the mission unit.
• They minimize meetings. Multiple ministries of parallel purpose are valued, and redundancy of action is no longer feared.
• They minimize bureaucracy. Mission units are simply obligated not to get in one another's way, not to work together in any prescribed manner.

The autonomy of the mission unit is given the highest priority, provided that the autonomous mission unit helps the congregation address the mission field targeted by the board, performs with constantly upgraded excellence, and functions within specific limitations of action that reflect the identity of the congregation. The unit is free to decide what needs to be done, how to do it, when to do it, and in what partnerships within or beyond the congregation that best ensure success.

Quadrant 4

The deployment of leaders in quadrant 4 will not only be extremely diverse, but the job description or mandate for each ministry leader or mission unit will be uniquely customized for the congregation's identity. However, to illustrate the proscriptive limitations that form these job descriptions and mandates, let us build some examples. Remember: This is only possible *after* the work of the other three quadrants has been accomplished. We will build job descriptions for the pastor, music coordinator, church secretary, and cell group shepherds, and mandates for a cell group and mission team.

The first step is to define the missional purpose. Remember that mission in the permission-giving organization of the thriving church emerges from below, it is not handed down from above. In other words, it emerges not from the strategic planning of a hierarchy of leaders, but from the disciplined spiritual growth of the congregational participants. Out of the personal and spiritual growth of the people, God calls individuals into mission. The role of the Stability Triangle is to help people define the nature of their calling and the point of their mission.

In the case of the call of a new pastor, and the formation of the job description that will be the basis of the search and interview process, the denominational judicatory may also play an important role. Judicatory leaders working with permission-giving congregational organizations must be aware, however, that standardized job descriptions will not work. The job description will be uniquely customized for the identity of the congregation. Traditionally organized congregations do not need any clarity about their mission, because the standard job description is really designed to guide pastors to fill only an institutional role. Permission-giving congregational organizations must have extraordinary clarity about their core values, beliefs, vision, and mission before they can even think of calling a pastor. Moreover, this consensus cannot be imposed by the denominational judicatory but must emerge from the spiritual discipline of the people.

The definition of missional purpose, rather than institutional role, lies at the heart of the job descriptions and mandates of the permission-giving organization. Every job description and mandate aims the task or ministry toward a specific mission result in keeping with the overall mission refined by the official board. This mission result *always* goes beyond the congregation to address the diverse publics of the community.

Pastor	Music Coordinator	Church Secretary
Missional Purpose	*Missional Purpose*	*Missional Purpose*
To motivate, coach, and train laity to grow in faith and live in Christian mission.	To design options and develop leaders for indigenous worship with music relevant to the publics within the mission field.	To facilitate ministries to accomplish their purpose, and help people to find their ministry.

Cell Group Shepherd	Cell Group	Mission Team
Missional Purpose	*Missional Purpose*	*Missional Purpose*
To coach people to build quality relationships, grow in faith, and discern calling.	To discover joy through our shared affinity, in good friendships and experience of God's love, which blesses others.	To better the quality of life for *these people* by doing *this service* and articulating *this message.*

Great care should be taken to state briefly and clearly the missional purpose of any leader or ministry. This is not an easy task. The stability triangle and the individuals called into ministry will need to link their missional purpose to the refined mission identified by the board, and consider how they can together measure their success. Missional purposes are understood as *proscriptive limitations* because in essence they state that "this specific purpose, *and none other,* is the mission of this person or ministry." This protects the leader or ministry from being intentionally or unintentionally diverted from their real purpose. Both the congregation as an institution and the general public will find it much more difficult to manipulate a church leader or ministry for other ends.

The second step is to define the boundaries for continuous learning, or the minimum methodology required to pursue excellence. Remember that the permission-giving organization will also need to provide funding in the budget adequate to these requirements. The individual mission leaders called into ministries will need to identify strengths, weaknesses, and hidden destructive habits that will positively or negatively influence the outcome of the mission. Of course, this is only possible because the congregation itself is regularly discerning strengths, weaknesses, and hidden corporate addictions that can influence their joint mission.

Pastor *Missional Purpose*	Music Coordinator *Missional Purpose*	Church Secretary *Missional Purpose*
To motivate, coach, and train laity to grow in faith and live in Christian mission.	To design options and develop leaders for indigenous worship with music relevant to the publics within the mission field.	To facilitate ministries to accomplish their purpose, and help people to find their ministry.
Continuous Learning	*Continuous Learning*	*Continuous Learning*
1. Cannot have unspent continuing education money at the end of the year.	1. Cannot have unspent continuing education money at the end of the year.	1. Cannot have unspent continuing education money at the end of the year.
2. Cannot spend less than 15 percent of work week among the unchurched public.	2. Cannot receive less than one hour of music training for every four hours of music teaching per week.	2. Cannot receive less than twenty hours training per year on computer related technology.
3. Cannot do more than 50 percent of formal continuing education in denominationally sponsored programs.	3. Cannot devote more than 50 percent formal music training to classical music and traditional hymnody.	3. Cannot do less than one formal training event per year in interpersonal relationships and crisis management.
4. Cannot fail to be in a cell group for personal growth.	4. Cannot be developing skills on fewer than three instruments.	4. Cannot fail to be in a cell group for personal growth.
And so on...	**And so on...**	**And so on...**

Cell Group Shepherd *Missional Purpose*	Cell Group *Missional Purpose*	Mission Team *Missional Purpose*
To coach people to build quality relationships, grow in faith, and discern calling.	To discover joy through our shared affinity, in good friendships and experience of God's love, that blesses others.	To better the quality of life for *these people* by doing *this service* and articulating *this message*.
Continuous Learning	*Continuous Learning*	*Continuous Learning*
1. Cannot lead a group without participating in the foundation training seminar of the church.	1. Cannot have a group spiritual discipline that excludes regular participation in weekly worship.	1. Cannot have a spiritual discipline that excludes weekly worship.
2. Cannot miss any of four upgrade seminars each year for any reason other than illness.	2. Cannot meet without reference to scripture in study or discussion.	2. Cannot work without a discipline of prayer and Bible study.
3. Cannot fail to participate in an ongoing mutual support for cell group shepherds.	3. Cannot meet indefinitely, or close the group without an individual assessment of future directions.	3. Cannot work without an intentional plan for skills development.
And so on ...	**And so on ...**	**And so on ...**

In section 2, it will become clearer that growth and learning in the permission-giving organization is a never-ending process that I compare to a modern "dance" involving constantly rotating partners. Congregational participants move at their own speed between personal growth opportunities, discernment opportunities, and practical mission opportunities. In other words, individuals will come to a place where they are as self-aware and spiritually knowledgeable as they can be at that given time—then move to processes through which they discover how God wants them to put their self-awareness and knowledge to good use—and then in the working experience of the mission field in the real world discover questions about themselves and God they never had before and which need to be addressed. And then the cycle starts all over again.

The third step is to define the boundaries for action. In part, these boundaries will reflect the policies identified in quadrants 1 and 2. If the congregation has developed these policies with care, it will be easier to identify the proscribed limits for action of any leader or group. In greater part, boundaries for action will simply reflect the management principles that the stability triangle thinks are necessary to measure the success of the ministries being released. The board and the stability triangle will need to exercise self-control. The more they intrude upon the work of the leader or group, the more they risk undermining motivation and creativity.

Remember that for clergy, the boundaries for action may also be shaped by denominational requirements. Special features of denominational polity should have been reflected in the policies identified in quadrants 1 and 2, and often touch upon issues related to sacraments, theological agreements, or pastoral care. The most radical change for the role of clergy in the permission-giving organization is that the missional purpose has shifted their energy from *doing* ministry to *equipping* for ministry. Ministry happens in the permission-giving organization through diverse *teams* of staff and volunteers, not through individuals supervised by committees.

Keep in mind that every congregational context will be unique. The limits of action suggested here are not intended to be exhaustive or comprehensive, and some may not be relevant. These are intended to provide a guide and inspiration for congregational planners. The one limitation that will be a constant is the very first: No leader or group can go beyond the boundaries of values, beliefs, vision, and mission that are the consensus of the congregation.

Pastor *Missional Purpose*	**Music Coordinator** *Missional Purpose*	**Church Secretary** *Missional Purpose*
To motivate, coach, and train laity to grow in faith and live in Christian mission.	To design options and develop leaders for indigenous worship with music relevant to the publics within the mission field.	To facilitate ministries to accomplish their purpose, and help people to find their ministry.
Continuous Learning	*Continuous Learning*	*Continuous Learning*
1. Cannot have unspent continuing education money at the end of the year.	1. Cannot have unspent continuing education money at the end of the year.	1. Cannot have unspent continuing education money at the end of the year.
2. Cannot spend less than 15 percent of work week among the unchurched public.	2. Cannot receive less than one hour of music training for every four hours of music teaching per week.	2. Cannot receive less than twenty hours training per year on computer related technology.
3. Cannot do more than 50 percent of formal continuing education in denominationally sponsored programs.	3. Cannot devote more than 50 percent formal music training to classical music and traditional hymnody.	3. Cannot do less than one formal training event per year in interpersonal relationships and crisis management.
4. Cannot fail to be in a cell group for personal growth.	4. Cannot be developing skills on fewer than three instruments.	4. Cannot fail to be in a cell group for personal growth.
Limits of Action 1. Cannot go beyond the bounds of values, beliefs, vision, and mission that are the consensus of the congregation.	*Limits of Action* 1. Cannot go beyond the bounds of values, beliefs, vision, and mission that are the consensus of the congregation.	*Limits of Action* 1. Cannot go beyond the bounds of values, beliefs, vision, and mission that are the consensus of the congregation.

2. Cannot accept fees for weddings and funerals for church members, or conduct either without an apprentice.	2. Cannot accept fees for wedding or funeral for church members, or work without an apprentice.	2. Cannot manage the office without training opportunities for volunteers.
3. Cannot celebrate Eucharist less than once per week, or offer the sacrament to the housebound or institutionalized less than once per month.	3. Cannot design music without teamwork to focus message and include drama or dance.	3. Cannot spend more than $500 for supplies without consulting the Administration Team.
4. Cannot visit home or hospital without an apprentice.	4. Cannot use organ more than 50 percent of the time.	4. Cannot allow voice-mail to have less than weekly update.
5. Cannot offer personal counseling beyond three sessions.	5. Cannot use the same choir or ensemble for more than one track of worship.	5. Cannot make fewer than two work stations available to volunteers.
And so on...	**And so on...**	**And so on...**

These limits of action for the pastor, music coordinator, and church secretary are by no means comprehensive, but they illustrate the point of proscriptive thinking. Both the freedom and responsibility of staff become apparent and measurable.

• The pastor and music coordinator can develop any wedding and funeral policy they choose, provided that fees are not charged for church members and they train volunteers to share in these ministries.

• The pastor can offer personal counseling using any resource, strategy, or focus she or he chooses, but cannot engage in long-term counseling that might divert energy from the missional purpose to equip *others* to do such ministries.

• The music coordinator can use any instruments or musical styles appropriate to the mission field, but cannot rely on traditional organ music more than 50 percent of the time.

• The music coordinator can develop any instrumental or vocal groups they wish, and budget to equip and train them, even if these groups happen to offend the aesthetic tastes of members of the board, but these groups cannot be used in more than one track of worship at any given time—and of course the music chosen cannot reflect values or beliefs that go beyond the consensus of the congregation.

• The church secretary can manage the office in any way that is found to be effective, provided that he or she equips workstations for volunteers and coaches them in their work.

• The church secretary can buy whatever office equipment he or she thinks best, provided that no more than $500 is spent without approval.

Careful thought by these leaders in cooperation with the teams of the stability triangle will obviously refine the perimeters of their work. The point is that leaders have greater freedom to work quickly, flexibly, and responsibly, and the teams of the stability triangle need not become burdened with relatively trivial management decisions related to the implementation of any given ministry.

The same strategy to define the limits of action can be applied to volunteer job descriptions and group mandates. Volunteers are allowed greater powers of initiative, and have clear performance criteria with which to measure their work. In the end, volunteers have more self-esteem and ownership for the overall mission of the church. They readily accept much higher expectations for ministry, and are willing to make more sacrifices of time and energy to implement ministry, because their spiritual calling has been respected and their training has earned them trust.

Cell Group Shepherd	Cell Group	Mission Team
Missional Purpose	*Missional Purpose*	*Missional Purpose*

To coach people to build quality relationships, grow in faith, and discern calling.

Continuous Learning

1. Cannot lead a group without participating in the foundation training seminar of the church.

2. Cannot miss any of four upgrade seminars each year for any reason other than illness.

3. Cannot fail to participate in an ongoing mutual support for cell group shepherds.

Action Limitations

1. Cannot go beyond the bounds of values, beliefs, vision, and mission that are the consensus of the congregation.

2. Cannot lead a group without mentoring a

To discover joy through our shared affinity, in good friendships and experience of God's love, that blesses others.

Continuous Learning

1. Cannot have a group spiritual discipline that excludes regular participation in weekly worship.

2. Cannot meet without reference to scripture in study or discussion.

3. Cannot meet indefinitely, or close the group without an individual assessment of future directions.

Action Limitations

1. Cannot go beyond the bounds of values, beliefs, vision, and mission that are the consensus of the congregation.

2. Cannot have more than twelve in the

To better the quality of life for *these people* by doing *this service* and articulating *this message.*

Continuous Learning

1. Cannot have a spiritual discipline that excludes weekly worship.

2. Cannot work without a discipline of prayer and Bible study.

3. Cannot work without an intentional plan for skills development.

Action Limitations

1. Cannot go beyond bounds of values, beliefs, vision, and mission that are the consensus of the congregation.

2. Cannot work without a strategic plan to

potential group leader.	group without forming another group.	address the mission.
3. Cannot fail to coach both faith and relationship building.	3. Cannot meet without a trained cell group leader present.	3. Cannot meet without a trained team leader.
4. Cannot lead a group without a personal strategy of prayer for each participant.	4. Cannot meet without a signed covenant for building friendship, faith, and a ministry result.	4. Cannot work without a plan for simultaneous beneficial social service and articulate faith witness.
5. Cannot change a group covenant without consensus.	5. Cannot meet without a specific timetable to close and help participants to choose options.	5. Cannot enter into debt without approval.
And so on...	**And so on...**	**And so on...**

Once again, these limits of action are not intended to be comprehensive. Unlike traditional organizations, which can impose a prescribed form of activity upon any committee or group, the permission-giving organization must customize the limits of action for every ministry. These limitations will be shaped by the policies of the church, but even more significantly by the specific affinity or mission which God calls forth from the people.

In our book *Growing Spiritual Redwoods*, Bill Easum and I described the cellular character of the permission-giving organization as a tension between freedom and covenant. Participants were free to think, speak, and consult, but only within covenants of mutual affirmation and acceptance. They could exercise their imaginations, make decisions, and take action, but only within covenants for learning and cooperation. They could share honestly, care compassionately, and critique objectively, but only within covenants of equal voice, shared values, and common missional purpose. The limits of action suggested in the foregoing boxes illustrate this tension.

• The cell group shepherd can use any resource and implement any group process, provided that there is a strategy for growth and prayer and participants can all share equally and honestly.

• Cell groups can share any affinity imaginable and attempt any mission result, provided that this is all done by consensus, with a clear covenant for time and place, and purpose, and guided by a trained leader.

• Mission teams can address any task or form any mission partnership—even if it seems "crazy" to individual members of the board—provided that they do not engage any debt without the approval of the Administration Team, that they develop a ministry plan that both concretely improves quality of life and witnesses to faith, and that the plan does not lead them beyond the core values, beliefs, vision, and mission of the congregation.

Once again, careful consideration by leaders, groups, and teams, in cooperation with the teams of the stability triangle, will obviously refine the perimeters of their work. The point is that the mission which emerges from the spiritual discipline of the congregation can be implemented quickly, flexibly, and responsibly, and the teams of the stability triangle need not become burdened with relatively trivial management decisions related to the implementation of any given ministry.

The fourth step is to define the limitations of confidentiality and personal safety. Since the thriving church system integrates personal development and action, and emphasizes quality interpersonal relationships as part of holistic relationship with God, the organization must protect the sacredness of the internal spiritual journey and the health of personal relationships. Even traditional organizations have found it necessary to articulate limitations for clergy and counselors with proscriptions not to violate the sacred confessional or reveal the content of counseling. The permission-giving organization must go even farther, however; it must be even more careful about all aspects of congregational life. Only then can they assure both congregational participants and the general public that they are *permission-giving*—but not *permissive*.

The core values identified in quadrant 1, the mission results refined in quadrant 2, and the standards of excellence identified in quadrant 3 have most likely all addressed the expectation for confidentiality and personal safety. Now, however, the organization can specify *how* confidentiality and safety can be protected in an environment of responsible risk-taking. It may seem odd that confidentiality and personal safety should be defined as *proscriptions*. After all, shouldn't the confidentiality of our conversations and the safety of our relationships always be *guaranteed?* A little reflection, however, reveals that the nature of growth and mission in itself places limits on the degree to which we can, and should, be protected. Risk is an inherent part of growth and mission. Information, for example, also needs to be transparent to the general public, and too much secrecy undermines credibility. Personal growth in faith and relationships, for example, also needs to be allowed the option to fail, experience pain, experience forgiveness, and learn from mistakes. In other words, there are boundaries to confidentiality and safety necessary for healthy growth and mission.

Pastor *Missional Purpose*	**Music Coordinator** *Missional Purpose*	**Church Secretary** *Missional Purpose*
To motivate, coach, and train laity to grow in faith and live in Christian mission.	To design options and develop leaders for indigenous worship with music relevant to the publics within the mission field.	To facilitate ministries to accomplish their purpose, and help people to find their ministry.
Continuous Learning 1, 2, 3, and so on…	*Continuous Learning* 1, 2, 3, and so on…	*Continuous Learning* 1, 2, 3, and so on…

Limits of Action 1, 2, 3, 4, 5, and so on…	*Limits of Action* 1, 2, 3, 4, 5, and so on…	*Limits of Action* 1, 2, 3, 4, 5, and so on…
Confidentiality and Safety Limitations	*Confidentiality and Safety Limitations*	*Confidentiality and Safety Limitations*
1. Cannot reveal confidences shared in context of sacraments. 2. Cannot reveal nature or direction of formal counseling with clients. 3. Cannot permit entrance or exit to pastor's office other than via the office of the secretary. 4. Cannot share visitation conversations with anyone other than the pastoral care teams of the church. 5. Cannot reveal the financial contributions of church members.	1. Cannot tutor minors without knowledge and cooperation of a parent or guardian. 2. Cannot share personal issues regarding choir/band members with anyone without their permission. 3. Cannot share personal issues regarding choir/band members with anyone other than the pastoral care teams of church. 4. Cannot refer anyone for counseling without the advice of the pastor.	1. Cannot release name, address, or telephone number of any participant beyond the church without their written consent. 2. Cannot store financial records of giving in a computer hard drive or unsecured cabinet. 3. Cannot allow anyone to wait in an isolated room or hall. 4. Cannot let the building entrance be unobserved. 5. Cannot reveal the pastor's counseling or visitation list.
And so on…	**And so on…**	**And so on…**

Both congregations and professional associations have lists of Do's and Don'ts to guide interaction with the public, and these can help the congregation define the limitations of confidentiality and safety. A proscriptive list, however, is ultimately more helpful. It forces the organization to identify their expectations very concretely, and it ultimately becomes a more flexible tool to address the unexpected diversity of everyday congregational life.

• The pastor can freely share all financial information related to the church, except information related to the specific givings of members. Congregational participants can expect the pastor to share health and family issues emerging among congregational participants with other members of the staff team, unless the participant specifically asks the pastor not to do so. Conversations in the supermarket can be shared to illustrate a sermon; conversations in the context of a sacrament cannot.

• The music coordinator can feel free to share concerns within the staff team, but not with the choir. He or she can tutor a child or teen in the community, within or beyond the church, but only with the knowledgeable support of a parent.

• The church secretary can provide a membership list to a stewardship committee, but not to the marketing representative of a Bible society. He or she can take a coffee break anytime, provided someone else observes who comes and goes from the building. Needy people can seek help from the food bank in the building, but they cannot approach other guests waiting for the pastor and ask for money.

The diversity and unexpectedness of daily congregational life will of course lead to many situations that require creativity that is mature, compassionate, and sensitive. Traditional organizations rely on generalized prescriptions for "common sense," "mature behavior," or "Christian attitude" to address the numerous gaps of ambiguity, plus a bureaucracy to gain approval before taking any action. This is too vague and too slow for the rapidly changing mission field of the twenty-first century. Permission-giving organizations rely on the intentional, continuous learning and cell group experiences of their leaders to provide them with the ability to react appropriately in ambiguous situations.

Similar confidentiality and safety limitations can be identified for volunteer leaders and groups. This significantly raises the expectation level for the personal performance of members of the board, the teams of the stability triangle, leaders of cell groups and mission teams, and all participants in the congregation. Confidentiality and safety are part of the environment of the organization as a whole, not just for the staff and elected volunteers.

Cell Group Shepherd	Cell Group	Mission Team
Missional Purpose	*Missional Purpose*	*Missional Purpose*
To coach people to build quality relationships, grow in faith, and discern calling.	To discover joy through our shared affinity, in good friendships and experience of God's love, that blesses others.	To better the quality of life for *these people* by doing *this service* and articulating *this message.*
Continuous Learning 1, 2, 3, and so on…	*Continuous Learning* 1, 2, 3, and so on…	*Continuous Learning* 1, 2, 3, and so on…
Limits of Action 1, 2, 3, 4, 5, and so on…	*Limits of Action* 1, 2, 3, 4, 5, and so on…	*Limits of Action* 1, 2, 3, 4, 5, and so on…
Confidentiality and Safety Limitations	*Confidentiality and Safety Limitations*	*Confidentiality and Safety Limitations*
1. Cannot reveal personal, relational, or spiritual growth matters pertaining to group members, except with pastor or staff team.	1. Cannot discuss personal, relational, or spiritual growth matters pertaining to group members beyond the group without permission of individual.	1. Cannot discuss personal, relational, or spiritual growth matters pertaining to members beyond the group without permission of the individual.

2. Cannot date any member of their group.	2. Cannot welcome new members to the group without providing easy, safe accessibility to the place of meeting.	2. Cannot deploy mission team members in the community in fewer than pairs.
3. Cannot arrange group covenants without appropriate child care approved by group members.	3. Cannot meet at night without arranging safe transportation home for every group member.	3. Cannot do labor with any less than full compliance with construction safety standards.
And so on...	**And so on...**	**And so on...**

Volunteer leaders and group participants now have greater clarity about the limits for their behavior. They may well liken such limitations to the proscriptions implied by the Ten Commandments, which generally governed the safety of individuals in the community of Israel, within the umbrella of values, beliefs, vision, and mission that was their clear consensus.

• Cell group shepherds know that they can discuss a group study or project in the supermarket, but can only discuss personal growth with the congregation's staff team. They also know they are free to date anyone they choose, except a member of their cell group.

• Cell group participants know that discussing the personal, relational, or spiritual growth of another, without permission, is unacceptable gossip. They also know that wherever people come from to attend, and however they choose to travel, the group has a responsibility to one another before and after the actual meeting time.

• Mission teams know that they can send people into the world in any number or configuration, but individuals cannot be sent alone even if it is only to put up posters in store windows. They also know that renovation work in the homes of the elderly, or automobile repair for the poor, cannot be done without hard hats, safety goggles, and whatever else professional safety codes require.

Volunteer leaders are also involved in continuous learning and cell groups, some of which is oriented to human relations. In other words, everyone in the congregation is aware of higher expectations for confidentiality and safety than ever before, and this gives the unchurched public confidence that they can participate in the congregation without fear of manipulation or abuse.

Generally speaking, *proscriptive thinking about accountability* and *proscriptive thinking about productivity* are all about setting limitations which define the boundaries beyond which staff and volunteers cannot go, but within which they are free to design and implement mission however they choose. Nonprofit, charitable, or service organizations will rely on a CEO to manage institutional life and direct volunteers. Christian congregations will rely on a simple Stability Triangle composed of three teams of staff and volunteers to manage institutional life, and cell groups or mission teams to implement the various ministries of the congregation. The teams of the stability triangle, and the assorted cell groups and mission teams that do ministry, are each granted significant autonomy within a framework of limitations. The nonprofit organization has the relatively "simple" task of linking with a CEO and recruiting volunteers to do very specific tasks. In a sense, there is one CEO and one basic "ministry." The Christian congregation has the relatively "complex" task of linking with management teams, and facilitating volunteers to give birth to the callings that God calls forth from them. In a sense, there is one mission, three vehicles to manage that mission, and innumerable ministries.

At the end of the foregoing chapter, on *prescriptive* thinking, I said that the art of governance for the Christian congregation is to develop policies for accountability and productivity which together shape an environment in which creative ministries can emerge. Now I can add that the art of governance for the Christian congregation is also to develop limitations for accountability and productivity which together guide the creative ministries that emerge, flourish, fade, and are replaced by more relevant ministries.

Earlier I used the metaphor of the birthing room to describe the permission-giving organization in *prescriptive thinking*, and the metaphor of the soda bottle to describe the organization in *proscriptive thinking*. The key to understanding both metaphors is to perceive the element of unpredictability or constant change implied in each. Traditional organizations pride themselves on their stability, tradition, and constancy. The organization looks and functions much the same today as it did one hundred years ago, and it is designed to look and function much the same way one hundred years from now. They understand themselves to be more like a *business franchise* than a *birthing room*, and more like a *fine wine* than a *soda bottle*. The business franchise of a denomination is basically the same anywhere in the world, producing the same product, in the same way, with the same technology. The fine wine of a denomination tastes best when delivered from the dustiest bottle on the shelf, in which the wine has slowly fermented in the wine cellar. Change is an enemy of both.

The death of Christendom and the emergence of the fast-paced mission field has changed the way Christian organizations address and deliver the gospel. The most important thing to know about birthing rooms is that they are noisy, messy, demanding, and have unpredictable outcomes which will affect the world in unpredictable ways. God alone knows what this ministry, born to these people, will ultimately do in the world. The most important thing to know about soda bottles is that *they are shaken*. Once the liquid is released, God alone knows who might get wet.

Earlier I said that the *prescriptive thinking* of the congregation helps congregation and public answer immediately, and with extraordinary clarity, these two questions:

Who in the name of God **are** *we?*
What in God's name are we **doing** *here?*

Now the *proscriptive thinking* of the congregation helps both congregation and public answer two more questions constantly, quickly, and with equal clarity:

Is God's world **really any different** *because we exist?*
How in God's name are we **to make real** *the realm of God?*

Having moved through all four quadrants of the organizational chart, the congregation can state succinctly what they are about.

"We are the people who live daily by these values, beliefs, vision, and mission, who are willing to sacrifice this much to achieve these results, who are determined to achieve those results to the best of our ability, and who are prepared to trust people to take the following risks for the sake of the gospel."

— 4 —

A Picture of the New
Organization

As with all snapshots, the perspective of the observer is distorted because the action is frozen in time. Traditional organizations tend to be true "snapshots" of organizational reality, because they celebrate the stability and constancy of organizational life. The picture of the organization tomorrow will be essentially the same as today's. Indeed, in the narthex of traditional church buildings one may often find photographs of the board dating back fifty years or more, and in each picture the board is posed in the same way, the photo is matted and framed in the same way, and the pictures may even be fixed by screws to the wall. This presentation is no accident. It reflects the obsession with *pre*scriptive thinking that is assumed by the congregation. Permission-giving organizations, however, experience constant change. I like to use the "life philosopher" Henri Bergson's metaphor, describing them as having a "cinematographic character." The snapshot of tomorrow will not be the same as the snapshot of today, but they will be linked by a flow of movement. Organizational *change* is the real constant.

The basic umbrella of congregational life is always evolving. The congregation continually refines their consensus about core values, bedrock beliefs, motivating vision, and key mission. Not only does God intervene in the life of the congregation to challenge them with new (and perhaps unsettling!) self-understanding, but God can carry them away in unexpected new directions. Moreover, the congregation *expects* that God will do this! That is the reason adult disciplines for spiritual formation are prized so highly. They may not know where they will go, but they do know that God will be sweeping them off their feet.

The board and the Stability Triangle are constantly reprioritizing their work. Their routines are always being adjusted as the changing mission field is interpreted, the mission focused, and the financial and volunteer energies of the congregation redeployed. This is not to say that there are no long-term plans. Indeed, long-range planning is as vital to the permission-giving organization as routine was to the traditional organization. Planning, however, assumes that ministry mapping will involve constant discovery. Strategies and tactics will change, some failure will be inevitable and instructive, and only the discipline of learning from mistakes will go on forever.

The cell groups and mission teams are constantly changing. Permanency is not highly valued, and no one expects that any group or mission team will survive forever. No energy will be given to recruit people to a denominational women's group, for example, simply to keep the women's group alive. As mission is revealed from "the bottom up" through spiritual disciplines of the church participants, groups and teams will continually be born, thrive, and die, so that new groups and teams can be born.

The staff configuration is always being modified. Staffing for the permission-giving organization is a *tactic,* not an *identity.* As the changing mission field is interpreted and the mission is refined, staffing will vary accordingly. The role of staff is to motivate, coach, and equip *others* to do ministry. As opportunities emerge to be seized, different leadership skills may be required. Therefore, staff may need to be retrained and redeployed, or different staff may be needed altogether.

The Organizational Calendar

The organizational chart of four quadrants is itself a dynamic movement of activity. It has a "cinematographic character." Let's look at what the various parts of the organization are actually doing through the year.

The Annual Congregational Meeting

The primary purpose of the annual congregational meeting is to regularly *define, refine,* and *celebrate* the basic umbrella of congregational life. In my book *Moving Off the Map: A Field Guide to Changing the Congregation,* the process described to obtain consensus around core values, bedrock beliefs, motivating vision, and key mission suggests the processes surrounding the annual meeting. Prior to, or during, the annual meeting there may well be focus groups, interview teams, marketing surveys, and listening-prayer triads, which together test the reality of the core values and open the congregation to the leading of the Spirit. Values, beliefs, vision, and mission will change over time as the mission field changes and newcomers mingle with church veterans. For example, more than one congregation has discovered that their original core value for "family life" needed to be changed to "healthy relationships" because more and more people within and beyond the church were, in fact, single and unlikely to associate in traditional family units.

Annual meetings do *not* do management. Many denominational polities will require the annual meeting to approve a budget and elect key officers, but if these tasks take longer than thirty minutes the congregation is no longer fulfilling their purpose. They are doing management, and the fact that they are doing management suggests that they no longer trust their board. The real point of bringing the budget and nominations to the annual meeting is not to approve the tactics and strategies of the board to pursue God's mission for the congregation, but simply to ensure that financial energy and board leadership are not going beyond the basic boundaries of congregational life.

• A budget is presented by the Administration Team and approved. It may or may not be formally recommended by the board. It may not be detailed, but it will be highlighted. In particular, denominational policies may require specific congregational votes regarding major capital expenditures, the purchase or lease of property, or other extraordinary budget items.

• A nominations slate will be presented for election. The slate is not long. Members of the board and the three teams of the stability triangle are elected in classes of three to four years, but neither the board nor the three teams require many people. (Some denominational polities may insist that members of the Administration Team also be designated "trustees.") The management principle is to trust a gifted, called few. The congregation knows that each nominee has participated in discernment processes, and would not have been nominated unless they had the relevant spiritual gifts, a clear sense of calling to this particular ministry, and a readiness to accept covenants of continuous learning.

• The leaders of groups and mission teams—the "ministers" of the church—are not elected. They are celebrated. This is because mission emerges from the gifting, calling, equipping of laity, not by institutional appointment. The congregation celebrates the leaders God has called forth, not bureaucrats provided with an institutional mandate. The congregation will pray for these leaders, consecrate these leaders, and support these leaders within the basic umbrella of congregational life, which forms the consensus boundary beyond which leaders cannot go.

• Pastoral-relations decisions regarding clergy may be made. Denominational polities may require that ordained, commissioned, or denominationally certified staff be formally approved or "called" by the congregation—or that significant change or termination of a pastoral relationship be formally approved by the congregation. Permission-giving organizations may, or may not, even have clergy or denominationally certified people on their staff, since staffing is a matter of tactics to achieve mission and not a necessity for congregational identity.

The point is that the involvement of the annual congregational meeting in management is sharply curtailed. Their job is to define, refine, and celebrate the basic umbrella of congregational life. They do not rely on clergy or denominational affiliation to shape their identity as a congregation. They shape their own identity, interpret their own mission field, focus their own mission, and rely on the denomination to provide them quality options that help motivate and equip them to do what they are called to do.

The annual congregational meeting is a unique Christian experience. It must be distinguished from other cultural gatherings.

• The annual congregational meeting is not the accountability forum of a charitable social service. It does not provide innumerable statistics or recruit volunteers to lobby other powerful public bodies for specific issues. It does celebrate the congregational vision and mission, and articulate their long-range plan to address their changing mission field.

• The annual congregational meeting is not the shareholders' meeting of a corporation. It does not reassure investors that they will eventually receive personal rewards for institutional support. It does celebrate the congregational values and beliefs, and tell stories of personal and social transformation.

• The annual congregational meeting is not the pep rally of a political convention. It does not make exaggerated promises to gain support for charismatic officers. It does celebrate gifted and called leadership, and motivate participants to form covenants for personal and spiritual growth, and make sacrifices for the gospel.

The annual congregational meeting has the intimacy of a banquet, the motivation of a crusade, and the celebration of a joyous party. The agenda might look like this:

Worship
Review of the basic umbrella of congregational life
Multimedia presentation of changing mission field and long-range
    plan
Prayers for vision and mission
Focus group conversations over dessert and coffee
Refinements for the values, beliefs, vision, and mission of the church
Celebration of missions and ministries
Elections for the board and stability triangle
    (changes regarding denominational pastoral relations, if necessary)
Laying on of hands and prayers for leaders

Approval of budget
(approval of extraordinary capital expenditures, if necessary)
Party! Including music, storytelling, dancing, and any activities
imaginable.

It may be that the pastor or key lay leaders may wish to share
important ideas or hopes for the congregation, or that certain issues
may emerge for discussion from the unique context of their community. The primary focus, however, is to define, refine, and celebrate the basic umbrella of congregational life.

The Official Board

The primary purpose of the official board is to focus the mission
and measure the overall success of the congregation in pursuing
God's vision for their church. In *Moving Off the Map*, I provided tools
for mission assessment, ministry mapping, and leadership development that a board might use. The first helps the board survey all
eleven subsystems of congregational life to discern strengths, weaknesses, and hidden addictions. The second helps the board interpret
the mission field, form creative partnerships, and develop a long-
range plan. The third helps the board develop healthy relationships
between leaders and congregational participants. The focus of the
board is *not* the daily management of the programs and ministries
of the congregation. Their focus is the long-term viability and mission of the congregation.

The official board may meet three or four times a year. Since their
work has more to do with planning and policy, rather than day-to-
day management of programs and ministries, they do not need to
meet frequently. They do need to spend time among the various
publics of the community listening to needs, observing trends, and
searching for potential, creative partnerships for mission. It is their
responsibility not only to attend a few meetings, but to initiate formal and informal conversations beyond the church with both identifiable organizations or agencies, and individuals on the street or in
the coffee shop.

*Pro*scriptive thinking forces the official board to step back from day-to-day management. The actual management of ministries is entrusted to mission leaders and mission teams, who have the power to design, implement, and evaluate whatever initiatives they believe best live out the congregational identity and mission. The agenda of the official board dramatically changes from traditional habits.

Traditional Board Agenda	*New Board Agenda*
Brief prayer	Extensive prayer
Treasurer's report	Scripture study and conversation
Budget review	
	Review of the basic umbrella
Review of the strategic plan	of congregational life
or multiyear work schedule	Development of strategies to define, refine, and celebrate
Program maintenance and	identity and mission
nominations	
Property maintenance decisions	Identification of emerging cultu-
Fund-raising planning	ral trends and mission opportunities
Reports on all activities	Sharpening of the point of mis-
of all offices and committees	sion or defining risk (as needed)
Approval or disapproval of	Review of processes for grow-
recent work	ing, equipping, and deploying leaders
	Clarification of limitations vis à
New business:	vis mission work (as needed)
Implementation of new work	Adjustments to policy (as needed)
(design, implementation,	Renewal of spiritual formation
evaluation)	covenant
Expert interpretation of values	
and beliefs	

Board meetings in the permission-giving organization are anything but routine. They do not review the budget, listen to reports, or approve work. Occasionally, they may be asked to make a decision as to whether a particular activity falls within or beyond the basic boundaries of values, beliefs, vision, and mission of the congregation. However, if the congregation itself has performed its role well, these boundaries are so transparent that such decisions will be exceedingly rare. The permission-giving board concentrates on the overall mission and long-term plan for the future.

The Stability Triangle

The primary purpose of the Stability Triangle is to grow, equip, and deploy ministers. They manage the process by which ministries are born and turned loose in the world. The Human Resources Team guides the processes of personal growth, spiritual discernment, and continuing education which lie behind leadership development and accountability. They monitor the expressions of discontent that inevitably emerge in a dynamic organization. The Staff Team guides the processes for training and coaching leaders for spiritual discipline and skills development. They equip leaders for excellence. The Administration Team manages the day-to-day life of the congregation. They administer the budget and manage resources to deploy ministries effectively within and beyond the church.

The three teams of the stability triangle will meet regularly, perhaps monthly, through the year. Their agendas will vary among congregations and communities, but will routinely include fundamental elements related to growing, equipping, and deploying ministry leaders.

Human Resources Team	Staff Team	Administration Team
Spiritual gifts and personality discernment processes	Discernment of call and opportunities for mission	Seeding and supporting programs and ministries
Options for counseling, education, and consultancy	Training and ongoing coaching for planning and skills development	Property and resource development
Healthy relationships between leaders and congregation and general public	Mutual support and team building among leaders and groups	Communication, marketing, and fund-raising

If the board has done its job well in clearly defining the limitations to measure success, the teams of the stability triangle can evaluate their own work, and help emerging cell groups, mission teams, and other ministries do the same. Congregations may hire staff directly related to any, or all, of these three teams, depending on the needs of the congregation.

Cell Groups and Mission Teams

Every Christian is called into ministry. The permission-giving organization is designed to help individual Christians discern their gifts and callings, equip them for excellence, and find personal fulfillment through the pursuit of that ministry. Most often, ministries are best fulfilled in partnerships or teams. There is no limit to the possible groups, teams, or individuals doing ministry, and the nature of these ministries will be constantly evolving and changing. This is the ferment of growth and action created by the permission-giving organization. The bureaucracy of board and stability triangle has been dramatically streamlined, specifically to free the laity to discern and pursue their ministries.

The most significant thing to remember in the permission-giving organization is that these groups and mission teams are trusted and equipped to manage their own mission. They do not depend on others to manage their mission for them. They discern, design, implement, and evaluate their own mission work. The teams of the stability triangle help them do this comprehensively and objectively, monitor mission and leadership in reference to the basic umbrella of congregational life, and help them address any emerging discontent. These groups, teams, or leaders, however, are the primary *doers* of mission and ministry.

The possibilities for work are endless, and it would be impossible to describe the agendas, methods, processes, tactics, or even goals that are possible for these leaders. Section 2 will describe how group leaders are identified, how group covenants are formed, and how group processes lead to beneficial action. My point here is that the possibilities for mission are limited not by the imaginations of the officers of the church, but only by the imaginations of the people of the congregation. The resources of the institution do not arbitrarily limit the possibilities for mission, but the emerging mission drives the resource development of the institution.

A creative idea, calling, or mission may emerge at any time, to any person, as individuals participate in disciplined personal and spiritual growth. The stability triangle helps the called Christian do ministry with excellence, learn from inevitable mistakes, work in effective partnerships, and integrate continuing growth and service. The official board helps the called Christian understand the mission field in order to stretch the mission's ability to effect personal and social transformation. The congregation helps the called Christian work with an integrity of clearly articulated values and beliefs, and integrate the mission in a broader corporate vision. The denomination helps the called Christian experience the best support possible from a congregation, and maximize the impact of their called ministry to the world. The foundation of ministry in the permission-giving organization is not the clergy, the heritage, or the institution, but the called Christian.

Addressing Discontent in Congregational Life

As the calendar of the permission-giving congregation unfolds, a clear strategy to address and reconcile discontent pervades the organization. Although this strategy is a policy of the board, it is usually developed and implemented by the human resources team of the stability triangle. This strategy is crucial for two reasons.

First, the shift from traditional to permission-giving organization is founded upon a clear commitment to systemic change. Many congregations recognize that systemic change is required for the spiritual organization to thrive in the twenty-first century. However, systemic change is more stressful than proactive or programmatic change. It is inevitable that congregational leaders will occasionally make mistakes, since risk-learn experimentation is the primary vehicle to explore creative ministry in a changing culture. It is also inevitable that expectations of leaders by congregational participants will occasionally be disappointed. Moreover, congregations engaged in systemic change can be vulnerable to dysfunctional leaders or congregational participants who manipulate the chaotic circumstances of systemic change, intentionally or unintentionally, for personal benefits.

Second, it is the nature of the permission-giving organization to be open to diversity and encourage multiple mission. Mission emerges from the spiritual growth of the participants, guided only by the basic umbrella of congregational life that is the congregational consensus. Not only are missions and ministries blossoming in both expected and unexpected directions, but these missions will be pursued with considerable passion. It is inevitable that frustrations or conflicts will emerge in an atmosphere of spiritually contained chaos. Permission-giving congregations that work within a denomination can also be vulnerable to discontent, because most denominations are hierarchical organizations that think only *prescriptively*. There will be gaps between what the denominational judicatory wants a congregation to do, and what congregational participants believe themselves to be called to do.

Traditional organizations have grievance procedures, too. These may be as simple as a complaint box, or as complex as a bureaucratic process. Frequently, however, their grievance processes are hidden or inaccessible to both members and the public. This inaccessibility is not really a coincidence. It is implied by the very nature of the traditional organization itself. At the heart of the traditional organization is the assumption that a serious grievance procedure in a Christian congregation *is not really needed.*

• The traditional, *prescriptive*, congregational organization relies on several layers of redundant management to create the greatest homogeneity possible in the congregation. Participants all "look alike." They tend to share the same culture, language, age, economic or educational background, and other common demographic features. To be discontented in such a congregation suggests that an individual does not really have a place. The hidden message is: *If you are discontented, don't complain. Leave.*

• The traditional congregational organization tends to assume that discontent is a result of misunderstanding. Therefore, they devote all their energy to clarifying *pre*scriptive mandates, multiplying meetings, and increasing administrative information to the congregation. To be discontented in such a congregation suggests that an individual is unwittingly or willfully ignorant. The hidden message is: *If you are discontented, don't complain. Join a committee.*

• The traditional congregational organization tends to be hierarchical or bureaucratically centralized. Power is judiciously passed on by one generation of controllers to another, not through discernment processes for gift and call, but through patronage. To be discontented in such a congregation suggests that an individual is inherently unfriendly. The hidden message is: *If you are discontented, don't complain. Make friends with the right people.*

The result is that the traditional congregation believes they do not really need a grievance procedure. The complaint box can be buried in the narthex, and the complex bureaucratic procedure need never be advertised or explained. The discontented either leave, join the management, or go to the right supper club.

Even if traditional congregations aggressively make their grievance procedures known and accessible, they are frequently inadequate. In part, this is because they are continually sabotaged by the assumptions just identified. The process becomes so burdensome that the discontented, who do not want to join a committee or befriend the right people, leave anyway. The deeper truth is that the grievance procedures of traditional organizations do not work in the post-Christendom era.

• Most traditional organizations develop grievance processes that are merely oriented to salaried staff. They have no effective way to address discontent with volunteer or lay leadership. However, in the post-Christendom era, most effective ministry and mission is done by volunteers. Discontent will frequently involve laity in mission, rather than staff in mission.

• Most traditional congregational organizations develop grievance processes that do not address the full range of discontent. Since they are oriented to staff only, they tend to be oriented to legal liabilities and lead to formal proceedings. This, of course, is important. However, in the post-Christendom era, most discontent has nothing to do with legal liabilities and does not require a formal proceeding. It will involve mission priorities and the limitations of excellence.

The grievance procedures of traditional organizations, therefore, are only salaried *personnel* procedures, and are usually placed in the hands of legal or counseling professionals. They may be effective if a staff person commits an illegal or immoral act, but they rarely address the myriad other sources of discontent which more surely damage a congregation than these occasional blunders. Traditional organizations tend either to under-react or over-react to discontent, but rarely seem to address it quickly, effectively, and directly.

In contrast, the permission-giving organization knows that a process to address discontent is absolutely vital to a congregation that encourages mission diversity. They establish processes that are clear, public, and accessible.

• The permission-giving organization creates the broadest heterogeneity possible within the basic umbrella of values, beliefs, vision, and mission shared by congregational participants. The public message is: *If you are discontented, you may have a different insight into mission we need to examine. We need to know it.*
• The permission-giving organization assumes that discontent is a legitimate expression of personal need. They have devoted all their energy to nurture disciplined spiritual formation and birth mission. The public message is: *If you are discontented, you may have a gift and calling we need to better nurture. We need to do it.*
• The permission-giving organization knows that mistakes will be inevitable, and that the organization will only grow if they can learn from mistakes. Correcting a problem is only a first step in addressing discontent. The real goal is credible, quality ministry. The public

message is: *If you are discontented, some activity or some leader may have gone beyond the policy boundaries or leadership limitations defined by the congregation and the board. We need to change it.*

The permission-giving organization develops a process to address discontent that pervades the daily life of the organization. They want you to be yourself, not leave. They want you to deepen your spiritual journey, not join a committee. They want you to support the mission of the church, not befriend the right people. Therefore, they design a process that addresses the full range of discontent, and which will be equally helpful to volunteers and staff.

The process for addressing discontent can be informed by similar processes in corporate and nonprofit sectors, but it will also need to be unique for the Christian and congregational context of the organization. Generally, the congregational process needs to be more vigilant to preserve confidentiality and spiritual integrity than even corporate and nonprofit processes. In addition, congregational processes need to:

- cut bureaucracy and shorten response times;
- respect the unique polities and personnel requirements of denominations related to ordained or commissioned personnel;
- acknowledge that divine grace, not merely education or counseling, is of equal relevance to healing.

Given the growing hostility of the twenty-first-century public to organized religion, it is even more important that congregational processes fully understand, and follow, stated human rights codes of Canada and the United States.

The Context to Effectively Address Discontent

There are three primary foundations for an effective process to address discontent. If any one of these foundations is weak, then the process to address discontent will be flawed regardless of the quality or professionalism of the persons seeking to intervene.

1) *Clarity and consensus about the Basic Umbrella of Congregational Life.* The umbrella consists of clear, shared understandings of core values, bedrock beliefs, motivating vision, and key mission.[1] This clarity must be readily transparent to all participants and newcomers to the congregation. It represents the boundaries beyond which leaders cannot go, but within which they are free to experiment creatively. The primary role of any annual congregational meeting is to define, refine, and celebrate this congregational identity.

2) *Regular work-plan reviews.* The regularity may be quarterly, annual, or semi-annual, depending on the experience of change *in the community as a whole,* and not just the congregation. The more rapid the change in the community as a whole, the more frequent should be the work-plan reviews. These are *not* strategic planning sessions, and are not intended to fix work plans for extended periods of time. Instead, these are opportunities for leaders to review the relevance of ministries and rapidly adjust ministries to seize new opportunities. Reviews allow the congregation to address emerging concerns about leader burnout, and make adjustments regarding team-based ministries.

3) *Regular performance reviews.* Annual performance reviews are usually the preference for congregations. Since many of the ministries in growing congregations are *team-based* ministries including staff and volunteers, and since the most effective teams have considerable autonomy to design and implement ministry, performance reviews primarily rely on peer evaluations—which, in turn, rely on the quality of partnered spiritual disciplines in the team. Performance reviews can address issues of competency *and* credibility. Among Christian congregations, both issues are equally important.

In addition to these three foundations, some congregations may wish to add a fourth related to specific behavioral expectations for leaders. If this is done, it is important that these behavior expectations be applied to *all* leaders (staff and volunteer alike), or the effectiveness of team-based ministries will be undermined. The decision to develop a fourth foundation for behavior expectations will largely depend on the nature of the consensus around the Basic Umbrella of Congregational Life. Denominational, cultural, or local concerns may drive the congregation to be more explicit about issues related to dress, speech, covenanted sexual relationships, leisure activities, and other lifestyle matters. It is crucial that any behavioral expectations be compared with existing human rights codes, and it should be recognized that thriving churches affirm the broadest diversity of lifestyle possible in communicating the gospel.

The Alternatives of Discontent

In Christian congregational life, the process to address discontent includes at least three basic options. The choice of which one to implement will be guided by the source of the discontent, but the final decision will be made by a committee appointed by the congregation. The decision will take into consideration both the urgency or alleged seriousness of the issue, *and* the result anticipated by the person or persons who are the source of the discontent.

1) Expressing Concern: When the object is to express a concern about leadership, the anticipated result is that the leader and the congregation will *listen* to advice and give such feedback serious reflection. It may, or may not, result in any change of behavior or action. It will result in clear communication to the source of discontent, and to the congregation as a whole. When a *concern* is expressed to staff, board, or group leaders in the church, their response will be:

a) Clarify (if possible) with the source of the discontent that this is a matter of *concern* which will result in reflection and communication, but not necessarily in action or changed behavior.
b) Consult with the team appointed by the congregation to receive the congregation's assessment of the seriousness or urgency of the issue, and confirm that the matter is best addressed as a *concern.*

c) The team can then raise the concern with the appropriate leader either privately, or in the context of performance review or work-plan review.
d) The leader takes responsibility to communicate with the source of discontent (if possible) and with the congregation to share the results of his or her reflection.

Note that in the context of addressing *concerns,* the staff person, board members, or group leader to whom the concern was first expressed *removes* himself or herself from any role as a mediator or communicator between the source of the discontent and the leader toward whom discontent is aimed. The source of discontent may be anonymous, but the primary goal is to bring the source of discontent and the specific leader into direct conversation.

Many concerns are actually not about leadership, but rather about the content or direction of ministry. Therefore, the real conversation that needs to take place is within a team in the context of their work plan. If the congregation develops job descriptions and ministry mandates *prescriptively,* the assessment of the concern will involve more time and bureaucracy as the team or board reviews the list of everything a leader can or should do, and appeals to ad hoc committees to get permission for innovation. If the congregation develops job descriptions and ministry mandates *proscriptively,* the assessment of the concern is much easier. The team or board can quickly discover if the leader has done something proscribed. If so, the leader can be blocked from doing it, or the job description or ministry mandate can be revised to address a changing community situation.

2) Expressing a Grievance: When the object is to express a grievance about leadership, the anticipated result is that a specific action or change in behavior will happen. A grievance may allege that a leader has failed to cooperate with a ministry team in the implementation of their work plan, or it may allege that a leader has failed to give serious consideration to the cumulative feedback provided through sharing "concerns." More often, however, a grievance may allege that a leader has intentionally, or unintentionally, gone *beyond* the boundaries of values, beliefs, vision, or mission that is the consensus of the congregation.

A grievance process is more formal, and *cannot* accept anonymity. Although unique situations may add details to the process, it will include at least the following:

a) A "Letter of Intent" must be sent by the source of discontent to the leader and to the team, defining the nature of the grievance and describing how the leader has been perceived to go beyond the boundaries of the Basic Umbrella of Congregational Life. (If the congregation has laid a fourth foundation of "behavioral expectations," the Letter of Intent must specify how the leader is alleged to have contradicted them.)

b) The team will arrange to meet with the affected parties within fourteen days of the receipt of the Letter of Intent. Both parties are given the option of being represented or accompanied by others, provided that these persons are *not* functioning as legal counsel. The team may also request additional documentation, witnesses, or the participation of other staff or volunteer leaders relevant to the issue.

c) The team may design the meeting, or meetings, in any way that helps participants jointly discover the truth, but they will ensure that the time, location, participation, and record of the meeting all combine to protect the confidentiality of all participants.

d) The team will give a written assessment and decision regarding the grievance to the affected parties within seven days of the conclusion of the meeting or meetings. *Only the decision* can be shared with the board and the pastor. The board and the pastor, with the advice of related ministry teams, will determine if or how the decision should be shared with the congregation and commu-nity.

e) The decision of the team will be binding, and cannot be reconsidered by the congregation itself. Any affected party has the right to appeal the decision to a formal hearing of the denomination or the civil courts. In either case, both the allegations toward the leader, and the integrity of the congregational grievance process, will be brought under scrutiny.

Note that refusal to accept the decision of the team can result in the board's withdrawal of the volunteer from their leadership role or termination of a staff person's employment through the personnel procedures approved by the denomination. It can also lead to the removal of lay volunteers from offices of the church. If the decision of the committee includes recommendations for continuing education or counseling, the congregation must be ready to at least subsidize the costs.

Some grievances are not primarily about leadership, but about the content or direction of ministry. As I stated, the manner and speed with which these grievances are addressed will largely depend on whether job descriptions and ministry mandates are developed *prescriptively* or *proscriptively*. The decision of the committee may actually have less impact on the changed behavior of specific leaders, and more impact on the skills enhancement and work plans of ministry teams. Their decision may also affect the continuing definition, refinement, and celebration of The Basic Umbrella of Congregational Life in future annual congregational meetings.

3) Seeking a Formal Hearing: When the object is to seek a formal hearing, the anticipated result is a disciplinary action that may affect employment and career, and may eventually lead to civil or financial obligations. Congregations that are part of a larger denomination will find that their personnel procedures will now serve as a guide. The congregational committee will support the process and help interpret it to the congregation. These processes may well involve legal counsel, and the costs are usually supported by denominational funds.

On the other hand, congregations that are independent will need to be prepared to offer a procedure for a formal hearing that has integrity, and which can be presented to affected parties as an alternative way to resolve a dispute outside the civil court. Indeed, even those denominational congregations which have denominational procedures for formal hearings involving salaried personnel, may still need to develop an internal procedure related to *volunteer leaders*. The congregation should obtain the advice of both legal counsel and risk-liability counsel in designing a procedure that has legal and financial integrity.

The formal hearing will certainly include the following elements:

a) Legal counsel that shapes the articulation of the complaint, and represents both the complainant and the leader about whom the complaint is made.

b) Legal counsel that guides the team seeking to adjudicate the complaint.

c) A process of inquiry that is reasonably rapid, involves clear documentation and witnesses, includes character references, and which *guarantees* the confidentiality of the proceedings.

d) Clear communication of the *process,* but not the *content* of the process, to the congregation and community.

e) The board (and the pastor if this person is not the leader involved), with the advice of legal counsel, will decide whether or how to communicate the decision of the formal hearing to the congregation and the community.

Note that any of the parties in the formal hearing may still appeal the decision to the civil courts. However, given the time, cost, and public visibility of such suits, a process that has integrity and can be contained within the congregation may be preferable to a resolution sought in civil court. If the congregation is linked to a denomination, the denominational process will take precedence over any congregational alternative.

This plan will need to be customized for different congregations and communities. Once the plan is defined, it should be communicated regularly to the congregation and be readily available to both congregation and community. Systemic change will bring stress to leadership, and the permission-giving organization will inevitably make mistakes. No plan in itself will be able to alleviate that stress. It must be part of the larger context of the thriving church system and the permission-giving organization.

• There will be multiple communication vehicles, focus groups, opportunities for conversation, and general sensitivity of congregational leadership to the diverse needs of congregational and community participants.

• There will be concentrated energy for disciplined spiritual formation that grows, trains, and deploys leaders and ministries.

• There will be a strong corporate continuity around values, beliefs, vision, and mission, plus strong shared spiritual disciplines among staff and ministry teams.

• There will be a shared passion for the gospel that welcomes creative experiments to address emerging needs in a changing culture.

The truth is that the permission-giving congregation believes some discontent to be a good thing. The fact that it exists in the congregation is not a sign of failure, but a sign that the organization is doing what it is designed to do. Discontent means that the grace of God is moving in the community of faith—disturbing, questioning, challenging the status quo and motivating continuing change. Discontent means that congregational participants and leaders are investing themselves in ministry—growing, risking, failing, and learning in their spiritual journeys and exploring new missions. This positive attitude toward discontent does not mean that the permission-giving organization will not work to *resolve* the issues of discontent. It means that the organization never assumes that contentment is the ideal state of being for the organization. The moment everyone in the organization is content, it loses spiritual depth and mission momentum and ceases to be truly "permission-giving."

— 5 —

LEADERSHIP AND
ORGANIZATIONAL CHANGE

The permission-giving organization of the thriving church system is very different from the traditional organizational model of many churches. Both lay and clergy leaders may find it exciting, but unfamiliar. They may be drawn to it because it maximizes spiritual growth and mission, rather than institutional management and survival. Yet they may be hesitant to embrace it, because it places high leadership expectations on laity and changes the organizational role of clergy.

Denominational polity is often given as an excuse not to embrace the permission-giving organization. The truth is that unique denominational polities are not the real barrier to organizational change. Most denominations (with few exceptions) are either hierarchies or centralized bureaucracies, and they will all alike struggle with the rise of the permission-giving congregational organization, but there is little that is unique to any particular denomination that would block a congregation from such change. It is fruitless to say, *"Because we are Lutheran (Methodist, Presbyterian, Episcopalian, Baptist, or whatever) we can't do it."* The identifying characteristics of most denominations or religious traditions can be incorporated into the permission-giving organization if these characteristics truly grow from the consensus of the congregational participants themselves around the basic umbrella of congregational life.

The truth is that what blocks leaders from organizational change is rarely what the denominational polity says, and almost always *what they think* the denominational polity says. It is habit that blocks change, not polity. Organizational habits, so ingrained as to become unthinking choices and spontaneous ways to interpret polity, are the real blocks to change. These habits have been formed over centuries of Christendom institutional church experience, and have been reinforced by borrowing organizational assumptions from the twentieth-century subcultures of business, government, social service, and charitable sectors. John and Miriam Mayhew Carver have attacked these habits for the nonprofit sector, regardless of the particular charity or service offered. I have been challenging these habits for the Christian congregation, regardless of the particular polity or tradition offered.

In a post-Christendom world, the traditional congregational organizations that worked well in the 1920s simply will not work in the 2020s. Congregations have been the first to realize this. Denominations are the last to realize this. Fortunately, however, both congregational and denominational leaders are awakening to the change and embracing the possibilities.

Advice for the Small Church—and Any-sized Church?

Small congregations will no doubt wonder how the permission-giving organization can be adapted to their context. These are congregations with a hundred or fewer participants, and fifty or fewer people in regular worship attendance. These congregations may be in rural or remote areas or areas with declining populations. They may also be in urban areas experiencing dramatic demographic changes. Some of these congregations may actually own large or historic properties and possess a glorious heritage that has faded over time.

These congregations often tend to be on the very edge of viability, but have no objective way to test that viability. Therefore, they long to continue as a congregation—but the slightest variation in financial income or expense can close them.

Income Variations	*Expense Variations*
Death or retirement of a single good giver	Unexpected damage to historic property

Scandal regarding a single prominent family

Economic downturn in a single industry area

Inability to obtain clergy leadership

Claims on inadequate liability insurance

Taxation of church property

Increased personnel costs for benefits

In addition, small congregations in changing demographic contexts may conflate congregational mission with community survival. This skews the precarious budget further, with financial priorities weighted to property maintenance and internal pastoral care. This forced financial expectation then skews the organization itself, and the board finds itself doing little more than raising funds, resolving conflicts, and facilitating frequent staff changes.

Clearly, the permission-giving organization that I have described here assumes that the board and the three teams of the stability triangle are distinct bodies. The board meets less frequently and is solely preoccupied with refining the point of mission and measuring the success of the congregation in achieving it. The teams of the stability triangle meet more regularly, each team designing and implementing strategies to grow, train, and deploy ministry leaders. A diversity of cell groups, mission teams, and individual ministries emerges as the Spirit leads through the growth disciplines of the participants. Although members of the board and the three teams of the stability triangle can, and should, be part of the diversity of missions and ministries emerging from the congregation, the board and the stability triangle remain distinct groups. In other words, the board is preoccupied with policy, mission targets, and monitoring for excellence, while the stability triangle fulfills the role of the designated CEO and is preoccupied with management.

Small congregations will initially wonder if they have enough people to form the board and three distinct teams. Indeed, the real question is whether they have sufficient gifted and called people who are prepared to be trained for these distinct bodies. The *number* of people linked to the congregation is really not the primary issue here. The primary issue is *readiness*.

• Spiritual gifts and personality inventories can determine whether the small congregation includes a diversity of gifts including administration, leadership, evangelism, helps, teaching, and so forth. If the small congregation is not ready to commit to such discernment, but simply wants to elect people to office who appear to have the time, financial and business skills, or traditional authority, then the congregation cannot build a permission-giving organization.

• Daily spiritual disciplines and partnerships for prayer and meditation can help small congregations discover if individuals genuinely feel called by God to the ministries of board leadership and management. However, if the small congregation is not ready to involve every member in daily spiritual disciplines, but just wants to worship Sundays and have clergy take care of it, it cannot build a permission-giving organization.

• Perhaps most important, commitment to risk and to learning is crucial. The small congregation needs to place itself on a high learning curve, studying the systems that work for thriving churches, preferably in continuing partnerships with other congregations or consultants. However, if the small congregation is not ready to risk failure and learn from experimentation, but simply wants to perpetuate a heritage in fearful competition with the other small, declining congregations in the community or judicatory, then it cannot build a permission-giving organization.

It may be that even when the small congregation is ready, it simply does not have enough people to do the work. Numbers alone, however, are not the first consideration. Gifts, calling, and commitment to learning are the first considerations, and until the congregation clearly knows its own potential for these it will never really know whether it is a viable organization.

It is important to note that if small congregations question their ability to support the permission-giving organization, they are already experiencing stress trying to support the traditional organizations demanded by their denominations. Already small congregations have a small number of individuals serving multiple offices.

As I have said in my book *Kicking Habits*, the reason for this is often ambiguous. Small-congregation leaders will likely say that no one else will volunteer, forcing a few people to do all the work. However, hidden behind this reality is often a hidden addiction for control. Some of these same leaders in fact believe that no one else can be *trusted* to lead the church where they think it needs to go. As the financial pressures we have named further skew the organizational priorities of the congregation, this addiction can become ever more severe.

I raise this point because the stress experienced by small congregations considering a transition to this permission-giving organizational model is not merely about numbers. It is about principles. The permission-giving organization is as much a *philosophy* as it is a *structure*, and therefore it is founded on a *lifestyle* rather than an *institution*. It is revealing that small congregations are often not alone in complaining that they do not have enough people to manage the church and lead the ministry programs. Middle-sized and large congregations echo the same complaint. All alike suffer from the same inability to see that behind their preoccupation with institutions and methods, there are hidden assumptions about Christian self-understanding and lifestyle which are inadequate to contemporary life. This suggests that the real issue is not how many people are available to serve, but how willing current congregational leaders are to relinquish control.

The good news is that the permission-giving organization described here usually requires *fewer* people to serve an office than the traditional organization. Traditional organizations built around unified boards, executives, committees, and constitutionally mandated groups may require 25 percent or more of the membership to serve some form of office or committee. The permission-giving organization may only require 5 percent of the membership to serve on the board and the three teams of the stability triangle. To this extent, the permission-giving organization may be welcome news to the burned out, overbureaucratized, small congregation.

The question of numbers has a new significance for the permission-giving organization, however, that challenges the small congregation. The traditional organization emphasized *offices* that needed to be filled. It did not really matter who filled these offices, since the work was prescribed in exhausting detail. Therefore, the concern was simply to find enough volunteers. If there were not enough volunteers, individuals would be forced to serve multiple offices. The permission-giving organization does not emphasize offices, but *ministries*. It matters who leads these ministries. They must be specifically gifted, called, and trainable. The authenticity of the personal growth and spiritual discipline is at least equal in importance to their specific skills. Therefore, it is much more difficult for individual leaders to lead multiple ministries. Obviously, this issue may become stressful for congregations of *any* size!

If the small congregation is *ready*, but does not have sufficient people to form a distinct board and three management teams, there are at least three options to consider. Each one contains its own perils and opportunities.

1) Conflate the Board and the Stability Triangle.

This option may seem the most natural to small congregations, because in a sense they have already been doing this for years. The same people who are on the board may serve on one of the teams of the stability triangle. Aside from the continuing dangers of lay leadership burnout, there are two great dangers associated with this option.

First, the small congregation may once again confuse policy formation and management. In the nonprofit organization, John and Miriam Mayhew Carver separate these functions between the board and the CEO. In the permission-giving congregational organization, these are separated between the board and the stability triangle. But if the same people are involved, the tendency is for the meeting agendas also to become confused. Management work drives out policy development. Meeting agendas become dominated by management issues, and the board never fulfills its real tasks to refine the point of ministry, target future missions, and measure the success of the church in achieving their mission. The congregation is apt to return to the old pattern of budget management without vision.

Moreover, the conflation of the board with the stability triangle (or the confusion of policy formation and management) may also set the stage for stress in pastoral relations. The clergy can quickly find themselves torn between conflicting demands. Are they visionaries or managers? Do they help shape policy, or merely implement policy? If they do both simultaneously, are they vulnerable to accusations of conflict of interest or institutional manipulation? In such confusion, small congregations that manage to keep clergy for at least five years are apt to treat their clergy as Chief Executive Officers. Small congregations that experience rapid turnover in clergy leadership are apt to treat their clergy as program chairpersons or chaplains. Visioning or policy formation is often forgotten entirely, or tacitly left to controlling matriarchs or patriarchs who may or may not have the spiritual discipline and insight to fulfill such a role.

Not only does the congregation lose its ability to refine mission and measure success, but it forms two unhealthy codependent relationships. The first unhealthy codependency is with a handful of matriarchs or patriarchs. The congregation needs to be told what direction to go in the future, and a handful of leaders have a need to control the destiny of an institution. The second unhealthy codependency is with the clergy. The congregation (including the controlling leaders) need someone to take care of them, and the clergy have a need to be loved. Occasionally the controlling leaders are genuine visionaries, the clergy are content with chaplaincy roles, everyone possesses more than a little common sense and diplomacy, and the organization is harmonious. The enduring codependencies, however, continue an unhealthy situation that will suddenly worsen if any of these factors is eliminated. More often than not, the unhealthy situation of two simultaneous codependencies leads to pastoral relations strife—and this only makes it harder to draw volunteers into the organizational structure.

—— 147 ——

All this is at risk when the congregation tries to conflate the distinct functions of the board with the stability triangle. In order to avoid this danger, the congregation must be very clear about all four quadrants describing congregational organization for the thriving church system. They must begin with a clear philosophical choice to pursue that system and adopt a permission-giving organization. Small-congregation leaders must be prepared to surrender control—and small-congregation participants must be prepared to engage in serious spiritual discipline. Here are four keys to successfully overcoming this danger and conflating the board and stability triangle.

• Establish extraordinary congregational clarity and consensus around the core values, bedrock beliefs, motivating vision, and key mission of the congregation that is annually defined and refined.
• Ensure that leaders are in fact gifted and called to specific ministries to grow, train, and deploy diverse missions, and that all leaders are carefully trained for their work.
• Keep the meeting times and agendas pertaining to policy formation and management completely distinct. The agenda of the board meeting is related to refining the point of mission (mapping future ministries and defining the sacrifices the congregation is willing to make) and to measuring success (ensuring excellence and monitoring boundaries). The agendas of the teams of the stability triangle involve the practical tasks of growing, training, and deploying ministries.
• Ensure that the chairperson of the board and team leaders understand the distinct roles implied by the quadrants of the permission-giving organization, and together regularly monitor their success in keeping agendas distinct.

Conflation of the board and stability triangle will be more successful if the congregation understands that *ministries* will emerge neither from the board nor from professional staff, but from the spiritual growth of the people themselves.

The second danger inherent in conflating the board and the stability triangle is that the congregation will diminish its ability to measure their success in pursuing the mission. The third quadrant assumes both competency and objectivity. The people who best measure success will have a detailed grasp of the point of mission, a clear overview of the mission field, and a personal objectivity toward the work. In the management of natural resources, for example, the best people to measure the success of a forestry project may *not* be the loggers and seeders who are cutting and planting trees. Different skills and a certain personal detachment from the work are required.

When the board and the stability triangle are conflated, the congregational leaders may lose the ability to seriously challenge their own mission. Less energy is devoted to surveying the mission field and refining the point of mission, and objectivity is lost as leaders personally invest themselves in specific aspects of the work. The potential for addictive behavior patterns to grip congregational life increases significantly. I described this issue at length in *Kicking Habits.* A corporate addiction is a self-defeating or self-destructive behavior pattern that a congregation chronically denies, but to which they habitually return in times of confusion or stress. If the role of the board implied by quadrant 3 is weakened, the risk of addiction increases.

In order to overcome this danger, the congregation must understand that the measurement of success *is* the primary function of the board, and that the small congregation may need help to do this. Here are three possibilities.

• The regional judicatory of the denomination may be able to assist. If they understand the thriving church system, and if they support the philosophy of the permission-giving organization, the regional judicatory may be able to provide an overview that helps the congregation challenge its addictions and measure the success of mission. Unfortunately, not all regional denominational judicatories fulfill these conditions. Sometimes the regular oversight required by the denomination is not aimed appropriately at the work of the board for policy development (refining mission and measuring success), but is inappropriately aimed at the management work associated with the three teams of the stability triangle (personnel issues, property issues, staff issues). This means that the judicatory oversight may not only fail to challenge hidden addictions, but unwittingly reinforce them. At its best, however, the regional judicatory may be able to engage the board in its overview and refinement of the mission field, standards of excellence, and deployment of ministries.

• Partner congregations may also be able to assist. These are congregations who share similar values, beliefs, vision, and mission. Such a congregation may be within the same denomination or not. The congregation may be in the same geographical region or not. Communication with the partner congregation may involve personal exchanges between leaders or the Internet. The point is that regular consultation with a partner congregation can utilize their distinct leadership skills and objectivity to challenge your congregation. Unfortunately, some partnerships among congregations involve only the sharing of resources or tactics related to specific ministries. Programmatic sharing is not helpful here. This partnership links board to board, not program to program. It is specifically designed to help a congregation see itself, and understand its mission, with clarity.

• Independent consultants may be able to assist. Today the role of congregational "interventionist" (to borrow a term from Lyle Schaller) or consultant in congregational life is growing. These are people with some expertise in systemic change and permission-giving organizations, who can both train congregational boards and assist congregational boards in the measurement of success. Such consultation, however, is most effective if it is seen as a continuing process rather than a once-in-a-lifetime experience. This means that congregations are building long-term relationships with consultants, and integrating such consultation into the fabric of their denominational experience. There is always a risk that consultant may not fully understand unique denominational policies or traditions, and the congregation will need to encourage communication and respect between consultant and regional denominational judicatory.

Conflation of the board and the stability triangle will be more successful if the congregation understands that the issue is not *if* they should be linked with other partners, but rather *how* they should be linked to those partners. If only programmatic change is at stake, traditional organizations can continue to borrow resources from various directions while remaining essentially aloof from any serious, continuing partnership. However, now that systemic change is at stake, permission-giving organizations must enter intentionally selected partnerships that touch the essence of their identity and mission. Even the nondenominational congregation now urgently seeks partnerships with others.

Having offered some advice to overcome the dangers of conflating the board and the stability triangle, let me encourage the small congregation not to be too hasty in assuming that they do *not* have sufficient gifted and called people to create a distinct board and three teams. Sometimes the leaders of small congregations *think* there are no potential volunteers . . .

• because congregational participants are still thinking that voluntarism means serving bureaucratic offices in the traditional model for which they have no interest;
• because congregational participants are not involved in spiritual disciplines to discern gifts and callings, and no one really has any idea what potential leadership God might elicit from the people;
• because congregational leaders are actually very controlling, and denying the leadership potential among youth, seniors, marginal members, or others who are outside the current congregational core is one way to maintain control.

Before the small congregation chooses to conflate the board and stability triangle, they should test their assumptions. Participants should be fully informed about the different kind of voluntarism implied by the permission-giving organization. It may well motivate surprising interest. Congregational participants should be challenged to engage in spiritual disciplines. God may reveal unexpected gifts and callings. Congregational leaders should investigate with great care the potential gifts and callings of youth, seniors, and anyone who was formerly marginal to congregational life. They may uncover talents hitherto unsuspected.

2) Amalgamate.

The ability to establish an effective organization is in itself a test of the viability of the congregation. Amalgamation does not mean failure. It means that the small congregation of faithful Christian people have realized that the best way to pursue the ministry of Jesus Christ in their community or region is in unity with another congregation. Amalgamation may be the necessary first step to the creation of an effective permission-giving organization if one or more of the following conditions are true:

• the congregation has clarity and consensus about values, beliefs, vision, and mission—but the mission which fills them with enthusiasm is simply too ambitious to accomplish alone;
• the congregation is simply unable to find the objectivity and competency needed to measure the success of the people in pursuing their mission within the congregation, and cannot obtain coaching in this from their regional denominational judicatory, other congregational partners, or available consultants;
• the congregation has motivated and coached participants to engage in spiritual disciplines to discern gifts and callings, including those marginal to the core congregation, and there are not enough people to form a board that refines mission and measures success, or form teams to grow, train, and deploy ministries.

If any of the above conditions is true, then amalgamation may be the best choice of the small congregation. Note that these conditions say nothing about property, financial strength, or community survival. Indeed, if none of the above conditions is true, then the congregation may well have the organizational power to engage significant capital redevelopment, overcome financial crises, and positively affect the quality of life of the community. The ability to establish an effective organization—not financial or membership strength—is the real test of congregational viability.

The small congregation may well discover that they are in fact not a "congregation" at all, but rather a cell group or a mission team. In other words, their entire energy is absorbed by quadrant 4 of the permission-giving organizational model. At most there may be two or three distinct cell groups or mission teams of no more than twelve persons each that currently constitute the "congregation." However, the capacity of these cell groups or mission teams to pursue their calling is limited because they are not linked to a permission-giving organization that can refine and guide their mission and measure their success. Eventually, frustration will undermine the remaining cell groups and mission teams.

Such small congregations are cell groups in search of a larger organization in which they can thrive. They cannot unite with a *traditional* congregational organization, because traditional organizations will only be interested in their assets and not their mission. This is why they resist denominational efforts to merge the small congregation with another congregation. They rightly perceive that the merger is a matter of expedience, not mission, and that their identity as a cell group or mission team will simply be lost in an organizational machine controlled by outsiders. However, such small "congregations" can joyfully unite with the permission-giving organization of the thriving church system. In these organizations, their mission is valued more than their assets. They not only find the freedom to pursue the mission of their group, but they find themselves empowered to do so by an effective board that can help them refine their mission and measure success. The opportunities for growth, training, and deployment dramatically increase.

It is crucial to understand that amalgamations occur with permission-giving organizations differently from how they occur with traditional organizations. Traditional organizations can be amalgamated by the hierarchical decision of a denominational middle judicatory or bishop, which can be successfully imposed because the traditional organizations of each of the amalgamating congregations depend upon *offices*, not *people*. The merger is simply a matter of making sure that every required office is filled so that the standardized organizational machinery will run smoothly. However, permission-giving organizations can be amalgamated only by consensus of the congregations involved. Amalgamation succeeds because the congregations share common values, beliefs, vision, and mission, and because the people involved have discovered they are walking similar paths of disciplined spiritual growth.

The amalgamation of permission-giving organizations will succeed if the following conditions are met. These conditions reflect the organizational requirements of the four quadrants of the permission-giving church.

1) Each congregation has clarity and consensus about values, beliefs, vision, and mission;
2) Each congregation has clarified the point of mission and defined the acceptable sacrifices to achieve personal and social change;
3) Each congregation understands, and is clearly committed to, regular measurements of success, which include a continuing quest for excellence;
4) Each congregation allows the mission of the church to emerge from the spiritual disciplines of the participants.

Traditional amalgamations begin with conversations about property, finances, and personnel, and end with adjustments to program. Their biggest anxiety concerns preserving a heritage. The amalgamations of permission-giving organizations begin with conversations about vision, mission, and disciplined spiritual formation, and end with adjustments to property and personnel. Their biggest anxiety concerns fulfilling a vision.

It probably goes without saying that permission-giving organizations will *not* be able to amalgamate with traditional organizations. The small church that is a permission-giving organization will not tolerate a middle judicatory or bishop who imposes such a merger. At best, the judicatory or bishop will need to sympathize with the different character of the small congregation, and creatively broker conversations with potential partners. Permission-giving congregations take initiative in their search for an amalgamation partner. This search may well break quaint geographical limitations of the past, burst artificial judicatory boundaries within a denomination, and even cross denominational boundaries. Such congregations will be the supreme test for denominational viability in the future, because they will challenge the openness of the judicatory and test the denomination's own clear passion for the ministry of Jesus Christ beyond institutional preservation. The permission-giving congregation will eventually demand a permission-giving judicatory.

3) Transform the congregation into a nonprofit organization.

A third option for the small congregation is that they cease trying to be a congregation and form a nonprofit organization. This may be a community center, charity, or social service agency. This option may be attractive if the real mission goal of the people is simply to preserve a rural or remote community where all other community services have closed, or if a particular social need is so poignant that all other interests become a distant consideration, or if the remaining participants do not feel motivated to undertake any daily spiritual disciplines.

They may choose to form a community center that provides space for important socializing, regional meetings, and the occasional funeral, wedding, or reception. They may choose to fund and staff an agency for personal counseling or financial support. They may establish a center for youth or seniors. They may choose to develop a clinic or residential housing for the elderly. The possibilities may be endless. Such a choice allows the congregation to:

• reduce the size of the board, and limit expectations of board members to specific skills or expertise;
• entrust management of the center or agency to a volunteer or salaried CEO;
• extend services to any individual or group, with no expectations regarding religion;
• obtain funding from government sources for the center or agency.

In short, the organization becomes much simpler and can now function fully with guidelines such as those described by John and Miriam Mayhew Carver for nonprofit organizations.

There are hazards to this option as well, and once considered the small congregation may hesitate to make such a choice. First, both the burden and the benefit of spiritual discipline are removed. There is no particular Christian witness in the community from the former congregation, nor do board members need to consider the radical inbreaking of God's grace when formulating long-range plans. It may be possible to design the core values of the agency or center with broad reference to Christian tradition, but bedrock beliefs will need to be replaced by a core ideology. The volunteer or salaried CEO will not offer ministries of personal support, visitation, and spiritual guidance formerly associated with a pastor.

Second, both the burden and the benefit of denominational involvement will be removed. It may prove difficult to obtain denominational approval to relinquish control of the property. Regardless of property control, denominations are increasingly reluctant to fund and maintain properties, or extend liability insurance for agencies that are disconnected from congregational life. The congregational participants may grow rapidly distant from denominational networks of communication and planning, and consequently from a church tradition once significant for their identity.

Third, even though the board of an agency or center may be smaller and less demanding, they may also require a level of expertise difficult to find among volunteers from the former congregation. As the center or agency becomes more dependent on funding from beyond community and denomination, and as expertise must be found beyond the former congregational participants, loss of control will be inevitable. Paradoxically, some small congregations choose to become nonprofit organizations in order to maintain control of their property and community, only to find that they lose that control even faster.

Finally, in these unpredictable times the long-term survival of nonprofit centers and agencies is also very uncertain. Government cutbacks, corporate business decisions, demographic shifts, and market trends beyond the influence of the local people may ultimately be more decisive for the survival of a rural or remote community, or for the survival of an urban neighborhood, than anything the small congregation can do.

In order to overcome these obstacles, and create a viable and enduring nonprofit organization, the small congregation should anticipate the following work.

1) Create a core ideology for the organization. Clarity about organizational values, working assumptions, and performance goals will be crucial not only to obtain future funding, but to establish credibility in the community.
2) Commit the organization to its mission purpose with single-minded tenacity. Do not allow the organization to be sidetracked by irrelevant concerns to protect property or heritage. Be prepared to advertise, renovate, raise funds, and aggressively present the mission to the world.
3) Develop a detailed, aggressive financial plan. Consider hiring a consultant to help you. The plan will take financial responsibility for the "hidden" costs of running a local institution that hitherto went unrecognized in denominational support (e.g., liability insurance or other subsidies) and clergy personnel expectations (e.g., overtime, property maintenance, and other extras). The financial plan will also need to include an aggressive marketing strategy.
4) Orient the board to volunteer leadership development. Even if the emerging agency or center is able to salary a CEO to monitor

and coordinate volunteers, enormous joint energy will be required to recruit and train volunteers.

As the nonprofit organization emerges, the members will likely discover that the permission-giving model of policy governance and executive limitations such as that described by John and Miriam Mayhew Carver will be most effective in minimizing bureaucracy and maximizing energy for the work itself. They will also find that, although the responsibilities of leadership may be different in a nonprofit organization than in a Christian congregation, the responsibilities are still very demanding.

There may be other options for the small congregation. Unlike some large congregations with greater human and financial resources, however, the one option small congregations probably do *not* have is to continue as they are. The traditional organization, oriented as it is to bureaucracy and institutional maintenance, is no longer working.

• Volunteer leaders are burning out;
• Professional staff are no longer affordable;
• Property and technology can no longer be maintained with quality.

Most important, authentic missions and ministries which transform individuals and society are no longer happening. The public has less and less respect for, or interest in, the traditional organizations of small congregations. Denominations have less patience with, or subsidies available for, traditionally organized small congregations, which do no more than survive. The real dilemma facing small congregations is not size, but organization. The ultimate choice facing small congregations is not about survival, but about mission.

The Role of the Pastor

I have chosen to address the role of the pastor in the permission-giving organization at the end, rather than at the beginning. This is not because the role of the pastor is unimportant, but because it is more important to have a sense of *priority* in building the permission-giving organization. As my friend Bill Easum and I described in *Growing Spiritual Redwoods,* a clearly identifiable spiritual leader is crucial to the success of the permission-giving organization.

Traditional church organizations tend to be shaped around the pastor. The pastor leads by the authority of his or her office and denominational certification. The pastor ensures that congregational organization conforms with the structures of every other denominational congregational unit as if it were a franchise of a larger corporation. The pastor imports his or her values, beliefs, and vision into the congregational identity. The pastor's mission priorities shift congregational energies. Fundamentally, and often with profound subtlety, the pastor controls the church.

This is why few meetings occur without the pastor's presence, and virtually no activities happen without the pastor's knowledge and approval. The primary link between congregation and denomination is *pastoral relations,* the key membership of the pastor is with the denominational judicatory, and the most powerful positions in congregation or judicatory are related to personnel. The judicatory knows that by controlling the pastor, it can control the congregation. The congregation knows that by controlling the pastor, they can manipulate the denominational system.

Obviously, the traditional church organization rapidly becomes a web of control in which the pastor finds himself or herself at the center. Sometimes the controller, and sometimes the controlled, the pastor begins to define himself or herself as a politician or a diplomat rather than a spiritual leader. It is no wonder that the temptation is so strong for both denominations and congregations to borrow organizational models from surrounding culture and regard the pastor as the tacit CEO of the organization. In the Christendom era, when the denominational machinery worked smoothly and there was enough money to add staff, the web of control was not only tolerable but even rewarding. In the post-Christendom era, when the denominational machinery is not working and there is barely enough money to pay for property maintenance, the web of control is intolerable.

True, denominational seminaries and theological colleges train candidates in the admirable self-understanding that the role of the pastor involves *word, sacrament, service,* and *pastoral care.* The problem is not with this self-understanding, but with the way in which the traditional church organization warps that self-understanding in the real world. The web of control, and being controlled, changes how ministries of word, sacrament, and pastoral care are actually experienced by the congregation and community.

• The ministry of the word quickly becomes a practice of jealously guarded pulpits, denominationally imposed lectionaries, and advocacy for whatever is considered to be politically correct or theologically pure.
• The ministry of the sacrament all too easily becomes a practice of carefully scrutinized admission to membership, corporate uniformity, and elite opinions about "good" or "bad" worship.
• The ministry of service quickly becomes a practice of factional financial budgeting, personal advocacy of unpopular causes, advertising, and institutional program maintenance.
• The ministry of pastoral care is rapidly reduced to keeping church insiders content, so that control of the organizational agenda can continue unimpeded.

Of course, this is *not* what seminaries teach as the traditional role of the pastor! It is what the traditional church organization in the post-Christendom era *does* to what the seminaries teach about the role of the pastor! Insofar as seminaries do not teach fresh organizational models, and denominations prohibit fresh organizational models, the ideal and reality of life as a pastor will grow ever more contradictory. Seminary graduates will increasingly complain that the training they received in college does not help them cope with the real expectations of the local church.

Permission-giving organizations are *not* shaped around the pastor. Instead, the pastor shapes his or her lifestyle and work schedule around the organization. The pastor leads not by the authority of an office or denominational certification, but by the authority of his or her own spiritual authenticity. That authenticity is transparent to the congregation and the public by their disciplines of spirituality and learning, and by their eagerness to help others give birth to the full potential of gifts and callings that God has given each human being.

• The permission-giving pastor does not ensure conformity, but encourages diversity.

• The permission-giving pastor does not impose his or her own values and beliefs on the organization, but aggressively articulates the values, beliefs, vision, and mission that reflect the consensus and calling of the congregation.

• The permission-giving pastor does not direct preconceived mission priorities toward his or her own goals, but encourages mission previously unimagined that pursues the goals of others.

The permission-giving pastor does *not* fundamentally control the church. Instead, the pastor pervades all four quadrants of the permission-giving organization as visionary, synthesizer, trainer, and midwife. We will explore each role in each quadrant shortly.

First, let me complete the contrast of the role of the pastor in traditional and permission-giving organizations. The permission-giving pastor will probably be absent from most meetings, and may not even know about many activities. The primary link between the congregation and denomination will not be pastoral relationships, but shared mission activities. The key membership for the pastor will not be with the judicatory, but with the congregation itself. The most powerful position in congregational life (if any position in the diffused authority of the permission-giving organization can be said to be more powerful than another) is not the personnel committee, but the visionary board. The denomination will soon realize that to influence the congregation, controlling the pastor will not help. The only way a denomination can influence a congregation is by sharing and facilitating their mission.

If you are building a traditional church organization, then you will *begin* with the role of the pastor and shape the organization around him. You will be convinced that clergy *professionalism* is the key to success in the organization, and you will concentrate on equipping that pastor with ecclesiastical skills approved by the hierarchy, relational skills certified by secular associations, and management skills equivalent to the CEO of the best nonprofit organizations. You will wait for the pastor to arrive, before you go in any new directions, because that pastor will be the professional who can show you where to go and how to get there.

On the other hand, if you are building a permission-giving organization, you will consider the role of the pastor *last* and shape the organization first. You will be convinced that the spiritual discipline of the congregation is the key to success in the organization. You will build clear consensus about the congregational identity of values, beliefs, vision, and mission. You will gather visionary leaders who can interpret the mission field, focus the mission, and define the level of sacrifice the people are prepared to make. You will create a Stability Triangle of a gifted, called, equipped few who share authority, a common quest for quality, and a passion for transforming people and society. You will look for mission to emerge from the interaction of the Holy Spirit and spiritually disciplined lives, and look for every way possible to coach and support it. And when you have done all these things, *only then* will you worry about salaried staff.

First, shape the organization. Once the congregation has a clear sense of identity and purpose, and once the congregation has itself taken responsibility for the privilege of ministry, only then will it be time to consider the call or appointment of clergy leaders. In an existing congregation, with a current pastor, both pastor and ongregation can work together to build the permission-giving organization. However, do not start by sending the pastor away for continuing education and then relying on him to design the organization. Instead, send teams of lay leaders away for continuing education (with or without the pastor) and rely on them to coach organizational change. Do not start by asking the pastor to define core values, bedrock beliefs, motivating vision, and key mission. Start by building congregational consensus for the basic umbrella of congregational life. In the foregoing paragraphs, I use the word "you." To whom do I refer? I refer to the laity, to the credible volunteer leaders, to the people themselves. The present clergyperson can be among them. She can encourage them, coach them, build new partnerships with them, and learn right alongside them. In the end, however, either the people create the permission-giving organization or it will never be created at all.

What, then, does the pastor actually *do* in the permission-giving organization? How does this organization put into practice the traditional pastoral identity of word, sacrament, pastoral care, and service? The pastor moves through the four quadrants of the permission-giving organization as visionary, synthesizer, trainer, and midwife. Generally speaking, her role is not to keep the organization running smoothly, but to facilitate the spiritual and personal growth of the people upon which the success of the organization depends.

The Pastor in Quadrant 1: Imagining Possibilities and Articulating Boundaries

The pastor helps the congregation answer the question *What are the boundaries?* As the congregation regularly defines, *refines*, and celebrates their consensus around core values, bedrock beliefs, motivating vision, and key mission, the pastor facilitates the spiritual discipline and purposeful conversation that is required for both discernment and consensus to be achieved. Keep in mind that this is a continuing task throughout the year, because that congregational consensus should be in continuous conversation. Two roles for the pastor as spiritual leader are particularly important, and will strongly influence the long-term success of the organization.

1) The spiritual leader must expand the imaginations of the congregational participants, and increase their sensitivity to the callings of God. The pastor speaks and acts from the visible context of his or her own spiritual discipline and lifestyle, and in response to the vision of mission she or he has experienced from God. The pastor also contributes to the conversation about boundaries from his or her own experience of interaction with the public. The pastor's credibility and leadership largely depend on the quality and reliability of the interface between vision and mission field that she or he presents.

2) The spiritual leader must make the values, beliefs, vision, and mission of the congregation transparent to the public. The pastor is not the originator of the core values, beliefs, vision, and mission of the congregation, but he or she must be the *chief articulator* of that basic umbrella of congregational life. The pastor "holds the umbrella up" over the heads of congregational participants to be as welcoming and inclusive as possible.

These two tasks indicate that the pastor consistently fills a necessary presence among both congregational participants and the various publics or cultures that form the wider community. Note, however, that this presence is not characterized by *doing ministries* such as visitation, advocacy, counseling, socializing, or office holding, but rather is characterized by the articulation of basic values, beliefs, vision, and mission through his or her own lifestyle. In other words, the interface between vision and mission field is not programmatic (scheduled into the pastor's work week), but behavioral (transparent in every moment of the pastor's lived week). As Bill Easum and I described in *Growing Spiritual Redwoods,* the spiritual leader becomes the "face in the tree" that personifies the identity of the congregation. The *doing* of ministry happens through gifted, called, equipped laity. The overall representation of these ministries, and the rationale of values, beliefs, vision, and mission that lies behind them, is the task of the pastor.

In classical terms, the pastor's work in quadrant 1 comes the closest to the "ministry of sacrament" described in historical Christian thought. A "sacrament" is any activity or event which renders ordinary living open to extraordinary grace, resulting in the redemption or blessing of people touched by the holy. The spiritual leader is not more pious or saintly than others, may or may not be ordained or certified by a denomination, and may or may not have received formal seminary training. Their leadership depends on the spiritual authenticity that allows them to open ordinary experience to the inbreaking of divine grace.

In current terms, the pastor is a *visionary*. A true visionary is more than someone who can anticipate the future and help others prepare for it. The pastor as a true visionary identifies for others the positive, redeeming possibilities that lie in an ambiguous future. The true visionary communicates the excitement and joy of those possibilities, and invites others to share in that joy. The true visionary allows others not only to see the vision, but also to shape and refine the vision. The true visionary is motivated by hope, and it is that hopefulness as much as the vision itself which captures the imaginations of others. The true visionary is motivated not by anger or judgment, but by genuine compassion for people.

The Pastor in Quadrant 2: Focusing Mission and Motivating Sacrifice

The pastor helps the congregation answer the question, *What is the point?* As the board focuses the community benefits and positive personal changes which the mission of the congregation seeks to achieve, the pastor helps the board interpret the mission field and anchor the mission response in scripture. Similarly, as the board defines the degree of sacrifice or risk that the congregation is willing to stake on achieving the mission, the pastor helps the board realistically evaluate the strength of the congregation and identify potential organizational partners who can help the congregation achieve their goals. This task, too, continues throughout the year. Note especially that while the success of this pastoral role depends on the quality and depth of the pastor's experience with both mission field and congregation, it also depends on the quality and depth of the board's experience with both church insiders and the publics of the community. While the scriptural knowledge of the pastor is important, the spiritual discipline of the board is equally important. Two pastoral roles in particular will strongly influence the long-term success of the organization.

1) The spiritual leader must build credibility among the publics of the community as a perceptive listener and trustworthy liaison to the church. The pastor's credibility depends on her or his ability to engage culture in reasonable dialogue, and not emotional confrontation. Such leadership is often quiet and rarely makes headlines, but in the long-term it builds confidence with the multicultural, interfaith, and spiritually hungry community. The pastor can be trusted to present accurate and fair interpretations of community life to the congregation, and help the congregation respond in the sincerity of their faith without judgmentalness or manipulation.

2) The spiritual leader must motivate congregational participants to prioritize their energy and resources for mission. The pastor leads people in mission, not survival. He or she helps spiritually disciplined congregational participants plainly perceive mission targets, understand the rationale for addressing these targets, and motivates them to make great sacrifices to achieve these targets. The ability to motivate is linked directly to the ability to coach others in spiritual growth. The pastor helps participants understand that generosity in mission brings self-fulfillment, and the experience of joy in the midst of sacrifice.

These two tasks indicate that the pastor consistently reveals by word and lifestyle perceptiveness, clarity of thought, and passion. Note, however, that no particular style, training, or personality is assumed by these tasks. Traditional academic and denominational training *may* sharpen the spiritual leaders perceptiveness, clarity of thought, and passion, but it may *also* cloud these abilities with irrelevant presuppositions, jargon, and mere emotion. The most effective spiritual leaders speak and live perceptively, clearly, and passionately, having reflected on their own experience of personal struggle and spiritual victory.

In classical terms, the pastor's work in quadrant 2 comes the closest to the "ministry of word" described in historical Christian thought. This does imply preaching, faith-sharing, and witnessing, just as it implies the ability to interpret and teach scripture. Much of the preaching and public speaking of the pastor will be related to the refinement of mission and motivation for sacrifice associated with this quadrant. However, classic terms really need to be expanded to "the ministry of word *and lifestyle*" which, in truth, is closer to historical Christian experience. The greatest preachers and teachers have always been leaders whose *lifestyle* reflects the content of their preaching and teaching. They are remarkably humble and unconscious of any "perks" or "privileges" associated with their role in the permission-giving organization. They "walk the talk"—and they "talk about the walk" with remarkable clarity and persuasiveness.

In current terms, the pastor is a *synthesizer*. A true synthesizer is more than a dilettante who dabbles with many ideas and mingles superficially with many cultures. A true synthesizer begins with a clear commitment to the values, beliefs, vision, and mission of the congregation, but then appreciates the smallest nuances of alternative points of view. The pastor as a true synthesizer is able to link seemingly contradictory ideas, and bridge seemingly incompatible cultures. He or she is able to gain the trust of people from many diverse cultures, and with many diverse lifestyles. A true synthesizer is not motivated by a desire to understand an enemy in order to defeat him, but by a desire to know someone who is different in order to learn from her. A true synthesizer does not learn about culture in order to manipulate it, but converses with culture confident that there is a deeper truth that can be discovered together.

The Pastor in Quadrant 3: Training Ministers and Equipping Ministries

The pastor helps the congregation answer the question *How is success measured?* As the board and the stability triangle define limitations for excellence, shared authority, and leadership development, the pastor supports management that grows, trains, and deploys ministers. From time to time, the pastor may offer advice when particular ministry ideas or activities appear to test the boundaries of values, beliefs, vision, and mission. The pastor may offer coaching to identify comprehensively the limitations that can both guide and free the teams of the stability triangle, or emerging mission teams in the congregation. He or she helps mission leaders and groups develop the focus of their missional purpose, and establish the working covenants, that will discipline their work.

Note that as pastoral work goes from *prescriptive* to *proscriptive* thinking, two changes occur in the role of the pastor. First, the role of the pastor becomes more practical. Specific skills for small group development, leadership support, communications, faith-sharing, and worship design become more important. These skills can be obtainable, trainable, even certifiable, but they may well not be the skills taught in traditional seminary or theological college curricula. Not only will the pastor train others to do ministries, but the pastor will train others, who in turn will train others, to do ministries. Second, in the transition to *proscriptive* thinking, the pastor's role also becomes even more limited. Perhaps the single greatest shift in pastoral leadership roles from the traditional to the permission-giving organization is that the pastor is no longer simply *doing ministry*. The laity are the ones doing the ministry. The pastor helps train and motivate them. If the pastor does ministry at all, the primary purpose is to model the ministry task so that others can take responsibility for it.

1) The spiritual leader must expect excellence, and help people achieve it. Upholding standards of excellence for both congregational membership and lay leadership is a distinctive mark of the pastor in a permission-giving church. Traditional pastors habitually accept mediocrity, and therefore rarely trust lay leaders to do ministry with integrity. They follow quietly behind laity cleaning up messes—and inevitably lower the standards of excellence that they apply to themselves! Permission-giving pastors demand quality, and are prepared to spend energy and money to get it. They then have ample reason to trust lay leaders—and to model the quest for quality in their own personal and professional lives.

2) The spiritual leader must let go of control. Although pastors will themselves participate in various ministry teams (most notably the worship team that coaches and motivates laity), their participation in teams will ebb, flow, and change over time. The ability to let go of control is another distinctive mark of the pastor in a permission-giving organization. There is absolutely nothing in the permission-giving congregation that a gifted, called, and equipped layperson cannot do—and perhaps do better. Even in denominations that limit the celebration of sacraments to designated priests, permission-giving pastors are relinquishing more and more control in order to involve volunteer men, women, and children in the sacramental act. The pastor models shared authority for everyone else in the church.

These two tasks indicate that the pastor articulates the high expectations for discipleship defined by the board both within and beyond the church—and applies them to his or her own leadership. The pastor has high standards for personal performance and integrity, which are publicly articulated, and the pastor is also clearly a *team player*, which is constantly modeled.

In classical terms, the pastor's work in quadrant 3 comes closest to the "ministry of pastoral care." Admittedly, this is stretching a point. As in the leadership style of Jesus himself, whose primary personal support was given to the Twelve, the permission-giving pastor offers personal support primarily to the core of leaders who constitute the board and stability triangle. After all, laity are grown, trained, and deployed to exercise the pastoral care ministries traditionally associated with the clergy. The fullness of "pastoral care" in historical Christian experience, however, was always associated with lay empowerment. In this sense, the permission-giving pastor is a "caregiver" because he or she coaches others to take responsibility for their own gifts and callings in order to fulfill their God-given potential.

In current terms, the pastor is a *trainer.* A true trainer not only teaches skills and techniques, but encourages mental stamina and spiritual fortitude. A true trainer feels the bruises and shares the victories of the spiritual athletes he or she is training. The pastor as a trainer helps others discern gifts and callings, and then develop and sharpen skills to achieve their best possible ministry performance. A true trainer balances growth and achievement in equipping ministry. Personal growth without achieving mission targets leads the trainer to help a volunteer learn from mistakes. Achievement of mission without personal growth leads the trainer to help the volunteer reexamine the fundamentals of living. The true trainer celebrates only when growth and success happen together, when the joy of self-fulfillment matches the healing of transformed persons or the justice of a changed society.

The Pastor in Quadrant 4: Birthing Missions and Coaching Missionaries

The pastor helps the congregation answer the question *How are leaders deployed?* As individuals, groups, and mission teams emerge from the personal and spiritual growth of the participants, the pastor coaches leaders to do effective ministries. This will involve coaching adjustments to the changing mission field, facilitation of continuous learning, and the development of new tactics for ministry. This work never ends and is never routine. Since mission emerges "from below," rather than being imposed "from above," there is an unpredictability about mission. The pastor is always challenged to learn and grow, so that she or he can coach others more effectively.

1) The spiritual leader must help others give birth to the full potential that is within them. The ability to challenge and cheer, confront and nurture, all at the appropriate times, is a distinctive mark of the pastor of a permission-giving organization. Traditional pastors recruit volunteers into the mission of the institution. In their need to fit individuals into organizational offices, they ignore or devalue the uniqueness of the individual. Permission-giving pastors help individuals discern their own calling. Since that calling is uniquely associated with individual identity and potential, they value uniqueness. Since that calling is given to another, they surrender responsibility for the newly born ministry to the unique individual who has given birth to it.

2) The spiritual leader must offer twenty-four-hour coaching support. The readiness to offer constant coaching support is a final distinctive mark of the permission-giving pastor. Traditional, professional pastors are preoccupied by "days off" and "vacation time." This is understandable, because in the traditional organization the burden of doing ministry is entirely the pastor's. In the permission-giving organization, this burden is borne by others who are gifted, called, and equipped to do it. True coaches offer twenty-four-hour support. True coaches are always available, on or off the field of play, every day of the week. As the organization grows, true coaches build coaching teams in order to make sure that players receive what they need, when they need it.

These two tasks indicate that the pastor will behave *purposefully* in devoting wholehearted attention to birthing the potential of others, and allow nothing—no program, no visitation request, no capital building campaign—to distract him from that goal. On the other hand, the pastor will behave *flexibly* to offer whatever coaching in whatever form, content, and direction the current circumstances require. If for the traditional pastor *routine* is crucial, for the permission-giving pastor *timing* is everything! The routine of the Christian year, the weekly program, or the bureaucratic calendar means little. The timeliness of personal interventions that may be challenging or nurturing—and which make all the difference for the birth or abortion of a creative idea, or hitting or missing the mission target—will determine the success of the congregation.

In classical terms, the pastor's work in quadrant 4 comes closest to the "ministry of service" described in historical Christian thought. Indeed, such pastors are often called "servant leaders." This can be misleading, however, because pastors in the "enabling model" of ministry associated with traditional organizations of the twentieth century also called themselves "servant leaders." The difference is *for whom* the leader is a servant. In traditional church organizations, the pastor is the servant of individual church members and programs. He or she does the ministry each member or committee requests. In the permission-giving organization, the pastor is the servant *of other leaders and the spiritually seeking public.* In other words, servanthood is not aimed toward church insiders as a privilege of membership, but toward the lay volunteers doing ministries and the church outsiders who are part of the mission field. Therefore, the permission-giving pastor does not do myriad *services,* but rather offers a single service of support to others who have been gifted, called, and equipped to do myriad services. This is why the "servant leader" of the twenty-first century is far more focused and purposeful than the "enabling pastor" of twentieth-century Christendom.

In current terms, the pastor is a *midwife.* My colleague Bill Easum and I introduced this term in *Growing Spiritual Redwoods.* A true midwife knows that every human being is gifted by God—pregnant with the possibilities of God—whether they admit it or not. A true midwife is driven by an urgency to do whatever it takes to help another give birth, knowing that the only alternative is death. The pastor as a midwife has the intuition of timeliness, and can be appropriately nurturing or challenging in order to cajole, guide, or do whatever else it takes for the potentialities of God to be born. A true midwife does not celebrate merely the doing of various ministry tasks, no matter how important they may seem. A true midwife celebrates the joyous fulfillment of another's life through the effective ministries they accomplish in God's name. Perhaps most significant, a true midwife always hands the "baby" back to the "mother." The pastor never assumes responsibility for another's God-given gift or ministry, but coaches them to care for that gift or ministry themselves.

As we follow the role of the pastor through all four quadrants of the permission-giving organization, you will have observed an important shift of emphasis. The *prescriptive thinking* that characterized the first two quadrants assumed the *spiritual authenticity* of the pastor. The *proscriptive thinking* that characterizes the last two quadrants assumes the *professionalism* of the pastor. The painful lesson for twentieth-century churches has been that exquisitely trained and competent clergy, who are not spiritually authentic leaders, cannot lead a permission-giving organization. The challenge to twenty-first-century churches is that profoundly spiritual pastors who are not on a quest for quality and who refuse to develop the skills needed to grow, train, and deploy ministries will not last long in a permission-giving congregation.

The unique, organic character of the permission-giving organization requires the pastor to have a unique spiritual authenticity. This authenticity is based on their own personal experience of life struggle and spiritual victory. What is more important, it is reflected in their spontaneous demonstration of core values, beliefs, vision, and mission in their daily lifestyle. The church is a "seven-day-a-week" church. The pastor's spirituality is a "twenty-four-hour-a-day" lifestyle. At the same time, the unique character of the permission-giving church also requires the pastor to have distinctly different professional skills. The old skills of ecclesiastical administration, command of denominational polity, expository preaching, large group development, one-to-one counseling, and member visitation are the *least* relevant to the organization. New skills for spiritual discernment, improvement of quality, training, coaching, small group development, demographic interpretation, cultural sensitivity, multimedia, and marketing are the *most* relevant to the organization.

This changes the structure of accountability which governs the pastor's career. In the traditional church organization, *pre*scriptive thinking assumed that accountability would be linear.

Denominational Certification

|

Regional Judicatory Administration

|

Congregational Personnel Supervision

|

Pastoral Office

—— 173 ——

Credentialing by a denomination certified the spiritual authenticity of the pastor, who then worked within broad personnel guidelines administered by a regional denominational judicatory. The judicatory's primary oversight of the congregation was through a congregation personnel committee, who perpetuated *pre*scriptive thinking by supervising long job descriptions of what the pastor could or should do. Accountability followed a direct line from congregational supervisors back to the bishop or judicatory, occasionally bypassing the middle judicatory altogether.

The accountability structure for the pastor in the permission-giving organization is quite different because it functions *pro*scriptively. The pastor's career is at the center of a triangle of influences.

Credibility for spiritual authenticity depends primarily on the depth, sincerity, and clarity of the pastor's own experience of life struggle and spiritual victory, and sense of calling. Accountability lies with the conscience of the pastor and the perception of the public. The Human Resources Team of the congregation can reflect back to the pastor the degree to which he or she has credibility for spiritual discipline and leadership, but the measurable accountability of the pastor to the congregation is about identity and purpose. The congregation holds the pastor accountable for living within their consensus for the basic umbrella of congregational life, and facilitating with excellence their mission purpose. This, too, can only be accomplished if the human resources team is particularly sensitive to the mission field, and not just to the membership. The role of the denomination is diminished, but still significant. That accountability measures the pastor's ability to develop quality professional skills and cooperate with other organizational partners to accomplish a larger purpose. The directions of accountability are balanced through the career of the pastor.

Several contrasts between accountability structures of traditional and permission-giving church organizations should be immediately apparent.

1) The accountability system of the permission-giving organization relies more heavily on clarity and consensus within the congregation for the basic umbrella of congregational life (core values, bedrock beliefs, motivating vision, key mission).

2) Permission-giving organizations link to the denomination through mission partnerships and continuing education, rather than through ordination and personnel supervision.

3) There is no longer any relevant role for the regional denominational judicatory in the supervision of personnel.

4) All three directions of accountability are open to the perspectives of the general public and mission partners unrelated to the "closed" denominational system.

5) The accountability system of the permission-giving organization is most effective with *long-term pastoral relations,* rather than with short-term denominational appointments.

The rise of the congregational permission-giving organization is rendering traditional denominational hierarchies obsolete. If denominations shift their role from spiritual certification and supervision of personnel, to professional development and partnership building, they will have a place in the accountability system of the permission-giving organization. If they do not shift, permission-giving congregations will fill the vacuum in their accountability system in the manner of other cultural groups. They will form "professional associations," the primary purpose of which will be to set standards of quality for professional skills and facilitate partnerships for larger, long-term ministries. The reason some independent "megachurches" have actually longed for some quasidenominational link, is precisely the same reason why other denominationally linked congregations have longed to sever their connection. They are looking for a reliable method to ensure the careful building of professional skills and enduring, global mission partnerships.

Perhaps the best illustration for the role of the pastor in a permission-giving organization is found in scripture itself. In Acts 18:24-27 and 1 Corinthians 3:5-6, 9, 16, and 21, the experience and self-understanding of Apollos not only hints at the way the spiritual leader moves through all four quadrants of the organization, but it also suggests the three directions of accountability which govern the pastor's career:

> Now there came to Ephesus a Jew named Apollos, a native of Alexandria. He was an eloquent man, well-versed in the scriptures. He had been instructed in the Way of the Lord; and he spoke with burning enthusiasm and taught accurately the things concerning Jesus....But when Priscilla and Aquila heard him, they took him aside and explained the Way of God to him more accurately. And when he wished to cross over to Achaia, the believers encouraged him....On his arrival he greatly helped those who through grace had become believers.

> What then is Apollos? What is Paul? Servants through whom you came to believe, as the Lord assigned to each. I planted, Apollos watered, but God gave the growth....For we are God's servants, working together; you are God's field, God's building....Do you not know that you are God's temple and that God's Spirit dwells in you?...So let no one boast about human leaders. For all things are yours, whether Paul or Apollos or Cephas or the world or life or death or the present or the future—all belong to you, and you belong to Christ, and Christ belongs to God.

II. TURNING THE LAITY LOOSE

ORGANIZATIONAL CHANGE THROUGH CELL GROUPS AND MISSION TEAMS

— 6 —
THE BASIC IDEA:
CELL GROUPS AND MISSION
TEAMS

There is nothing more exciting in organized Christian life, nor more powerful in changing society, than *ordinary people living a Christian lifestyle*. This joy and power is magnified exponentially when these ordinary Christian people are:

• *linked* together in partnerships of shared learning and mutual support;
• *focused* on the mission field that starts just outside their own backdoor;
• *expectant* for the transforming power of God to grasp them, mold them, and use them to expand the realm of God on earth.

Linked, focused, and *expectant*—the whole purpose of the permission-giving organization is to make that happen.

The first section of this book provided a theoretical overview of the organization in the thriving church system. As we surveyed the organization, it became clear that the real *ministries* of the church do not happen among salaried staff, board members, or even the three management teams of the Stability Triangle. Missions and ministries happen in quadrant 4 with the ferment of growth and mission done by the congregational participants themselves. It is here that people experience personal and spiritual growth, discern calling, and initiate mission in the world.

This section of the book examines *from within* the organization just how ministries and mission erupt from congregational life. This section is not written from the perspective of a congregational leader already committed to the church and eager for the church to become more effective. It is written from the perspective of the seeker who has come to an organized Christian congregation for the first time. What does the seeker see?

1) The seeker sees immediately a clear consensus and enthusiasm for an "umbrella" of core values, bedrock beliefs, motivating vision, and key mission. This umbrella is more than seen. It is experienced in every conversation, in every activity in which the seeker finds herself—no matter how simple or complex. This "umbrella" is integrated into the *lifestyle* of the congregational participants.
2) The seeker sees people moving in, out, and between innumerable partnerships for growth and mission. These cell groups and mission teams may be simple or complex, informal or formal, but they are happening everywhere, all the time, and include everybody.
3) The seeker sees opportunities in which he or she can worship, grow relationally and spiritually, experiment with original ideas, and do something satisfyingly good for other human beings. All these opportunities are given twenty-four-hour support, and they all have a "safety net" of acceptance and learning in case he or she makes a mistake.

In general, the seeker sees a spiritually contained anarchy. The seeker experiences a ferment of growth and mission that is institutionally untidy and joyous, leads in unexpected directions, and requires no institutional burdens. The seeker sees mission emerging from spiritual growth of the people.

If the seeker sees mission emerging "from below," rather than "from above," then it is worth mentioning what the seeker *does not* see.

1) The seeker does *not* see a preponderance of salaried staff. Yes, there is a pastor or spiritual leader, along with other staff who equip ministries, but the staff are generally in the background. Activities do not depend upon them, and they do not attend all congregational activities.

2) The seeker does *not* see a financial statement. Yes, there is a budget and stewardship of money is clearly articulated, but the truth is that the financial life of the institution is generally in the background. No one hounds them about offerings, forces them to face deficit statistics, or insists that they worry about office supplies.

3) The seeker does *not* see a bureaucracy. Yes, there is a board and management teams, but they are in the background. Nominations committees are not continually begging for volunteers, no one pushes the seeker onto a committee for possessing a professional skill needed by the institution, and property is not sacred.

The seeker does not see the organizational infrastructure. It is there, of course. We have described it in section 1. Yet the seeker does not see it. Why? First, the organizational infrastructure has been *streamlined*. It is not as large as the traditional congregation organization. Second, the infrastructure has been *redeployed*. It is no longer doing ministry, but facilitating ministry done by others. Third, the infrastructure has been *reoriented*. It is freeing people within boundaries, not telling people what to do. The seeker does not see the infrastructure, because in the permission-giving organization the infrastructure is not important. What is important is the disciplined spiritual growth of the people.

This section is written from an insider's experience of the permission-giving organization. As the seeker participates in the congregation, he or she will eventually come to know the infrastructure of the church. However, seekers may never care much about it, invest much energy in it, or serve in any offices. They will come to care passionately about the basic umbrella of congregational life and the opportunities they have for personal and spiritual growth, and the success of the various missions and ministries will transform people and benefit the community. As the seeker becomes a disciplined Christian, he or she may never receive a visit from the pastor (even in hospital), serve on the board, or read a denominational magazine. She or he will certainly value many deep, trusted Christian friends (who do visit in hospitals), always participate in a cell group or mission team, and use any and every resource that aids growth and discernment of calling.

The seeker's experience of the permission-giving congregation is a world of personal opportunity. When asked by their next-door neighbor to talk about their church, what do they say? They don't talk about the beauty of their building, the clever preaching of their clergy, or the purity of their denominational polity. They don't talk about the pleasantries of their supper club, or the squabbles of their committees, or the regrettable financial deficit. They talk about the growth they experience, the training they receive, and the ministries that they are doing. They talk about what really fills the horizon of the church experience: *their cell groups and mission teams.*

Why Cell Group Ministry?

Cell Group Ministry is the cornerstone of adult faith and spirituality development in thriving churches on the brink of the twenty-first century. The strategy is adaptable to large, medium, or small churches. The strategy requires nothing of participants except a *desire to grow* in self-understanding, personal relationships, and connection with God.

The term "cell group" is not a political metaphor, but a biological metaphor. Bill Easum and I spoke of "cell groups" in the context of "growing the Spiritual Redwood."[1] The organic nature of the permission-giving organization is cellular, much like the many microscopic cells which together form a tree. Each cell is stamped with a similar genetic code, and works with other cells to allow the tree to grow tall and send roots in all directions.

In thriving churches, more than 80 percent of the adults will be involved in some form of faith development or spiritual discipline through the week. For many of these adults, participation in a cell group will be a central part of their discipline. Nurturing adult faith produces positive results:

• growth in motivated lay leadership
• growth in local, regional, and world mission

• growth in Sunday school for children
• growth in youth ministries among teenagers
• growth in worship attendance
• growth in new participation in the whole life of the church.

Why? Because cell group ministry helps people change. It helps them overcome their addictions and burdens, discover new life, and discern their place in God's loving work. Positive change is contagious. When people are changed, they live differently. When others see them live differently, they begin to believe change is possible for them as well.

It *is* possible to rejoice in yourself and have positive self-esteem.
It *is* possible to have deep, deep personal relationships with intimate
 friends.
It *is* possible to have a profound connection with God.
It *is* possible to have an achievable purpose for living.

Who? Cell group ministry helps people who are currently *beyond* the church to explore their connections with God in an unpressured, highly motivating experience of intimacy. It helps people *on the margins* of the church to deepen their spirituality and become personally involved in mission. It helps people *already active* in the church to rejuvenate their energy and fulfill themselves in clearly beneficial ministries. North American culture on the brink of the twenty-first century is ready for a different kind of church.

The public has a deep spiritual yearning.
Marginal church people have a profound desire to walk daily with
 Christ.
Active church people are eager to be turned loose for productive,
 quality ministries.

The spiritually yearning, institutionally alienated public are the "Gentile mission" of the twenty-first century, to which the church is called to be "all things to all people, that [it] might by all means [rescue] some" (1 Cor. 9:22).

Cell Group Ministry Involves Organizational Change

Cell group ministry is a very simple strategy—with far-reaching organizational implications. There are many resources on the market today for cell group development. Some are quite easy, others are quite sophisticated, and most are very good. The difficulty with all of them is that they do not quite prepare a traditional congregational organization for the changes that cell group ministry will require.

Traditionally organized congregations may discover that "cell groups" are already emerging in their church experience—usually on the fringes of church life. Such groups may not be formally initiated or "authorized" by the official board. They just seem to "happen," and usually they are welcomed. Unless these spontaneous groups become part of an intentional strategy, however, they eventually fade.

• The group may share an affinity that upsets church leaders, so the church discourages or rejects the cell group;
• The church may regard cell group participation as an "extra" which should not take energy away from the official committees and task groups of the church;
• The cell group leaders may not be truly gifted or trained, so group participation is not ultimately fulfilling, or the group fails to overcome inevitable obstacles in building relationships or faith.

Even when traditionally organized congregations embrace the strategy of cell group ministry wholeheartedly, they commonly become preoccupied with cell group "management" and ultimately complain that cell group growth has "plateaued" for some unknown reason. As soon as cell groups fail to replicate themselves, the strategy itself begins to die.

The difficulty is that traditional congregational organizations cannot help perceiving cell group life as another form of committee structure. The diversity and experimentation of cell group life challenges any imposed structure, and the traditional organization compensates by institutional management. Now there are many reasons why cell groups may experience difficulties, and many good resources can help the congregation address issues of group growth. It is best at the very beginning, however, to recognize one fundamental truth. *The number 1 reason cell group growth fails is that the traditional congregational organization refuses to change!*

Some congregations will approach cell group ministry from a plan devised to transform themselves into a permission-giving organization. They will embrace the thriving church system and carefully develop the organization through quadrants 1, 2, and 3. They will define the boundaries of congregational life, refine the point of mission, and develop measurements for success. The more carefully they do this work, the more easily cell groups and mission teams can grow.

Many congregations, however, will approach cell group ministry without clearly embracing systemic change, or with only partial preparation in the first three quadrants. There is nothing wrong with this, provided that they recognize the reasons for the inevitable stress to come. Development of the ministries of quadrant 4 will bring pressure on the church to clarify quadrants 1, 2, and 3. If congregational leadership recognizes this need, and works to define boundaries, refine mission, and measure success, then the cell groups will have patience and continue to grow. It does not have to happen immediately. All that is required is for the congregation to be credibly progressing through the first three quadrants.

Cell group ministry will have patience and flourish if the congregation is seen to commit itself to organizational change by doing four things: *forethought, planning, leadership preparation, constant prayer support.*

Forethought may be *afterthought* in some cases, but the church must capture the real vision and essential attitude necessary for cell group ministry. These groups are not simply "pleasant extras" for church involvement. They are the core experience of church participation, and the chief vehicle through which ministry is expressed in the church.

Planning needs to become more deliberate, so that the diversity of cell group life shares the harmony of the basic beliefs, values, and vision of the church. The church can understand how the various "pieces" of cell group ministry "fit together" in the overall life and mission of the congregation.

Leadership preparation becomes prioritized, so that cell groups can truly fulfill their potential for personal discovery and mission. The best way to expand cell group ministry is to constantly improve the quality of cell group experience.

Constant prayer support is crucial for the Holy Spirit to bring cell group experience to full flower. It helps group leaders to face all the challenges, and identify all the opportunities, cell group life brings.

Cell Group Ministry Requires Stress Management

You will find that nurturing cell groups is like raising rabbits. They multiply! At first, it seems very simple to raise a rabbit—and indeed it is! Before very long, however, you will begin to discover that there is more stress involved than you might have expected.

Stress #1: Raising rabbits is not the same as raising dogs.

Churches soon learn that cell groups are not the same as program committees. Most mainstream churches are very good at starting, organizing, and guiding committees based on an institutional agenda provided to the committee. Committee skills have become a kind of ingrained habit for many mainstream church leaders—a habit they repeat automatically with any group that forms. There is always unconscious pressure from mainstream church leaders to transform any group into a committee.

The organizational model for many mainstream churches is one of high bureaucracy. At least four layers of administration are required to manage the church:

numerous standing program committees
an executive of the official board
the official board itself
regular congregational meetings.

No ministry happens unless it is controlled by
a committee, and supervised by these layers of management. What is important
to these churches is that every committee have a chairperson, an
agenda, and a prescriptive mandate that lists everything they
can or should do. The committee is like a trained
dog ("guide dog" or
"retriever"). It obeys
the commands of its
owner, and it does
only that which it has been
trained to do. Its whole purpose in life is to achieve the goals of
another—the institutional church. It is their way to get the work of
Christ done.

Unfortunately, it is not a way that works well on the brink of the
twenty-first century. Frustrating bureaucracies, stagnating institutions, unfulfilling offices, and exhausted leaders repel newcomers
and discourage veteran church participants. People are looking for
a better way to get the work of Christ done.

Small spirituality cell groups are different from committees. There
is no chairperson, but there is a group leader who guides and mentors participants to build healthy relationships and grow in faith.
There is no agenda, but there is a "flow" to group experience. There
is no mandate beckoning people to do their duty, but there is a
group affinity based on a common enthusiasm. And instead of
deploying four redundant layers of management to watch over
their work, the board tries its best to get out of their way. Cell groups
are like rabbits. They hop wherever they want to hop, eat whatever

they happen to find nourishing, and befriend whomever they wish. They sniff every changing breeze of culture, sneak into unlikely places in the community, and hate being confined in a building.

The first stress that traditional, mainstream churches experience in cell group ministry is that it is simply foreign to their experience. *Excellent dog-owners do not necessarily make excellent rabbit-raisers.* Cell groups (like rabbits) not only demand a different kind of food, but they require a whole different routine of nurture. To say it simply, cell groups are truly a different species of animal. And this means that mainstream church leaders not only need to learn new skills, but they need to learn new habits. Cell groups require a different *attitude* on the part of the church.

The cell group "attitude" or "habit" is gained only through experimentation. You don't just read about it, intellectually comprehend it, and then do it right the first time. You try, you fail, you try again, and you fail again—each time laughing at yourself and learning from your mistakes. The reason you try and fail is that the habits of owning "dogs" are difficult to overcome when you want to raise "rabbits." Don't be surprised if new attitudes take a while to form. But don't give up. The benefits will be great!

Stress #2: Raising rabbits requires more attention than raising dogs.

Churches also learn that cell groups demand more time from the Pastoral Leadership Team. The ministers (i.e., pastoral leaders) will need to reprioritize their weekly agenda to give significant attention to the nurture of the cell groups. This time will likely be taken from other tasks, such as administration or visitation. Those churches who expect their ministers to take sole responsibility for pastoral care, and those churches for whom the minister is the only guide through the labyrinth of denominational polity and congregational bureaucracy, will experience stress as the pastor reprioritizes time. These other tasks will need to be done by gifted and called lay leaders.

In the same way, cell groups will demand different skills of the church leaders. The skills to "mentor," "coach," and "shepherd" are quite different from the skills to "teach," "administrate," and "manage." Continuing education for the staff, and for church personnel committees, may be necessary. Churches that are "dog-owners" tell their committees what to do, and then watch to see that they do it right. Churches that are "rabbit-raisers" turn their cell groups loose, "shepherd" them to discover their own callings, and then "coach" them to overcome obstacles and do ministry with excellence.

The pastoral leader (or leadership team) will not only spend time developing the first cell group. They will find that they must begin immediately to train and coach potential cell group leaders for cell groups that will emerge. When the rabbits start to multiply, they quickly outnumber the pastoral leaders available. The minister will not lead all the cell groups. In time, the minister will not have time to lead *any* of the cell groups. The energies of the pastoral leadership team will be devoted to training leaders. Don't burn out! Start now to train the cell group leaders of the future!

Stress #3: Rabbits soon take over the backyard.

Finally, be prepared for the rabbits to take over the backyard—and the frontyard, and the house, and the barn! They will transform your living space. In the same way, cell groups will transform your congregation's life and mission.

The strategy of cell group ministry is not a program to be incorporated into a traditionally organized congregation. It is a system of spiritual growth and ministry that ultimately *replaces* the traditionally organized congregation. We call this *systemic change*.

• The clergy invest time training and motivating laity, and the laity invest time actually doing the ministry;

• Program committees rapidly become superfluous, and mission is accomplished by cell groups;
• Nominations processes are replaced by spiritual gifts discernment processes, as fewer people are recruited for the institutional agenda, and more people are motivated to fulfill their own callings;
• Sunday morning worship motivates weeklong discipleship;
• Congregational life becomes extraordinarily diverse, and erupts in more mission, than could ever be "controlled" by the bureaucracy.

Just as rabbits soon multiply to take over the backyard, so also cell group ministries soon multiply to the point that the organizational model of the mainstream church dramatically changes. This can be very stressful.

The first thing that happens is that church organization becomes streamlined. The cell groups multiply too fast for the slow bureaucracy of the church. The ministries that emerge from cell groups are too dynamic for the hierarchical supervision of the church, and are constantly being adapted and customized to changing circumstances. And the enthusiasm of the people involved in cell groups parallels their growing frustration with being "sidetracked" into all kinds of administrative, reporting, and miscellaneous bureaucratic activities.

The second thing that happens is that the mission agenda of the church is set "from below," rather than "from above." No longer does the official board define the mission agenda for the coming year, and then recruit dutiful members to implement their mission plan through committees. Instead, cell groups discover the missions they are called to do, and they inform the board of their plans. The role of the official board changes. No longer do they tell people what to do. Now they equip and assist people to do whatever it is they are called to do.

In both ways, church leaders begin to fear that they are "losing control." Indeed, "control" will become the most stressful issue as the cell groups multiply. The issues of control will be addressed in detail later, but it is good to be aware of this stress now. The *prescriptive* thinking of the traditional church organization is like a magnet that can subtly draw the organization away from its per-mission-giving purpose.

Look at it this way: Dog-owners are used to putting their dogs on a leash. Supervision is direct and constant. If ever the dog is let off the leash, it is given verbal commands which are instantly obeyed. But you can't put a *leash* on a *rabbit!* They have to be free to follow their noses, and hop in any direction they choose. A rabbit on a leash will die. It is the same difference between a committee and a cell group.

This fear among church leaders who are in the habit of owning dogs (i.e., supervising committees) can become a serious problem. In fact, your very success in multiplying cell groups can raise the stress level of some church leaders. This is part of the challenge of systemic change. The cell groups soon take over the mission agenda of the church, just as rabbits take over the frontyard.

How do you reduce your organizational stress?

Remind your church leaders that "control" and "accountability" are two different things. Even when raising rabbits, there are methods of accountability. They are just different.

1) *Define the boundaries beyond which they cannot go.* The rabbit run is surrounded by a fence. Cell groups are surrounded by the boundaries of basic beliefs, values, and vision that form the identity of the church. They can roam wherever they wish within the boundaries, but they cannot go beyond.

2) *Equip and coach cell groups for excellence.* Rabbits will go their own way, but they can be helped to do it well. Cell groups can be trained for excellence, and coached by pastors and lay leaders to do whatever it is they do with quality.

3) *Select, train, and support cell group leaders with care.* Cell group leaders must be gifted and called. They need to be given initial training, plus regular opportunities to mutually mentor one another and upgrade skills.

Although the official board may not play the same role of giving or withholding permission to do ministries anymore, they do play an important role in coordinating and monitoring the performance of cell groups.

In the end, a yard full of rabbits hopping in diverse directions may seem more chaotic than a yard with only a few well-trained dogs on tethers. The cell group strategy in all its fullness may seem equally wild. Cheer up! No one need be hurt, everyone will have more fun, and many more helpful ministries will be deployed in the community.

Cell Groups Function with Clear Assumptions

Cell group ministry is based on key principles. Whatever the specific resource a congregation uses, simple or sophisticated, these principles are an integral part of the permission-giving organization itself. In *Growing Spiritual Redwoods,* my colleague Bill Easum and I described these principles as the DNA (genetic code) with which every cell of the organization is stamped. No matter how diverse the cell groups may be, no matter how many different kinds of cell group styles and activities may emerge, the cell groups all share the same basic assumptions. Every cell group leader is trained with these principles in mind.

Theological Assumptions

Any profound experience of faith must include:

1. An experience of the Holy that questions, deepens, changes, and enriches

God's power needs to be felt in the heart, in order to change the motivation and behavior of individuals. It needs to enrich their lives, and open them to mystery. It needs to invite constant questioning and dialogue, and allow them to interpret for themselves who this God is, and what this God is doing with their lives.

2. An experience of deep, healthy relationships with partners on a journey

Faith development needs quality intimacy with people who

---

share one's desire for God. Mutual support, honesty, respect, and prayer help people find their way through ambiguity.

3. An experience of self-discovery and maturing self-esteem
Faith development needs a foundation of positive self-worth, and a readiness to discover whatever lies hidden within oneself. It requires confidence that beneath all the vices and failings, there is a person who is essentially lovable.

4. An experience of deep, sensitive compassion for strangers
Spiritual growth deepens when one's attention transcends self to recognize the needs and yearnings of others. Faith and hospitality to strangers are two sides of the same coin.

5. An experience of humility, growth, and celebration
Enduring faith confronts all obstacles with hope. One must be always open to learning new things and playing diverse personal roles. Thanksgiving and celebration lie at the heart of a deep faith.

Mission Assumptions

Effective and enduring mission requires:

1. The timely release of one's spiritual gifts
Faithful Christians must know and exercise the spiritual gifts with which God created them, and do so courageously when the time seems right.

2. Maximum confidence to share faith and take risks in service
The Faithful Christian must not only do good deeds, but be able to articulate the religious motivation for those deeds to others. Witness and service must go together.

3. Responsibility for mission by the people who are called to do it
Effective mission results only when one moves beyond supervision and administration, to personally participate in the work of ministry.

4. Mutual accountability in a quest for excellence
Enduring mission results only when the participants work as a team with others, and demand of themselves the highest standards.

Educational Assumptions

Profound personal growth requires:

1. *Learning through intimate, challenging, and informed conversation*
Dialogue that is honest and knowledgeable helps every participant form interpretations of the world with integrity and respect.

2. *Learning through problem solving and development of practical life skills*
Growth begins by addressing pressing issues and questions, and equips individuals to overcome obstacles.

3. *Learning and work in dynamic tension*
Activity and reflection reinforce each other. Personal growth should be revealed through behavioral change.

4. *Learning that integrates intellectual, emotional, and spiritual dimensions*
Profound growth unites the whole person. It blends body, mind, heart, and soul. Discoveries in one dimension affect all other dimensions.

5. *Learning through laughter and experimentation*
Profound growth cultivates the ability to laugh at oneself, and to risk failure or the appearance of foolishness.

Pastoral Assumptions

Sensitive pastoral care requires:

1. *Mutual support for healing and personal change*
Only constant, committed group support can help individuals overcome destructive addictions to find healing.

2. *The encouragement of healthy intimacy and personal significance*
Honest, respectful sharing should reinforce each individual's self-worth. The well-being of each participant should matter to every other participant.

3. *The discovery of meaning through doing*
People find meaning in life through involvement in activities that have clear, practical, and significant benefits.

4. *The conviction that those who seek life must give life away*
The true affirmation of oneself does not come through self-centeredness, but through self-surrender to a higher purpose.

This genetic code imprinted on each cell group is directly linked to the core values, bedrock beliefs, motivating vision, and key mission that is the consensus of the congregation. The cell may be distinct in its missional purpose, covenant, and leadership, but it will share with every other cell these assumptions. The basic umbrella of congregational life is taken into the heart of cell group life.

Cell Group Ministry Is Part of a Larger System

Cell group ministry plays an important part in a larger system of thriving church life. It will not be the only way adult faith development is encouraged by the church, but it may well be the primary way adults from the cultures beyond the institutional church participate in Christian growth.

The pentagon-shaped model illustrates the complete system of the thriving church. People who come to the church do so motivated by a desire to be changed or to be different. This yearning may be motivated by a desire to break free of destructive addictions, or simply by a desire to find purposefulness and meaning. Whatever the degree of urgency, adults come to the church seeking "to be changed" and not simply "to belong to an institution." For a complete description of the system of the Thriving Church, refer to my book *Kicking Habits: Welcome Relief for Addicted Churches*, published by Abingdon Press.

Many adults will find their way into church life through participation in some opportunity for worship. Thriving churches seek to diversify the opportunities for worship so that individuals can worship at the time, and in the style, that is most meaningful to them. Some adults will find their way into church life directly through a cell group. It is the specific affinity (shared enthusiasm) of a group that attracts their interest, plus the opportunity to pursue that interest in a spiritual context that encourages informal, unhurried dialogue.

THRIVING CHURCH

Called

MATURITY   MEANING

Equipped   Gifted

SERVANT
EMPOWERMENT

MINISTRY   MEMBERSHIP

Sent   Changed

MISSION

THE PUBLIC:
LOCAL & GLOBAL

Cell group ministry lies at the heart of each of the five subsystems of the pentagon model. This key organizational change is the cause of much of the stress congregations will experience in the development of cell group ministry. Failure to understand this key change will cause premature "plateaus" in cell group multiplication. However, since experience is the best guide to understanding, we will return to this point in the *last* chapter. At this point, simply refer to the five sides of the pentagon model:

1) As people begin to sense themselves changing through a worshipful connection with God...
2) they covenant with the church to go deeper into their faith and personal relationships...

3) they discern their opportunities to fulfill themselves in God's greater plan of love...

4) they are equipped and coached to exercise their callings with excellence...

5) and they enter partnerships with others, free to do what they are called to do.

Cell group ministry is really a *Dance!* It is a constantly repeated movement of the human spirit that moves from personal growth, to discernment of destiny, to active service—and then right back into more personal growth. It is like a waltz with three steps: *1, 2, 3...and 1, 2, 3...and 1, 2, 3.* The "dance" itself is coached or encouraged by teams of staff and volunteers, particularly in the two places of *transforming worship* and *training for excellence.*

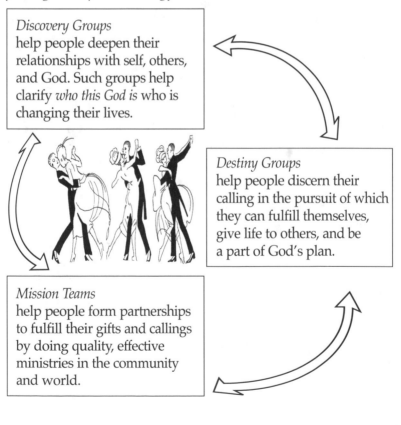

Discovery Groups help people deepen their relationships with self, others, and God. Such groups help clarify *who this God is* who is changing their lives.

Destiny Groups help people discern their calling in the pursuit of which they can fulfill themselves, give life to others, and be a part of God's plan.

Mission Teams help people form partnerships to fulfill their gifts and callings by doing quality, effective ministries in the community and world.

Discovery Groups, Destiny Groups, and Mission Teams are composed entirely of volunteers. Laypeople provide the leadership for these groups, and laypeople participate in these groups. Individuals move from one group to another as they spiritually grow, change, evolve, and explore—their faith, their relationships, and themselves. Each type of group is associated with one of the five subsystems of the thriving church:

From "membership" to "meaning"—Discovery Groups
From "meaning" to "maturity"—Destiny Groups
From "ministry" to "mission"—Mission Teams

This "dance" is repeated over and over again, in a manner and speed that is unique to every person. The partners in each group are ever changing, and the groups themselves are ever changing. This also means that the mission of the church is ever changing! The mission agenda of the church is determined by the spiritual growth of individual participants, not by an institutional hierarchy.

However, two other types of cell groups help coach, equip, and encourage this movement of human spirit. In order to help people move

from "maturity" to "ministry"

training teams of salaried staff and volunteers help those who have been changed, gifted, and called to now exercise their gifts with excellence. These same teams provide twenty-four-hour coaching support for the Mission Teams as they do their ministries.

A second type of team composed of salaried staff and volunteers also works to motivate and encourage participants in their "dance" of personal growth and ministry. In order to help people move

from "mission" to "membership"

worship teams design multiple opportunities for newcomers and church participants to experience and give thanks for God's contin-

THRIVING CHURCH

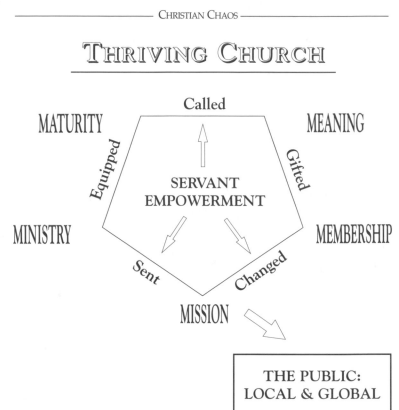

uing grace. These teams design and lead the worship services of the church, and provide twenty-four-hour prayer support of participants in all the other groups of the church.

Cell group ministry not only transforms the organization of the church, but it also changes the leadership roles of staff and volunteers. Salaried staff and volunteer leaders also function together in cell groups, in a manner described more fully in the next chapter. They are enabled to spiritually grow, change, evolve, and explore in the same way as participants in every other group. Their role in the system, however, is not to *do* ministries, but rather to equip, coach, and encourage *others* to do ministry.

In the end, seekers and participants in a thriving church system do not experience the congregation as an organization at all. They experience it as a flow of activity, a movement of spirit, a journey of faith, a quest of mission. No institution demands their allegiance: no committee, no budget, no structure, no building, no denomination, no heritage, no office. There is only *the dance*—and an appreciation for quality coaching.

There is the **Dance:**

And there are the **Dance Coaches:**

— 7 —

CELL GROUP AND MISSION
TEAM LIFE

Cell groups are an expression of—or an instrument for—systemic change. If the congregation has developed carefully the first three quadrants of the permission-giving organization, cell groups will express the core identity of values, beliefs, vision, and mission in the DNA of emerging mission. If the congregation has yet to transform its organizational structure, cell groups will become an instrument that brings stress to the organization until it does define identity, refine mission, and commit to excellence.

Now let us take a closer look at the internal workings of cell groups themselves. When we speak of *Cell Groups* we do not mean just any kind of group with a limited number of people. We are speaking of a specific, detailed strategy of adult personal growth and faith development. This strategy has emerged through the practical experience of many congregations from many denominations and traditions, and from the practical experience of Twelve-Step and other self-help programs around the world. Cell group life can be enormously diverse, and yet at the same time value redundancy. Cell groups can be utterly unique, or remarkably repetitive. Whether they explore new territory, or walk participants down a well-trodden path, they deepen an individual's values and beliefs through the mutual support of intimate colleagues in grace, and enable the individual to overcome obstacles to find new hope and life. Although there is almost infinite variety in cell group activity, there is a basic pattern to success—they multiply constantly. Here I call them simply *P.A.L.S. Groups.*

P.A.L.S. Group Essentials

Every *P.A.L.S.* group does four essential things, regardless of its individual character, content, or direction.

1. **P**RAYER: Prayer for others will always be a part of the group process. Prayer might be as informal as a few moments of silence, or a brief spoken word by the participants; or it might involve a major block of time using the aid of liturgy, singing, or meditative disciplines like Tai Chi or Yoga.

2. **A**CTIVITY: Some group activity will always be a part of the group process. Everyone will participate, and the activity is often the primary purpose for being there. Initially, the activity is simply that which the participants most enjoy doing. This is their shared enthusiasm or affinity. Eventually, the activity is expanded to be of some concrete benefit to others beyond the group. It becomes a form of *mission*.

3. **L**EARNING: Two kinds of learning will be a part of every group process.
   First, participants will learn more about themselves. They may discover their spiritual gifts, personality types, or simply clarify their own feelings, hurts, hopes, and dreams.
   Second, participants learn about God. This may be as simple as discussing a Bible passage for a few minutes or sharing personal experiences, or as complex as Bible *study* or research into comparative religions.

4. **S**HARING: Intimate, honest, personally revealing conversation will always be a part of the group process. Participants bond together in a context of trust, and share in confidence and respect whatever is in their hearts or minds.

Cell group life will have endless variety. The only limits are those of your imagination. Nevertheless, each group will include these four basic themes.

P.A.L.S. Group Organization

Since group *life* will have endless variety, group *organization* will also be very diverse. The shape of the organization will depend on the affinity that binds the group together, and the unique preferences of the participants of each group. Groups may be highly structured or incredibly unstructured. Only four constant factors will be true for every P.A.L.S. group.

1) Trained Leaders: The church trains a leader for every group, who guides the flow of relationship building and faith development. This leader may be called a "Shepherd," "Pastor," "Elder," or simply the "Group Leader." Selection, training, and accountability are so important that chapter 8 is devoted to leadership entirely.
2) Limited Numbers: Groups will never have more than twelve participants, in order to maximize intimacy. Groups may "band together" for larger projects, but if any one group grows beyond twelve persons the church will help them form a second group.
3) Self-determination: Each group decides for itself how it will be organized. Organization is not imposed by the institutional church, and regular "reports" are not required by an official board. No group representative is needed to attend another group or committee for "liaison" purposes.
4) Consensus: Decisions in groups are always made by *consensus,* and not by majority vote. The trained leaders help build consensus. If a direction for group activity cannot gain consensus, the church will help them form a second group.

Most traditionally organized churches worry excessively about *accountability.* P.A.L.S. groups are remarkably independent and creative, and are not designed to respond to the directives of higher institutional authority. Like rabbits, they are free to roam, explore, and generally "poke their noses" into anything they wish. However, there *is* a method of accountability. It involves:

- the selection, training, and regular sharing of the P.A.L.S. group *leaders* regarding the relationship-building and faith-building flows of group life;
- clarity about the basic boundaries of values, beliefs, vision, and mission that is the consensus of the whole church.

The issue of *accountability* will be discussed in greater depth in chapter 8, and the larger issue of institutional *control* will be discussed in chapter 10. The freedom of the cell group is one of the most exciting—and stressful—aspects of cell group ministry!

P.A.L.S. Group Covenant

Every P.A.L.S. group will have a covenant. The covenant outlines the basic organization of the group, key expectations of the participants, timelines, gathering places, and any other details unique to the group. The covenant of the group will be determined by the affinity which binds the group together. For example, a mutual support group for addictions will have a very different covenant than a hobby group for gardening. Not only will the time and location of the mutual support group emphasize regularity and confidentiality, but the covenant may also specify that new members cannot join after the first few meetings. The covenant may be initially prepared by the trained group leader, but it may be changed, shaped, or perfected by group consensus. On pages 207-8 are some examples.

The covenant of the group is the primary vehicle for mutual accountability. If people are regularly absent or late for gatherings, or if individuals wish to carry the group in a direction other than the stated purpose, or if individuals somehow contradict the expectations of the group, this covenant is the vehicle for group participants to evaluate group participation. Potential group members can know in advance the expectations of group participation, and decide whether any conditions of time or interest block their involvement.

COVENANT
Cell Group Participation

Yes!
I am ready to go deeper into my awareness
of self, others, and God!
I am eager to enjoy our common affinity!
I am committed to participation with this group as indicated below.

Purpose
The enthusiasm we share is:
Freedom from addiction to prescription drugs.

Time Limits
Our group will gather: *Every Monday night.*
At the following times: *7:00 P.M.–9:30 P.M.*
This covenant ends: *June 1st (after nine months).*

Location
Our group will gather at: *Church lounge.*

Membership
New members may join: *In the first 3 meetings.*
The total group will not exceed: *12 persons.*

Key Expectations
Commitment to confidentiality and honesty.
Willingness to listen.

Group Leader
Our group leader is: *Elder Smith*
Once our covenant is completed,
I will feel free to explore whatever future path of growth I wish.

Signature: _____

COVENANT
Cell Group Participation

Yes!
I am ready to go deeper into my awareness
of self, others, and God!
I am eager to enjoy our common affinity!
I am committed to participation with this group as indicated below.

Purpose
The enthusiasm we share is: *Gardening!*

Time Limits
Our group will gather: *Every other Saturday morning.*
At the following times: *7:00 A.M.–11:30 A.M.*
This covenant ends: *April 1–September 1 (after five months).*

Location
Our group will gather at: *Participants' backyards.*

Membership
New members may join: *Anytime.*
The total group will not exceed: *12 persons,*
but the truth is guests are always welcome.

Key Expectations
Bring your own gardening gloves.
Readiness to have fun rain or shine.

Group Leader
Our group leader is: *Sally and Fred.*
Once our covenant is completed,
I will feel free to explore whatever future path of growth I wish.

Signature: _____

P.A.L.S. Group Multiplication

P.A.L.S. groups are like single cell creatures that constantly divide and multiply. In fact, it is the replication or multiplication of these cells which makes that whole organism of the church grow. The trained leader of the group helps birth new groups. (See our book *Growing Spiritual Redwoods.*) Groups multiply for a variety of reasons:

1) The group has fulfilled the time limit of its covenant, and participants may recovenant with a group of similar purpose, or move on to some other group or spiritual discipline;

2) The group has grown too large (usually to more than twelve), so that full sharing is hindered by the size of the group and must be divided into two groups with the same purpose;

3) Some participants of a group have grown in a distinct direction, and want to pursue an activity which does not have the consensus of the whole group;

4) Practical considerations (such as time and place) unexpectedly change for some group participants, causing two groups to form with the same purpose.

Whenever a group multiplies, a new trained leader must be part of the nucleus for the new cell. These new leaders may emerge from within the first group, or from the whole church. They will be trained by the church in a manner to be described.

Completely new groups, of course, may emerge at any time. The partnerships people form with others for intimacy and spiritual growth will be ever changing. Any comprehensive church list of cell groups will become quickly out-of-date—just as any comprehensive list of church ministries will become quickly out-of-date.

1) Some new groups will form as a trained leader gathers people around a new enthusiasm or interest.

2) Other new groups will form as spontaneous clusters of church participants seek the help of a trained leader to consolidate and expand their enthusiasm or interest.

3) Still other new groups will form as a surprising offshoot of the growth that has been experienced in an existing "Discovery Group," "Destiny Group," or "Mission Team."

In order for new groups to form and existing groups to multiply, however, it is crucial to realize that all groups have a specific life span. *Groups must also come to an end.* Groups that never end soon stagnate. The participants may love one another deeply—but they stop growing—and their stagnation blocks the growth of future groups. Trained group leaders help their group overcome the sadness of closure, so that they can experience the joy and challenge of new opportunities for growth.

P.A.L.S. Group "Dance"

I indicated earlier that cell group ministry is part of a larger *system* of church life in which people are changed, gifted, called, equipped,

THRIVING CHURCH

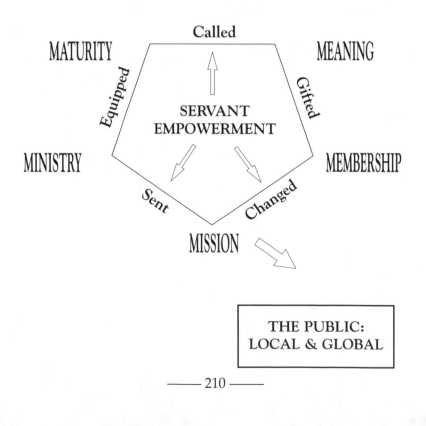

and sent into ministry. The pentagon-shaped model illustrates the changing *orientation* of P.A.L.S. groups as people experience life in the church over an extended time.

One of the great contrasts between a traditional church and a church emphasizing cell group ministry, is that the latter is in constant movement. Change is not only welcome—it lies at the heart of church life.

In a traditional church, life is relatively static. What is important is whether or not you are a *member*—whether or not you are *in* or *out*. Individuals tend to locate themselves in the organization (on a committee, official board, permanent fellowship group, etc.) and never leave it. The church leaders actually appreciate the static nature of church life, because at any given time they know who is doing what.

In a thriving church emphasizing cell groups, life is always dynamic. What is important is whether or not an individual participant is *growing*. Individuals are in constant movement (within themselves, in their relationships with others, and in the roles they play in church life). Communications systems must be very good, and church leaders must constantly be "on their toes," because at any given time laity might be doing something completely different!

(For a complete discussion of this contrast between two church systems, again see *Kicking Habits: Welcome Relief for Addicted Churches* and *Growing Spiritual Redwoods*.)

The dynamic church life that emerges from cell group ministry may seem chaotic, and perhaps even random. It makes doing strategic planning in the traditional way difficult. However, a closer look at this dynamic church life reveals predictable patterns and a strategy for growth and group multiplication.

The metaphor of dance is helpful. Picture in your mind a teenage dance: loud music, heavy rhythm, a packed dance floor, and teens moving and swaying in seemingly infinite ways. To many traditional adult chaperones, it looks like chaos. Yet there are hidden patterns crucial to the dance.

1) *It is always better to attend the dance in a group, than to come alone.* People almost always come in a group. During the dance, the group serves as a center from which individuals come and go, but within which they can converse, joke, and evaluate their experiences. In the same way, cell groups are crucial to dynamic church life.

2) *It is always better to have a partner, than to dance alone.* Although at various times individuals may well dance alone, primarily they dance with partners. The partners may change, and occasionally there may be more than one. In the same way, personal spiritual growth is best accomplished in relationship with others.

3) *Every dance includes repeatable "steps."* These "steps" may be bodily movements, and they may encourage innovative gyrations, but for a dance to be a dance (and to be fun) there must be a repeatable pattern. The waltz is the most obvious example, but the most modern dances follow the same principle. In the same way, personal spiritual growth follows a distinct pattern: discovery of self, discernment of purpose, living out a mission... and back to discovery of self once more, reassessment of purpose, revised mission service... and back to deeper discovery once more. As in a dance, it is 1, 2, 3... and 1, 2, 3... and 1, 2, 3... over and over again.

4) *The most important thing is to lose yourself in the rhythm!* Once the rhythm has penetrated one's mind and heart, the body is free to move on its own. Dancing is not done well as a strategic plan. It happens spontaneously and enthusiastically. In the same way, the *vision* of the church for spiritual growth permeates every cell group. However diverse groups may be, they are all dancing to the same not-so-distant drummer.

I should probably add that in *modern* dance, innovation is especially prized. No dance remains static, but the dance itself evolves as individuals experiment with it. In the same way, cell group ministry accelerates change in the church, and diversifies the possibilities in church life. If you look out on the teenage dance floor, it may look like total chaos. Many adults itch to organize everyone into a nice, understandable, tidy *square* dance—or at least control movement

1
Discovery Groups
Individuals discover themselves:
their gifts, personalities,
beliefs, values, and self-worth
and
they discover their
connection with God:
the Person of Christ, and the
touch of the Holy.

What Discovery Groups Are Not!	What Discovery Groups Really Are!
1. They are not mere "Fellowship Gatherings" (pleasant times over coffee and idle chatter).	1. They are times of intimate conversation (purposeful, confidential, honest sharing that reveals attitudes, values, and beliefs).
2. They are not mere "Information Sessions" (raising awareness about issues).	2. They are strategies of self-discernment (of hidden obstacles and opportunities, gifts, personalities, talents, feelings).
3. They are not "Administration Teams" (exercising a committee mandate).	3. They are enthusiasm for an activity (doing what it is they love to do).
4. They are not "Power Cliques" (controlling areas of church life).	4. They are an internal, limited consensus (expressing their united enthusiasm).
5. They are not "Sunday school Classes" (studying doctrine, history, or polity).	5. They are creative expressions of spirituality (understanding the Bible as it applies to their own daily living).

with a slow polka—but it cannot be done. Just try to impose such control, and watch the participants leave!

There *is* a pattern, and there *is* a predictability to the dance. Identify it and build upon it, and not only will everyone have a great time, but more and more people will join the dance!

Discovery Groups provide an environment in which people can explore life, relationships, and faith. They have freedom to question, experiment, and grow. The mutual support of the group, and the coaching and encouragement of the group leader, allow participants to risk or invest themselves in introspection, relationships, or spirituality. Depending on the nature of the group, this may be very informal and easygoing, or more serious and intense. Examples of discovery groups might include gardening, furniture repair, theater, reading, cooking, or conversation, diet support, physiotherapy, sports, or addiction release. The possible affinities are endless. The point is that the orientation of a discovery group is to "discover" meaning in life in new ways.

A common mistake in the development of discovery groups is the imposition of some form of "curriculum" or "study guide" on the discovery group by the official board or pastor of the church. *Some* groups may welcome a more formal study guide if it is appropriate to their shared enthusiasm and agreed organization. Other groups find such structure inhibiting. Imposed curricula too often function as a "control" mechanism of the church that forces uniformity of theological perspective or ideological opinion on group participants. If any "study guide" is used, it must be chosen through the consensus of the group, and it must be built into their covenant.

Remember, cell groups are "rabbits," which must have freedom to wander and roam. In order to let this happen with safety and integrity

• the congregation must have clarity about its own basic boundaries of core values, bedrock beliefs, motivating vision, and key mission;
• the congregation must provide quality group leadership that can coach and encourage personal and spiritual growth.

We will discuss quality leadership and appropriate organization in later chapters of this book.

2 **Destiny Groups** Individuals listen for their callings to use their gifts in ways that benefit others; and they discern their place in God's greater purpose of healing and grace in the world.

Destiny Groups provide an opportunity for people to discern their place in God's unfolding plan for the universe. These groups are designed for people who are aware of their gifts, but do not know what to do with them. God calls every Christian into ministry, and these groups help individuals discover what that calling might be. Once again, these groups might be very unstructured and informal, or they might be quite disciplined and intense. Examples of such groups might include conversation, camping, walking, motorcycle maintenance, or prayer—or Bible study, guided Ignatian prayer, yoga, reading great spiritual texts, or relaxation exercises. Again, the possibilities are infinite. The point is that the orientation of a destiny group is to help participants discern how they can fulfill themselves in God's service.

What Destiny Groups Are Not!	What Destiny Groups Really Are!
1. *They are not "House Churches"* (independent centers of spirituality).	1. *They are spiritual disciplines linked to regular worship* (helping individuals listen for personal callings).
2. *They are not "Task Groups"* (groups assigned to implement a program).	2. *They are discernment opportunities* (motivating people to do their own mission).
3. *They are not "Membership Classes"* (training people to join the church).	3. *They are prayer groups* (locating people in the ministry of Christ).
4. *They are not "Nominations Processes"* (recruiting people to serve offices).	4. *They are meditation processes* (guiding people into God's plan for ministry).
5. *They are not "Power Cliques"* (controlling areas of church mission).	5. *They are Bible studies* (building ownership for the mission of the church).

A common mistake in the development of destiny groups is the imposition of some form of "committee mandate" or "nominations process" on the destiny group by the official board or pastor of the church. This is not a process to fill vacancies for offices of the institution. *Some* individuals or groups may find themselves called to a ministry or task that fits neatly into the nominations needs of the church. *Most* individuals or groups will not. Instead, the offices of the church will need to be flexibly adapted to *their* sense of emerging destiny.

Remember, cell group ministry flourishes in streamlined, permission-giving organizations. In these organizations

• the "mission agenda" is determined by the emerging spiritual callings of the participants;

• the volunteer "offices" are constantly being reshaped to fit the unexpected callings discerned by the participants.

We will return to the description of this organization in the last chapter of this book.

3
Mission Teams
Individuals form partnerships
to accomplish particular strategic
projects, tasks, or ministries
and
they support and coach one another
in a shared quest for quality.

Mission Teams involve people in activities with a specific purpose of ministry. These groups are designed for people who are aware of their gifts, and who have discerned the calling which will allow them to use those gifts, but who cannot fulfill their calling *with excellence* without partnerships with similarly motivated people. The stress on excellence is important. Mission teams are not merely about doing a task which is too large for a single person. They are about personal growth, and help individuals to constantly improve the quality of their ministry singly and together. Mission teams do more than accomplish projects. They build personal confidence. As always, the possible projects, tasks, or ministries are endless. They may be very simple and require no budget, or complex with a large budget. Examples of mission teams might include worship, visitation, care and counseling, teaching—or building "Habitats for Humanity," child or elder care, social advocacy, evangelism, or world outreach. The point is that the orientation of a mission team is to help gifted and called people exercise effective ministry in and beyond the church with excellence.

What Mission Teams Are Not!	What Mission Teams Really Are!
1. *They are not "committees"* (appointed representatives implementing an institutional agenda).	1. *They are partnerships forged by a leader* (coworkers invited by a leader to implement a shared mission).
2. *They are not "fund-raisers"* (soliciting financial contributions to pay other experts to do ministry).	2. *They are action teams* (doing the ministry and raising money to do it whenever necessary).
3. *They are not "study groups"* (merely learning about community needs).	3. *They are activities* (accomplishing a project from research through to ultimate completion).
4. *They are not "service clubs"* (providing funding or leadership to a variety of charitable causes for philanthropic reasons).	4. *They are project teams* (pursuing a specific mission motivated by Christian faith).
5. *They are not "administration centers"* (administrating or governing multiple charitable organizations).	5. *They are self-directed cells of mission* (designing and doing a single ministry for the practical benefit of others).

There are two mistakes commonly made in developing mission teams. The first mistake is that the members of the team are chosen by the official board or pastor (often as representatives of various other church organizations). Effective mission teams are always formed by the group leader personally as she or he invites individuals to join the team. These individuals do not represent any constituency. They are chosen because of their skills or gifts, which will enhance the work of the team.

The second mistake is that mission teams are often merely "task groups," their only goal being to complete a specific job. Effective mission teams also understand themselves to be "growth groups," working to improve the gifts and skills of the team members. Not only is a project accomplished, but the team members have grown in confidence and competence.

Remember, cell groups are all about personal and spiritual growth, the fulfillment of which is generosity to others. The ministries and missions of the church grow and multiply, not because a central board or denominational body believes projects to be worthwhile, but because

• individual, growing Christians are motivated to pass life on to others;

• the congregational system is committed first and foremost to mission.

You may wish to refer to the first part of this book, or to the larger discussion of systemic change in *Kicking Habits: Welcome Relief for Addicted Churches* or *Growing Spiritual Redwoods*.

P.A.L.S. Group Growth

Affinity Is the Bond!

"Affinity" is the "glue" which holds the group together. An "affinity" is any passion, interest, or enthusiasm that is shared by a group of people. This may be a hobby, activity, issue, life experience, problem, obstacle, addiction, identity trait, goal, or task. The affinity may seem trivial or unimportant to those outside the group, but to those inside the group the affinity is a number-one priority or enthusiasm in their lives.

The question is, If you could spend your spare time doing anything at all that was really important, enjoyable, or interesting, *What would it be? That* becomes the affinity which bonds a group together. It is this passion or interest that motivates participants to set aside time to spend with others in the group.

Notice that this affinity is not determined in advance by the church. It is not a program committee or task group. The church does not say, "This is important, and you should be recruited to join a group to address it." No, the church asks, "What is really important to you? We will help you find like-minded people who share your enthusiasm, and help you spend quality time together."

In the initial "wave" of *P.A.L.S.* groups, the affinity may be related to sports, hobbies, or music. Another "wave" of *P.A.L.S.* groups may be related to community services or tasks. Yet another "wave" of groups may be related to personal needs, such as addiction relief or interpersonal relationships. The affinity can be anything at all a group of people might share with keen interest and enthusiasm.

Readiness Is the Spark!

The church can never really predict what the affinity of cell groups might be. However, there will be a clear and spiritual purpose that is also shared by every group. The church uses the affinity as a vehicle to help people go deeper into themselves, their relationship with others, and their relationship with God. This motivation to "go deeper" is best described as a "spiritual readiness."

It may be an "electricity" of curiosity within the group, or an eagerness to ask questions and to engage in dialogue about deeper subjects of personal concern. Or it may be a "magnetism" that seems to draw people to issues of universal significance or fundamental values. Or it may be a passion to do something worthwhile for others. In a Discovery Group, the participants share a spiritual readiness to discover more about themselves and their meaningful connection with God. In a Destiny Group, the participants also share a spiritual readiness to discern their appropriate place or work in the larger plan of Christ for ministry. In a Mission Team, the participants share a spiritual readiness to invest their time and energy in a worthwhile purpose.

This "spiritual readiness" is a clear assumption communicated to prospective participants in a group. The spiritual environment in which the affinity is placed is never a surprise to newcomers in the group, and is often greeted with welcome relief—or as an exciting opportunity to be seized!

Many people are "ready" for the spirituality of a P.A.L.S. group directly from their own personal or community experience. The spiritual yearning of the public is surprisingly intense. Many people who may be profoundly alienated from the institutional church, will leap at the chance to participate in an informal, nonthreatening, unpressured group that talks openly about God. They have a yearning to be changed or different, and look for a higher Power to help them accomplish it.

Many other people are "ready" for the spirituality of a P.A.L.S. group after they have begun to sense the power of God in their lives through worship. They sense themselves changing, and want to understand why, how, by whom—and what lies at the end of the change! The opportunity to reflect upon all of this in the context of an affinity they enjoy, and with a group of enjoyable people, can come as a miracle in their busy lives.

However their "readiness" emerges, participants will always find the focus of the group to be their affinity, and the environment will be very informal. The leader will help the group find their way toward personal discovery and spiritual depth as they share their common interest.

Process Is the Key

Every *P.A.L.S.* group, whether it be a Discovery Group, Destiny Group, or Mission Team, will unfold in similar ways. There are two, simultaneous "flows" to a group, and the group leader will help the group move in each.

Think of each "flow" as a current in a river. The current may be swift or slow, or it may be choppy or calm. Some boats on the river may move quickly and easily through the current, and others may move slowly and with more difficulty. Yet in each boat there will be someone "at the helm" who will steer the boat forward into the current.

The *first* "current" to every *P.A.L.S.* group is the "flow" of *relationship-building*. Note that at each stage of progress, there are risks to be avoided. The group may move through this process more than once in its life, but each time the conversation becomes deeper and richer. People grow in confidence and self-esteem, friendship and intimacy.

Relationship-building

1. *Conversation* — the risk for which is boredom
2. *Information Sharing* — the risk for which is competition
3. *Ideas and Opinions* — the risk for which is disagreement
4. *Shared Feelings* — the risk for which is personality conflict
5. *Dreams and Fears* — the risk for which is shock
6. *Team Vision and Action* — the risk for which is stagnation
7. *Multiplication* — the risk for which is grief.

Conversation begins the group experience. Since participants may be complete strangers, it tends to be introductory and perhaps superficial. The leader helps everyone to express themselves and feel comfortable, but knows that the group must move to a deeper communication level if participants are to avoid boredom.

Sharing information is the natural next step in their affinity. They talk about what they love, or the affinity that has motivated their presence in the first place. People reveal their knowledge, special interests, and questions. The leader helps the group avoid mere competition, in which individuals begin to try to dominate conversation or position themselves to be "experts" who might "tell" people what to think.

Shared ideas and opinions emerge as the group builds trust. They risk sharing their perspectives and revealing their ignorance. Conversation becomes more fascinating and even heated. The leader encourages disagreements to emerge, but helps participants find common ground. The greatest challenge is to help the group accept and respect disagreement that remains unresolved.

It is often at this point that many groups reach a crisis and thus the skill of the group leader becomes vital. Ordinary groups will often break up once disagreements cannot be reconciled. Individuals may abandon the group with hurt feelings, or splinter from the group with an alienated "minority opinion." At this critical stage, the group leader must move the flow of relationship-building forward.

Shared feelings is the next necessary step to deepen relationships. Individuals are encouraged to share their feelings (hurts, joys, tears, laughter) and to recognize irony and mystery. They begin to identify and describe their personalities, perhaps even using a distinct personality inventory. The group leader helps them understand, accept, and move beyond their personality conflicts.

Sharing deeper dreams and fears brings the group to a new level of trust and bonding. Although the original affinity is still their primary focus of conversation, participants discover they have much more to talk about in, through, and beyond their affinity. They begin to understand *why* their affinity is so important to them, and probe *where* their interest or enthusiasm might take them. They may use a spiritual gifts inventory. Prayer becomes more significant. These discoveries may sometimes be jarring times of self-awareness or revelation. The group leader will preserve confidentiality and move the group to deeper acceptance and mutual support.

Team vision and common action result from the relationship-building process. The combination of enthusiastic affinity, and the new spirit of partnership and unity, leads the group beyond just talk to action. The group leader helps them build consensus about an activity which celebrates their unity, and which benefits others beyond the group.

Multiplication brings the group to a close, with the positive motivation for participants to move on to other groups, personal disciplines, or ministries. If the group remains intact for too long, their relationship-building will plateau and personal growth will stagnate. The group leader helps people address the sadness of "goodbye," by celebrating past group relationships and future opportunities for growth and service.

The *second* "current" to every *P.A.L.S.* group is the "flow" of *faith-building*. Once again, at this stage of progress, there are risks to be avoided. The group may also move through this process more than once in its life, but each time the conversation becomes deeper and richer. People grow in joy and a deeper sense of God's presence.

Faith-building		
1. Covenant	the risk for which is	indiscipline
2. Curiosity	the risk for which is	consternation
3. Bible Awareness	the risk for which is	competition
4. Trust	the risk for which is	dependence
5. Questioning	the risk for which is	fear
6. Action	the risk for which is	judgment
7. Holy Discontent	the risk for which is	self-doubt.

Covenant begins the group process. It builds on the *readiness to go deeper* that is a part of the individual participant's expectation. The covenant may be formal or informal, but it implies a commitment to the group process and the overall environment of spirituality in which the affinity group is based. The leader helps participants understand the importance of commitment.

Curiosity about the spiritual context of the group is often the initial attitude of participants. They need to know that it is informal, unpressured, nonmanipulative, and wide-open to personal perspective. The group leader assures the group that participation does not assume any religious knowledge, nor even require any commitments to the church. The only commitment is to the group itself, and to the opportunity for personal depth.

Awareness of the Bible anchors the spirituality of the group, not denominational polity, tradition, or ideology. In Discovery Groups, it is simply a process of becoming acquainted with basic scriptural passages to test their relevance to daily living. In Destiny Groups, it is a more deliberate process of broadening biblical knowledge. In Mission Teams, it is the application of scripture to a particular ministry. The group leader helps people move beyond competition as to who is more "spiritual" or "biblically literate," to focus conversation on practical relevance to living.

> *It is often at this point that many groups reach a crisis.* Ordinary groups will often break up once disagreements over Scripture cannot be reconciled. Individuals may abandon the group with hurt feelings, or splinter from the group with an alienated perspective. At this critical stage, the group leader moves the flow of faith-building forward.

Trust becomes crucial to the future of the group. The legitimacy of multiple interpretations and acceptance of disagreement are combined with recognition of the inner worth of each person and affirmation of the inclusive love of God. The group leader helps people gain confidence in their own quest and avoid dependence on any one authority for the "right" answers.

Questioning emerges from the deeper trust uncovered by the group. Participants begin to articulate their doubts and questions, and to engage in dialogue without judgment. They learn to value both clarity and mystery, and understand the meaning of humility. They position themselves for lifelong learning. The group leader helps them overcome their fears of appearing foolish, making mistakes, or failure.

Action results from the faith-building process. Once again, the group moves beyond talk to mission. They are motivated by greater clarity about each one's own experience of God, and respect for the diverse experiences of others. Together they want to share the joy of their deeper connection with God beyond the group in some practical way. The group leader helps them build consensus for a common mission.

Holy discontent brings the group to a close. Participants become clearer about the individual spiritual paths they need to explore, and become restless to move forward. If the group stays together too long, their faith-building will plateau, and their spirituality will stagnate. The group leader helps people find the self-confidence to move forward in their personal faith journeys.

The *"Dance"* continues throughout the experience of church life. As individuals bring one *P.A.L.S.* group experience to a close, they begin another. Discovery of both self and God leads to discernment of calling for God's plan of ministry. A clear discernment of calling motivates participation in partnerships for mission. Participation in mission leads one to address further questions and mysteries about self and God, and therefore returns individuals to discovery.

And yes, just as in dancing there must be opportunities to pause and rest, so also in the *P.A.L.S.* group strategy individuals may cease involvement in any group for a period of time. When they are ready to continue once more, they themselves can choose the method and the direction of their growth.

P.A.L.S. Group Stories

Sally's Story

Meet Sally. Sally had just turned thirty when her beloved parent died. She is now thirty-three and has yet to get over it. Her inability to cope with her grief eventually led her to church, where she began to find healing through worship. As she began to sense the power of God to change her life, she covenanted with the church to go deeper into herself and her faith.

Sally joined a discovery group of ten persons who were all wrestling with their grief over the terminal illness or recent death of a loved one. The group leader (called the "Shepherd") helped the participants bond with one another. As they forged a deeper trust, they supported one another to address the grief each experienced. They began to pray for one another, and for those sick in hospital. They read portions of Scripture, and discussed how it helped or did not help them. The group helped participants explore their feelings and uncover (sometimes painfully) the roots of their reactions. Together the group became involved in assisting in funeral services and visiting people following funerals, as a meaningful activity.

Nine months later, Sally believed she hadn't been this whole, healthy, and satisfied in years. Yet she was restless. She wanted to have a greater purpose in life. So she joined a destiny group. The group leader (called an "Elder") guided five persons through a discipline of Ignatian Prayer and meditation. Sometimes they would go on a weekend retreat, and sometimes devote time to silence and solitude. Sally discovered that she had gifts in counseling and healing. She found great personal satisfaction in helping others face great challenges of life and health. Eventually, as she reflected on her personal experience, Sally became convinced that Jesus called her to a ministry among the terminally ill.

Sally discovered she was not alone. Another person who shared her enthusiasm in ministry was a nurse in a local seniors home. The church had trained her to be a group leader, and now she invited Sally to join her mission team. With the pastor's assistance, the team arranged for hospice volunteers to help train them in their ministry. Sally found personal fulfillment in ministry, and she participated in a partnership that gave her emotional support and constant training. The church regularly celebrates and prays for the ministry of the team.

Two years passed. Sally's experiences in ministry among the terminally ill have been profoundly enriching, and often quite stressful. The personal support and opportunities for training offered in her team have been crucial for her continued high-energy involvement in ministry. The team regularly sat together in worship, and found that their faith and compassion were powerfully renewed. Nevertheless, Sally's experiences raised many new questions about herself, her relationships with her family, and her relationship with God. She decided to leave the mission team and to join another discovery group to address these new questions.

Bob's Story

Bob came to worship primarily because his wife insisted she would not go alone. He was curious, but not deeply interested in religion. He was aware, however, of a certain emptiness inside. His life was dominated by work, he had few close friends, and he often complained of a general boredom. He did love model railroading. When he was invited to join a discovery group of seven other men who also loved railroads, he gladly accepted.

The group met every week, but because Bob enjoyed it so much he made time to attend. Mostly, they talked about railroading. The group leader (laughingly called "the Conductor") helped Bob fit right in. They would begin with a brief prayer and Bible reading. As time passed, the friendships deepened. When a group member appeared one night quite upset over a quarrel with his teenage son, the group set aside railroad conversation to support the friend. Together they prayed for him and his son. Bob's deepening sensitivity helped him gain insight into himself, his needs, and his relationship with God. Eventually the group as a whole decided to obtain space, and invite all the neighborhood children to help them build a huge model railroad. For years to come, kids came to a safe and fun activity, and the group members enjoyed nurturing them in modeling skills—*and life skills.*

Bob felt more contented than ever before—and he never failed to thank God for this in worship on Sunday. But he also felt a new kind of discontent. His heart ached for young teens he had met who were struggling with drug addictions. He decided to leave the railroading group and invest his time in a Bible study group that met early every Saturday morning in a local restaurant. The group leader (called an "Elder") led them through an intensive study of Luke-Acts. Eventually, Bob became convinced that Christ called him to a ministry among teenagers with drug addictions.

The church paid for Bob's community college training in drug abuse counseling. Conscious that such a challenging ministry would be most effective in partnership with others, Bob carefully gathered a team of five persons who shared his enthusiasm. One team member was skilled in public speaking and often addressed high school assemblies. Bob and another team member were particularly skilled in one-to-one counseling. The other team members built connections with the medical and law enforcement networks in the community for further consultation or referral.

The church regularly celebrates and prays for the mission of the team.

The Story of George S.

George will tell you frankly that he is an alcoholic. His Higher Power had guided him into Alcoholics Anonymous, and he had been sober for two years. He was also frank about his suspicion of organized religion, and he rarely attended worship. However, he felt a need to learn more about himself, and more about this mysterious higher Power. When he heard about a church discovery group offering support for alcoholics, he joined.

George attended both AA and discovery group meetings each week, making time in his busy schedule because it was worthwhile. The discovery group allowed him to achieve a deeper intimacy with others who shared his problem. The group leader (called simply "the Group Leader") helped them discuss and debate many diverse perspectives about God. They experimented with prayer. Most of all, they talked about the burdens of alcoholism and the challenges each faced every day. Together they helped inform the public about addiction, and build public support for Alcoholics Anonymous.

George gained a clearer understanding of himself and his religious beliefs than ever before. Although he never attended the liturgical worship on Sunday morning, he often attended the Saturday night contemporary worship service. Having overcome his past, and increasingly puzzled by his future, George leaped at the chance to join a destiny group formed by the pastor of the Saturday night service. Together they read books and discussed ideas. They would go in pairs to local bars, sipping soda pop and conversing with people, and then return as a group to pray for the individuals they had met.

George became convinced that God called him to lead discovery groups such as the one he had enjoyed. The church equipped him as a cell group leader, and George joined a mission team of similarly trained group leaders. In addition to their particular groups, George's team meets quarterly through the year for a "day apart" with the pastor. They trade stories, coach each other through difficult problems, and help each other identify weaknesses and upgrade their skills. The church commissioned George as a lay pastor, and regularly celebrates and prays for his ministry.

All of these stories reflect the *dance* of personal and spiritual growth. The exact pattern, timing, and movement can have infinite variety, but people are in a constant movement of growth and experimentation. And this growth and experimentation is most effectively, and most enjoyably, done with others.

Discovery Groups

help people deepen their relationships with self, others, and God. Such groups help clarify *who this God is* who is changing their lives.

Destiny Groups

help people discern their calling in the pursuit of which they can fulfill themselves, give life to others, and be a part of God's plan.

Mission Teams

help people form partnerships to fulfill their gifts and callings by doing quality, effective ministries in the community and world.

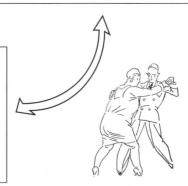

---- 8 ----

CELL GROUP AND MISSION TEAM LEADERSHIP

Twenty-first-century Expectations of Religious Leadership

I n order to identify and train *P.A.L.S.* group leaders, it is crucial to understand the dramatic shift in leadership expectations on the brink of the twenty-first century. The profile of the "credible Christian" has dramatically changed.

In the twentieth century, the "credible Christian" was defined by the experience and needs of a society that was identifiably Christian. This society was called Christendom. The public all had a basic understanding of Scripture and doctrine and were all generally sympathetic to the institutional church. The credible Christian was a professional, salaried priest or pastor.

Twentieth Century

A *Clergyperson* with denominational and academic credentials...

• was *oriented* around the *polity and doctrine of a church institution;*

• had been *trained to manage ecclesiastical work* and *take care of people;*

• had been *equipped with liturgical skills* and *historical perspectives;*

• was *professionally authoritative* and *knowledgeable of "eternal truths";*

• and was *supported by a denominational association.*

As we begin the twenty-first century, however, this society has disappeared. Today society is no longer identifiably Christian. The public does not have even the most basic understanding of Scripture or doctrine. They are not only unsympathetic with the institutional church but generally hostile to it. The credibility of leaders described in the box is sinking fast.

In the twenty-first century, the credible Christian is now defined by the experience and needs of a public that is profoundly spiritually yearning, and yet deeply alienated from the institutional church. The emerging credible Christian for the twenty-first century is a lay volunteer who is prepared, equipped, and motivated to share faith and help others in practical ways.

Twenty-first Century

A *Layperson* with personal authenticity and spiritual integrity...

- has *answered* for herself or himself *the key question, What is it about my experience with Jesus that this community cannot live without?*
- exercises *spiritual gifts from God* to *relate in healthy ways* to others;
- has been *equipped* by the church with *interpersonal skills and biblical insight;*
- is personally *humble and on a high "learning curve";*
- and is *supported by trusted, intimate colleagues.*

It is this version of the credible Christian that is the core vision for *P.A.L.S.* group leadership. This is the kind of leader you need to find and nurture within the church.

Finding such leadership will require some patience and care, and you will likely need to look, not among the core institutional church managers who serve standing committees and official boards, but among the informal and fringe networks of church life.

The Profile of the P.A.L.S. Group Leader

It is vital to understand that the cell group leader is *not* merely a facilitator, nor is this leader necessarily an "expert" in biblical interpretation, liturgy and worship, psychotherapy, or group process. The cell group leader is simply the effective "Pastor" or "Shepherd" of the group. The layperson who is a *P.A.L.S.* group leader is to the twenty-first-century cell group what the pastor of the twentieth century was to the congregation.

Their leadership affects the lives of participants beyond the group meeting. They are available to "coach" and "support" individual participants throughout the week, and may be the first person contacted by a group participant in the event of personal crisis. The cell group leader may even become the key worship leader for funerals, weddings, and other special occasions for group participants. The authenticity of their faith, the depth of their compassion, and the clarity of their vision help people find their way through the ambiguities of daily life.

No specific personality type is required for cell group leadership. However, cell group leaders will *know* their personality type, and use that knowledge to interact effectively with group participants. The primary issue in selecting cell group leaders is not personality

P.A.L.S. Group Leadership Integrity	
Deep, Daily Spirituality	Has clearly focused faith that pervades both personal and professional life.
Intentional Confidentiality	Invites immediate trust, gives reliable guarantees to preserve secrets.
Unswerving Fidelity	Exhibits loyalty in personal relationships, no hint of sexual exploitation, or flirtatious and abusive behavior.
Commitment to Equality	Avoids stereotypes of race, gender, generation, lifestyle. Encourages respect, treats others with fairness.
Personal Humility	Is always eager to learn and grow. Does not fear ambiguity or paradox.
Self-directed, Self-disciplined	Works hard, toward clear goals, with internalized motivation for excellence.

but integrity and style. *These leaders are "mentors" and "midwives" whose wholehearted and sole purpose is to help others give birth to the potential God has given to each person.*

In the twenty-first century, the public looks for authentic mentors and midwives who can support and guide them through the ambiguities of life. Such mentors may not be learned, but they are regarded as wise. They may not be articulate orators, but they are effective one-to-one communicators. They are absolutely trustworthy; their company is safe and reliable; they take care to be respectful of others. They never rely on authorities to direct their course, but possess an inner compass that directs their living. Their whole purpose is to help others give birth to the potential God has given each person—to free that person to raise their "child within" as they choose, and to coach that person to nurture life in love and integrity.

P.A.L.S. Group Leadership Style

Habitual Patience	Waits and prays for the work of the Holy Spirit; does not rush people or prematurely resolve differences.
Broad Vision	Locates experiences in a broader context of culture and history; discerns experience in a broader flow of purpose; celebrates diversity of lifestyle and opinion.
Gentleness	Is kind, sympathetic; recognizes and assists others to overcome obstacles.
Courageous Perception	Sees the point, faces contradiction, identifies the crux of decision making.
People Focus	Prioritizes persons above issues, dialogue above agendas, growth above success.
Inclusive Behavior	Is sensitive to silence, invites people to participate, is alert to the fringes of groups.

In the twenty-first century, the public looks for spiritual midwives who can help them birth their dreams and hopes into reality. Such midwives may not be accredited professionals or office-holders, but they are regarded as transformers. They may not be managers or administrators, but they are effective motivators for personal growth. They wait for truth to emerge from within, without imposing truth from beyond. They simultaneously nurture and challenge the individual.

The Search for the P.A.L.S. Group Leaders

The church may now have a clearer idea of the kind of person for whom they are searching—but they often leap to the conclusion that their congregation does not contain such leaders! The reason they may at first have difficulty identifying potential P.A.L.S. group leaders is that these people may well be on the fringes of church life.

The truth is that the qualities and skills important for P.A.L.S. group leadership are not necessarily the qualities and skills the traditional church organization has valued in the past. Remember, these potential leaders are *not* primarily committee members, committee chairpersons, managers, administrators, supervisors, financiers, liturgists, preachers, editors, musicians, social activists, politicians, or evangelists.

Look at it this way. If your church organization raises dogs, it values people who can train and control dogs. People who can nurture and shepherd rabbits will probably not be present among the core leadership of your church.

However, the fact that they are not among your present official board members does not mean they are not in your church. Indeed, although the board may not want to admit it, the unassuming presence and quiet leadership of these mentors and midwives among the congregation has probably been more significant to church life than any number of committee and board meetings. They are there. How do you find them?

Strategy One: The Pastor Looks at the Congregation with Different Eyes

If the pastor has been with the church for more than five years, he or she may already have an intuitive awareness of potential *P.A.L.S.* group leaders. In order for the pastor to identify these leaders, two things must happen.

First, the pastor will need to survey the congregation with new eyes. The old nominations and pastoral care lists will be ineffective. Potential leaders may be on inactive lists, or infrequently attending worship. They may be between the ages of eighteen and thirty-five and not visible in current church life.

Second, the church must free the pastor to spend significant time with people who might not ordinarily get priority for pastoral visitation. It will take time and personal conversation to share the vision of the *P.A.L.S.* group strategy, and to build excitement for training.

If the pastor has not been with the congregation very long, it may be better to rely on the following two strategies.

Strategy Two: Confidential Recommendations from the People

In any large and diverse gathering of the congregation, invite participants to think of, and anonymously write down, the names of persons they feel are the most widely respected as credible, persuasive, wise, faith-filled, and compassionate members of the church. Such gatherings might include congregational suppers, picnics, worship services, or Sunday school pageants—events in which the greatest diversity of people tend to participate and in which marginally active members of the church are well represented.

Collect these names, review the "*P.A.L.S.* Group Leader Profile," and compile a short list of those persons who are mentioned most. This becomes the prioritized visitation list for the pastor. Spend time with these people, sharing the vision of cell group ministry and encouraging their participation in the project.

Strategy Three: Spiritual Gifts Inventory

Discernment of spiritual gifts is rooted in the experience of the New Testament church (Romans 12, 1 Corinthians 12, and Ephesians 4). *Generally speaking, a "spiritual gift" is linked to whatever you profoundly enjoy doing, and which you deeply desire to do with excellence.* The Bible lists more than twenty such gifts, including:

Discernment	Mercy
Teaching	Giving
Serving	Administration
Leadership	Prophecy
Healing	Hospitality
Exhortation	Practical Helping
Evangelism	Knowledge
Prayer	Shepherding
Wisdom	Intercession
Counseling	Faith

If you are involved in doing any of these activities, and find that participation intensely fulfilling and meaningful, then you are probably doing what God created you to do.

This is why spiritual gifts discernment may intentionally become a part of the life of both discovery and destiny P.A.L.S. groups. The process helps individuals uncover and affirm their identities as God truly created them.

In the search for cell group leaders, however, many churches may focus on spiritual gifts discernment as a foundational ministry of the church. (It literally replaces much of the old "Nominations Process" required for the administrative bureaucracy of church leadership.) They involve as many church participants as possible in this discernment, and look especially for those individuals with spiritual gifts in *shepherding, counseling,* or *hospitality.* The names of these persons become the short list for the pastor, who may then approach them about the opportunities of P.A.L.S. group leadership.

In the earliest church, Christians first discerned the gifts God had given to them, and then served offices of the church to express their gifts. Centuries later, however, many churches today neglect spiritual gifts discernment, and simply nominate or recruit people to dutifully perform institutional tasks. Modern church priorities have reversed ancient church priorities. They emphasize the duty of par-

---

Spiritual Gifts Inventories

There are many spiritual gifts inventories available today, which list and define the spiritual gifts in various ways. Many churches will define the list in their own words, and customize the inventory and counseling process to fit their church experience. A spiritual gifts discernment process is similar to personality discernment processes such as the Myers-Briggs test or "Enniograms":

• Participants answer an extensive list of carefully prepared questions about their attitudes, feelings, and behavior;
• Their responses are categorized;
• Participants then spend time with a counselor skilled in the use of the process in order to interpret and apply these insights to their lives.

In a personality inventory, participants learn their personality *type* and discover how this influences their many personal relationships. In a spiritual gifts inventory, participants learn the gifts with which God created them and discover how exercising them can give personal satisfaction and joy.

In the search for potential cell group leaders, spiritual gifts discernment processes are particularly effective when they involve as many *marginal* members or *"fringe"* participants as possible. Therefore, it is more important to start the process among groups and fellowship gatherings, than among official boards and program committees.

Remember, the people who love to train dogs are likely the most conspicuous church participants at the center of administration; but the people who love to shepherd rabbits are less conspicuously moving at the fringes of institutional church life!

---

ticipants to fulfill the mission agenda of the institution, rather than emphasize the opportunity for individuals to fulfill themselves.

For this reason, many veteran church leaders may find spiritual gifts discernment a real puzzle. It makes sense for them to utilize the professional training of individuals for the purposes of the institution—but it seems wasteful to spend the energies of the institution simply helping individuals discover and do whatever it is they really enjoy. In the modern church, "enjoyment" and "calling" have been separated and even opposed. In the earliest church, however, "enjoyment" and "calling" were held together.

One test to determine whether or not you are really doing what Christ called you to do, is to discern *if you truly and deeply enjoy doing it!* Does this activity give life to you or rob life from you? energize you or spiritually exhaust you? lead you to laugh or lead you to sigh? fill you with joy or leave you with unresolved anger? For first-century Christians, authentic callings always, always led to joy.

Lay leadership "burnout" is not a biblical church issue. It is a modern church issue. It has become an issue because modern churches habitually motivate people to act out of duty, rather than out of joy. They continually remind people of their obligations, but fail to assist people in affirming themselves.

You can encourage your veteran church leaders to consider using a spiritual gifts discernment process by pointing out that current nominations processes are breaking down and that lay leader burnout is becoming a chronic problem. This process not only can help the church find the cell group leaders they need, but it can also help the church address serious burnout among core leaders.

Once you have compiled a short list of people who may be gifted to lead a *P.A.L.S.* group, the pastor (or other church leader who shares the vision of this ministry) begins to talk to those individuals face-to-face. *What do they talk about?*

Question One: Do you share the vision?

Conversation with potential *P.A.L.S.* group leaders should reveal that the person intuitively knows what you are talking about! At some point in the conversation, their eyes should light up with recognition and excitement. They may tell you that this is precisely the kind of group in which they are already participating elsewhere in the community during the week. Or they may say that this is the kind of activity they always longed to experience, or to create for others.

Not only do they grow excited by the vision, but they intuitively comprehend the skills or behavior patterns such a vision requires. These skills seem to come "naturally" to them. They may readily acknowledge mistakes, of course, but what is important is that they are capable of discerning "mistakes." Their clarity about the vision helps them evaluate and correct their behavior. They know that

• "Midwives" and "mentors" are *visionaries*. They have an inner compass that guides them in the right direction. They are convinced that real truth lies beyond themselves, and feel free to play many roles, knowing that their real self will never be lost.
• Midwives and mentors are *synthesizers*. They have an ability to build team visions among a group of people. They can bring together seemingly opposite perspectives to create unity, and they integrate diverse personalities and points of view to create harmony.
• Midwives and mentors are *motivators*. They teach by example, and they know that persuasiveness is more important than authority. They can motivate the most diverse people to move in a direction on their own initiative, and their own excitement is large enough to include others.

P.A.L.S. Group Leadership Qualities and Skills	
Qualities	*Skills*
Intuitively grasps shared vision	Synthesizes into a "both-and," integrates complexity
Is persuasive and motivating	Communicates excitement as well as knowledge
Is convinced of a truth beyond self	Is versatile, comfortable in both foreground and background, can play multiple "roles."

Question Two: Do you use your gift in daily living?

Conversation with the potential *P.A.L.S.* group leader should reveal that the use of their gifts has become a habit in daily living. At work or at play, at home or on the job, among neighbors or family, it is the same. They are mentors and midwives in all the relationships in which they participate.

P.A.L.S. Group Mentors and Midwives	
The Person	*The Connection*
Authentic	Spiritual bond: Clearly articulates own faith and faith journey
Vulnerable	Personal bond: Equal relationships that risk change to benefit others
Wise	Open to ambiguity: Guides people in uncertainty, toward unknown destiny
Compassionate	Confirms, celebrates, interprets healing: Helps people through stress of transformation
Dedicated to a direction, will not take over another's burden and destiny	Elicits personal mission; equips others to bear their own burden and to pursue their own destiny

• Mentors and midwives are always authentic. There is no pretense or charade, no projection of false images. They make quiet spiritual bonds with others by clearly articulating their own faith in simple and honest ways.

• Mentors and midwives are always vulnerable. There is no crust or defensiveness, no boasting of unrealistic power. They treat others as true equals, and are prepared to allow others to influence their feelings and behavior.

• Mentors and midwives are wise. They know the limitations of their knowledge, and can live with ambiguity. They reassure others in the midst of their mysteries, and by their own example can guide others to move forward with confidence.

• Mentors and midwives are always compassionate. They rarely focus attention on themselves. They help people identify and address stress in their own lives, always seeking to encourage opportunities for healing.

• Mentors and midwives are profoundly self-directed. They never surrender their own destiny to carry the problems of another. Instead, they help equip others to bear their own burdens and pursue their own journey.

Question Three: Are you committed to excellence?

Conversation with the potential *P.A.L.S.* group leader should reveal a readiness to be trained, coached, and generally pursue a quest for quality. The joy they feel in using their gifts increases as they exercise their gifts with ever greater excellence. Therefore, they see themselves as perpetually learning—and they see opportunities for learning in unexpected places.

P.A.L.S. Group Quest for Quality	
Qualities	*Skills*
Flexible	Revises plans quickly, easily
A continuous learner	Uses all media, open to all information
Clearly focused	Sticks to priorities
Belief in excellence	Always upgrades, refines

• Midwives and mentors know that they must always be flexible. Dogmatism, narrow-mindedness, or addictive behavior will not build cell groups. They know they must revise their plans and expectations frequently and spontaneously.

• Midwives and mentors know that they must continue to learn. No body of information or knowledge deserves their exclusive attention. They are open to all varieties of experience, digest all manner of information, through all media.

• Midwives and mentors know that they must have clear goals. Their ultimate direction and key priorities are never lost amid confusion. They opportunely grasp any vehicle to move the group forward.

• Midwives and mentors believe in excellence. Self-affirmation is never complacency with what you are now, but it is the desire to become the best you can be. Only through personal growth will the group grow.

Question Four: Do you feel Jesus calls you to this ministry, at this time?

Conversation with the potential *P.A.L.S.* group leader should reveal a conviction that God calls them to this ministry at this particular moment of their lives. It may be that there are present circumstances in a person's life to which God is calling for immediate attention and energy. Or, it may be that a person feels God calls them to exercise some other spiritual gift with which they were created.

The answer to this question will be deeply personal. Once made, it should not be questioned. At another time in the future, the opportunity can be presented once again. It is *vitally important* that people become P.A.L.S. group leaders motivated by personal calling, rather than by an obligation to fulfill an institutional task.

The decision can be made in the following way.

Prayer
The potential leader and pastor pray together over an extended period of time, keeping in mind that God's will is ever directed toward personal growth and ministry, never toward complacency or self-indulgence. The choice before Christians is never, "Should I be in ministry?" but rather, "In what ministry should I be active at this time?"

Bible Study
It is particularly helpful to read and discuss the Acts of the Apostles together. A potential leader and pastor may covenant to read the entire book over a limited period of time. Stories such as the birth of the Church of Philippi (Acts 16) illustrate the power of cell group ministries to transform people and communities, and motivate interest in their deployment in the church.

Assurance

The potential leader will require assurance from the pastor at several levels. This is especially true if small group ministry is a new initiative of the church, or if the potential leader has been a marginal member or fringe participant in the church. They will ask:

1) Will I receive quality training to begin, and continuing coaching and support during this ministry? The pastor will explain the training and support offered, and covenant to be available to the leader at all times.

2) Will I be sidetracked into administration, and required to attend committee meetings and complete reports? The pastor must assure them that no "hidden" administration is required, and that they will be free from bureaucracy.

3) Will the church truly value what I am doing with my cell group? The pastor will give evidence of the readiness of the congregation to continually pray for the cell group ministry, and regularly celebrate and promote participation in discovery groups, destiny groups, and mission teams.

This assurance should not be given lightly. Traditional congregations often celebrate cell group ministry at the beginning, and welcome new group leaders from the fringes or margins of congregational life with enthusiasm. However, as the "rabbits" start to multiply, as creativity begins to test the boundaries of values, belief, and vision of the congregation, and as leaders and groups take initiative for unexpected projects and missions, some traditional churches begin to panic. "Control" is imposed, and group leaders often find themselves sidetracked into committee meetings, with less time to spend in upgrading skills. Group passions are held in check by hierarchy, and groups and their leaders experience rising frustration. The new group leaders may feel tempted to exit the church once again to live on the fringes and margins of congregational life. They need to have the congregation's assurance—and they need to believe in it!

Training for the P.A.L.S. Group Leaders

Once potential cell group leaders are identified, they must be trained for excellence. The training methods, time lines, and the details of the training program will vary. There is no single "blueprint" for doing it right.

• The *context* and the *culture* of the community and congregation will shape the training discipline;
• The *affinity* of the projected *P.A.L.S.* group will shape the content of the training.

No matter what the professional or personal experience of potential leaders may be, however, *they must be trained by the church.*

• They must link the skills gained from beyond the church, to the unique life and mission of the church.
• They need to exercise their skills within the basic boundaries of core values, bedrock beliefs, motivating vision, and key mission, which are the consensus of the church.
• They need to establish a habitual pattern of risk, experimentation, and questing after excellence.

Training helps group leaders integrate their ministry into the larger ministry of Christ that is unfolding within the life of the congregation.

Most churches train their *P.A.L.S.* group leaders in some combination of the following three methods.

Pastor-centered Training

The pastor becomes a *P.A.L.S.* group leader, and the affinity of the group is that they are all training for *P.A.L.S.* group leadership. Not only does the pastor *teach* the skills of cell group leadership, but the pastor also *models* the skills of cell group leadership. The method resembles the discipling process Jesus himself used. Jesus discipled the Twelve, who in turn initiated ministry among the Seventy, who in turn initiated ministry in the world. This method requires two things:

1) The pastor must reveal the qualities of "mentorship" or "midwifing." In other words, the pastor must be personally gifted and skilled to be a cell group leader, exhibiting the qualities we have named earlier in this chapter.

2) The pastor must prioritize time to disciple the few. Just as Jesus frequently took time apart with the Twelve, so also the pastor must prioritize time for the cell group. This may require the church to readjust expectations of his or her weekly agenda.

As the *P.A.L.S.* group strategy unfolds, this method may become overwhelmed by demand. One option will be to add to the staff a designated person to train, coach, and develop *P.A.L.S.* group leaders. A less expensive, and perhaps more enduringly effective option, will be to turn to the following two methods.

Apprentice Training

Active *P.A.L.S.* group leaders add to their leadership responsibilities the task of mentoring an apprentice. The person being trained literally joins a *P.A.L.S.* group with the additional goal of observing the leader. Before and after group gatherings, the leader and apprentice talk about the goals, skills, and strategies the leader seeks to employ. The apprentice can take a leadership role and test the development of his or her own skills. This method also requires two things:

1) *The apprentice must share the affinity of the group joined.* Unless the apprentice truly shares the enthusiasm of the group, the flow of group energy will be diverted, and the nuances of group leadership will not be noticed.
2) *Leader and apprentice must have a bond of trust.* Unless they have such a bond of trust, they will not have the confidence to endure the honesty of their mutual sharing.

In many cases, this method happens naturally as a potential cell group leader is identified as a current participant of a *P.A.L.S.* group. The natural bond between that active leader and this emerging apprentice becomes the foundation for learning.

Mission Team Training

The church assembles various configurations of "trainers," who pool their time and skills to work as a team. The team members may include salaried staff, volunteers from within the church, and consultants from beyond the church. Each team member may bring expertise in various themes, such as prayer, biblical interpretation, group process, conflict management, culturally specific expectations for hospitality, and so forth. Again, this method requires two things:

1) *There must be a mission team leader.* A person takes responsibility to invite team members, design team responsibilities, and match schedules for training among all the participants.
2) *The church needs to budget for consultancy.* Money must be available to contract for expertise beyond the local church in order to pay for travel expenses and honoraria.

This method may be helpful both in the early and later stages of the cell group ministry strategy. In the early stages, it allows the church to provide expertise that may not yet be part of the pastor's skills. In the later stages, it allows the church to both train leaders more quickly and customize training for unique directions of ministry.

The Content of the Training

The details of the training given to cell group leaders will vary from context to context. There is no common "core curriculum" that one must master in order to become a *P.A.L.S.* group leader. Indeed, if churches become too demanding, they may discourage volunteers for group leadership. They may also inadvertently impose so many restrictions that the creativity and spontaneity so crucial to *P.A.L.S.* groups is undermined. On the other hand, the congregation must have a commitment to excellence. Their training budget will allow them to engage consultants or other professional trainers as needed.

Generally speaking, the content of the training will include:

1) The Key Question:
Leaders will be helped to discern and articulate their personal answer to the question, "What is it about my experience with Jesus that this community cannot live without?"
2) Systemic Vision:
Leaders will learn how *P.A.L.S.* groups participate in, and advance, the whole flow of church life and mission within the identifiable boundaries of congregational beliefs and values.
3) Cellular DNA:
Leaders will understand the theological, missional, educational, and pastoral assumptions of cell group life, and link it to the core identity of the congregation.
4) Integrity, Style, Skills:
Leaders will review the profile of leadership identified earlier, and practice through experimentation or role-playing to strengthen or focus their abilities.

5) Biblical Insight:
Leaders will learn the basics of Scripture, methods of interpretation, and multiple perspectives on key doctrines. Primary emphasis will usually be given to the great visioning passages of Scripture, the Gospels, and the Acts of the Apostles. Leaders devise their own Bible reading discipline.

6) The Relationship-building Flow:
Leaders will learn the fundamentals of group dynamics, group life cycle, and conflict resolution, and develop skills in listening and communicating. They may reflect on apprenticeship experiences or case studies, and experiment with role-playing.

7) The Faith-building Flow:
Leaders will learn the fundamentals of prayer or discernment of spiritual gifts, identify and discuss their own doubts and questions, and practice skills in dialogue.

8) Planning and Covenant Organization:
Leaders will learn how to build an affinity group: invite and assimilate newcomers, design group covenants, build consensus for mission, and discern when it is time to multiply. They develop their own plan to upgrade for excellence.

A Common Pattern of Training

Each congregation will customize its own system for training P.A.L.S. group leaders. However, a common pattern might look like this:

1) Initial Training:
The foregoing topics are addressed during a two-day to three-day retreat, or over a period of four to six weeks (one evening per week). An additional learning experience related to special knowledge or skills demanded by the specific group affinity may be designed within or beyond the church.

2) Coaching:
Once the leader begins her or his ministry, the pastor or other guides are readily available to the leaders to help them address unexpected obstacles, or respond quickly to sudden opportunities.

3) Formal "Upgrades":
Two or three times a year, the pastor or staff team takes *P.A.L.S.* group leaders on a one-day to two-day retreat. They support one another in prayer, the foregoing topics are reviewed, and they mutually "mentor" one another through emerging issues.

Accountability

Accountability is crucial to effective and enduring cell group ministry. The continuing coaching and formal "upgrades" for leadership support and development provide regular opportunities to critique leadership performance. The pastor and the human resources team will facilitate this regular process, but it is primarily a *peer supervision* experience. Cell group leaders support and critique themselves.

In cell group ministry, accountability is not an involved bureaucratic process. Leaders are explicitly *not* asked to attend numerous administrative meetings, complete long reports, or submit work plans to higher authorities. In every way possible, they are freed to do their ministry in the manner they believe it must be done.

The Difference Between "Control" and "Accountability"

Control keeps leaders on a leash, manipulating them to do what higher authorities decide should be done, in the way higher authorities want to do it.
Accountability allows leaders freedom to do what they choose, in the way they choose to do it, but *within* the normative boundaries of values, beliefs, vision, and mission, which are the consensus of the church.

In part, cell group leaders (with the help of the pastor and human resources team) will review and address any emerging discontent. Earlier, I outlined the continuing process the permission-giving organization deploys to address discontent. Much of this can be addressed within the team. However, if emerging discontent leads to a formal hearing or litigation, other denominational and civil processes will drive the process. If continuing coaching and formal "upgrades" are done well, discontent may well be resolved long before any denominational or civil intervention is required.

Mostly, cell group leaders (with the help of the pastor and human resources team) will review the effectiveness of their leadership and the impact of their mission. *First,* the process of personal and spiritual growth, and the quest for excellence, must be encouraged. *Second,* cell group activities must remain within the basic boundaries of core values, bedrock beliefs, motivating vision, and key mission, which are the identity of the congregation. *Third,* cell group mission must help the congregation achieve the mission result that is their reason for being. Note that obedience to a long list of prescriptive management goals is not part of the accountability process. So long as group leaders cooperate with the work of the Stability Triangle as they seek to grow, train, and deploy mission leaders— and so long as group leaders stay within the boundaries of congregational identity and group covenant—they are free to act.

There are four basic questions every group leader must answer. The questions may be asked by anyone, including the pastor, the human resources team, other group leaders, any individual in the congregation, and any individual among the general public. The permission-giving organization creates an environment in which these four questions can be asked clearly by *anyone,* and an expectation that every congregational leader should be able to readily *answer* the questions.

1) Is there any way in which the leader has gone beyond the boundaries of core values, bedrock beliefs, motivating vision, or key mission, which are the consensus of the congregation?

Traditional organizations cannot ask this question clearly, because they live in an ambiguity dominated by the personal tastes, opinions, and perspectives of matriarchs and patriarchs, or the tension between denominational requirements and local expectations. Permission-giving organizations can ask this question because they regularly define, refine, and celebrate their congregational identity in quadrant 1.

Leaders in the permission-giving organization can answer this question with equal clarity because the boundaries are transparent to all, and their performance is regularly reviewed. Note that in answering this question, the leader is speaking not only about his or her group or *church* activity, but also about her or his own *lifestyle*. If a leader has gone beyond the boundaries, there must be a correction or the leader can no longer be sponsored by the church.

2) Is the group accomplishing the mission of the congregation by changing lives and benefiting the community, to the sacrificial standard acceptable to the congregation?

Traditional organizations cannot ask this question, because their primary mission is to themselves. They are preoccupied with maintaining the institution and taking care of members, and offer only what energy is left over for outreach into the world. The primary measurements of commitment are financial offerings for property and program maintenance, management time, and leftover financial support for generic missions undertaken by other people.

Group leaders in the permission-giving organization can answer this question because the board has refined the point of mission, and the degree of sacrifice acceptable to achieve it. Their primary mission is beyond the church, and they can measure their success in achieving it. If the quality of life is not being improved either for individuals or society, there must be a correction or the group will no longer be sponsored by the church.

3) Are individuals growing relationally and spiritually in the group?

Traditional organizations cannot ask this question, because their real concern is that individuals fit into the homogeneity of the institution and keep the committee structures going. They want to be sure that the institutional agenda moves forward, and personal growth is merely a means to that end.

Group leaders in the permission-giving organization can answer this question clearly: Personal growth is essential for the emerging missions of the congregation. They can monitor the progess of the relationship-building and faith-building flows of group life which bear fruits that bless family, neighborhood, community, and world. If personal growth has stopped for the group as a whole, or any individual in the group, the group must refocus its energies and the leader must gain whatever additional skill or knowledge is necessary for the group to move forward.

4) Are the leader and the group cooperating with the management teams of the congregation to grow, train, and deploy mission?

Traditional organizations cannot ask this question, because their preoccupation with management is not really about growing, training, and deploying mission. They are concerned to minimize creativity and reduce risks so that the institution will not be embarrassed and its survival threatened.

Group leaders in the permission-giving organization can answer this question clearly. They have a clear covenant within the group to measure their performance. They have clear boundaries to which they can compare group activities. They have the Stability Triangle to measure mission development. The proscriptive nature of the organization does not require them to form a liaison with anyone in particular, but it does require them not to block anyone else in their personal or group growth.

These four simple questions are the foundation for the accountability of group leadership. They open the door for the pastor, human resources team, and group leaders themselves to explore four aspects of leadership:

Lifestyle: Leadership style to incorporate congregational core values into daily behavior, congregational bedrock beliefs into practical spiritual strength, congregational motivating vision into personal enthusiasm, and congregational key mission into weekly agenda priorities.

Competence: Leadership skills to help people grow relationally and spiritually, and to help people discern calling and take responsibility for mission.

Mission Effectiveness: Leadership knowledge to focus group energies to influence personal and social transformation, learn from mistakes, improve performance, and measure success.

Team Cooperation: Leadership qualities to develop healthy partnerships among group members, between groups, among congregational participants, and with the diverse publics of the community.

The public, the congregation, and the group leaders themselves have the assurance that this regular and intentional review of leadership performance will deepen, enrich, and improve both the personal and professional dimensions of congregational leadership.

The old saying is, "The proof is in the pudding." For a traditional congregational organization, the proof that the system of accountability works is that no mistakes have been made, everybody is happy, and no leader is being sued. For the permission-giving organization, this level of accountability is not nearly enough. For them, the proof of accountability is *credibility.* Mistakes will be inevitable, *but leaders learn from their mistakes.* Discontent will be inevitable, *but leaders have an accessible vehicle to address it.* Risks will be taken, *but leaders have integrity in taking them.* The real proof of a system of accountability is that the public and the congregation have confidence in the leaders, and the leaders have confidence in themselves and the commitment of the team to stand with them.

• The public has confidence that congregational leaders operate from transparent values and beliefs, remain open to real diversity, are dedicated to improving the quality of life of the community, are equipped to do quality work, and are linked to a feedback loop that is safe, sensitive, and accessible.

• The congregation has confidence that congregational leaders have been identified through disciplines of spiritual growth and discernment, are both trained and trainable, share a quest for quality, and are enthusiastic in both lifestyle and leadership for the identity and mission of the church.

• Leaders have confidence in themselves because their deep spirituality gives them strength, their training gives them the best skills possible, the pastor and other staff are available for twenty-four-hour coaching support, the congregation trusts them enough to take risks, and their colleagues are ready to go to extraordinary lengths to support them.

This accountability system may not be as secure as the one used by a traditional organization. It certainly will not guarantee freedom from stress. Yet it has the one quality traditional organizations lack: *credibility*.

Among P.A.L.S. group leaders,
Accountability assumes Trust, and Trust is based on the

Quest for Excellence.

P.A.L.S.
Group Stories

Gwynn's Story

Gwynn was eighteen and in her last year of high school when the pastor approached her to consider *P.A.L.S.* group leadership. She had been confirmed several years before, and had quickly drifted to the margins of the congregation. She had no interest in being a token youth member of a committee, and considered Sunday services to be dull. However, as the pastor surveyed the congregation with new eyes, she discovered that Gwynn knew more about the Bible than many veteran members. Gwynn often participated in Christian gatherings beyond the local congregation. And Gwynn's positive attitude and personal support were always mentioned by other youth in the church.

At first, Gwynn thought she was being recruited to lead a Junior Youth Group or teach Sunday school. However, when the pastor began to share the *P.A.L.S.* group vision, she grew excited. She and her pastor covenanted with each other to pray about it over a period of weeks, and met frequently to talk about "open doors to follow Christ." She accepted only with the assurance that the church would especially upgrade her skills for counseling.

Committed and trained, Gwynn simply identified the enthusiasm that most excited her: popular music. She began to invite individuals from her school, extended family, neighborhood, and church to participate in a discovery group oriented around listening to, and performing, various musical styles (rock, jazz, blues, and rap). Eventually she gathered ten other teens who shared her enthusiasm, and who were ready to explore their curiosity about God.

During the next nine months, Gwynn often sought help from her pastor. Most often, she needed help to overcome some odd personalities in her group. Occasionally, she asked for guidance about prayer. Once, she sought clarification about a Bible passage. She wept openly with the pastor several times, and felt foolish more than once. On the other hand, she never laughed so hard in her life on many occasions, thoroughly enjoyed the music, and felt that everyone (including herself) had really grown. She was ready to lead another group—and do it better.

Doris's Story

Doris was forty-five and had been a member of the church all her life. Very quiet and reserved, she avoided public speaking like the plague. She helped in the nursery, but never thought she knew enough to teach Sunday school. She was a member of the membership committee but rarely attended and never contributed. And yet, Doris always attended worship and carried a ragged Bible that she would be observed to read during coffee breaks at work. She always seemed to know when someone was in trouble, and often sent flowers for no reason at all. Colleagues at work, and friends at church, would seek her out if they had something on their mind. When the pastor visited a family who had left the church angry, she was greeted with the words, "It's O.K. Reverend, we talked with Doris." It was no surprise that her name kept being repeated when a confidential survey sought to identify potential P.A.L.S. group leaders.

Doris knew instantly what the pastor was talking about. Unknown to the church, she had hosted a gathering of friends and neighbors every Tuesday morning for tea and Bible study for some time. Her eyes flashed, however, when she realized that she could have an opportunity to be equipped to do better what she most loved to do. And her eyes grew moist when she was told that the whole church would pray regularly for her ministry.

Doris created a destiny group, gathering participants from her original Bible group and the church. Her greatest challenge, about which she talked to her pastor and other P.A.L.S. group leaders many times, was to move participants beyond personality conflicts and heated opinionating, to respect for diversity.

The destiny P.A.L.S. group came to be so intimate that it was difficult to multiply the group. The pastor helped Doris emphasize the need for growth beyond the group, and another *P.A.L.S.* group leader coached Doris in addressing the parting grief everyone felt. In the end, several participants initiated new ministries through the church, and several others decided to form a different destiny group oriented around prayer. A month later, Doris welcomed three church newcomers into her living room to form the nucleus of another Bible study group.

The Continued Story of George S.

Remember George S., the recovering alcoholic? You will recall that he was very cynical about organized religion but had a deep spiritual yearning. A discovery group for seeking alcoholics helped him to find deeper meaning in life, and clarity in faith. A destiny group with the pastor of the Saturday night contemporary worship service helped him reflect on his calling for ministry. In fact, it was the spiritual gifts inventory used by the destiny group that first alerted George to his gifts in mentoring others.

You will recall that George became convinced that Christ had called him to lead another discovery group for alcoholics. At first George thought he had all the training he needed, and resisted spending time in further leadership training. However, the church insisted, and George later confirmed this was wise. George's training emphasized the development of strong listening skills that his ministry would require. The church also paid his tuition in a regional workshop focusing on addiction research. Added to his spiritual growth and personal experience, George S. was able to form a most effective alcoholics' support group.

The greatest challenge for George did not come from within the group, but from beyond the group. Circumstances dictated that his group had to meet in the church building. The stench of tobacco smoke, and the presence of some wild-looking strangers on Thursday evenings, led some church members to complain to the board. George (you recall) was cynical about organized religion anyway, and he became furious. Conflict threatened the future of his ministry.

The board acted quickly, with the advice of the pastor and other *P.A.L.S.* group leaders:

1) They made it clear to those making complaint that George's group had *not* gone beyond the boundaries of the values, beliefs, vision, or mission of the congregation—and therefore deserved support.
2) They stepped up communications explaining the origins and purpose of the group to the congregation.
3) They brought this ministry into the congregational prayers for four consecutive weeks.

In the end, George S. and the group felt reassured and affirmed. The church spent extra money installing air recycling equipment and improving security. One church member left church. And today, in addition to groups led by George S., there is a recovering alcoholics' group for teenagers, and a P.D.A. (Prescription Drug Abuse) group for seniors.

Brenda and Lynn's Story

Brenda and Lynn are sisters in their early twenties. They were baptized as infants, dropped out of Sunday school in grade 7, only attended worship on Christmas Eve, and lived quietly on the fringes of church life. Their most frequent complaint about church was that worship was incredibly boring. When the congregation became serious about systemic change, they began to experiment with contemporary worship with a transforming missional focus. The pastor convinced Brenda and Lynn to join some others in visiting another congregation's model for worship, hoping that together they might gain inspiration for their own church.

Brenda and Lynn were overwhelmed and excited. They experienced God—and church—in a way they never thought possible. Hoping to gain some clarity about just what this grace of God was doing in their lives, they joined a discovery group. Since they loved "New Country" music and were (in the words of one song) "girls with guitars," they joined an informal band that played, discussed, and listened to music. As they grew in awareness of themselves, their new relationships, and God, the group seemed naturally to evolve into a destiny group. They prayed and searched for a way to use their passion for music and God in a way that would benefit other people.

Ultimately, Brenda and Lynn believed God called them to design and implement an additional, contemporary worship service in their church on Friday nights. The music would be all country or rhythm and blues, and the missional purpose would be healing. The church had never done such a thing before, but since they had gained some clarity about their "basic umbrella" of values, beliefs, vision, and mission they could tell that Brenda and Lynn's mission might be different and that it did *not* go beyond the boundaries. The church trained Brenda and Lynn in group leadership, and they formed a mission team.

Brenda and Lynn invited specific individuals to be a part of their team. Each had expertise or experience needed to design and lead the worship. Some members of the team had instrumental or vocal skills needed for the band. Other members of the team had confidence and talent in public speaking, and could recruit and train others in faith-sharing. Yet another member of the team was gifted in prayer, and could organize the prayer and technical support that would lie behind every worship experience. *All* members of the team shared the vision of the healing service, a sincere Christian faith, and a willingness to cooperate with others. It took a few months for the mission team to prepare themselves for a quality worship experience, and even then they began only with monthly worship. After each worship experience, they would critique the mission and redesign it.

Eventually, it became a regular weekly service of the church. When the time period in the cell group covenant finished, most team members recovenanted, and some new team members were invited to join with new skills needed to expand the mission. The pastor rarely attended these services, mostly because he *hated* "New Country" music! He helped train Brenda and Lynn, however, and was always available for coaching to any member of the team. At one point someone asked Brenda how her band could sustain the energy and commitment to design and lead the worship service week after week. Brenda replied, "We can do it because we are not just a band. We are a spiritual growth group. And this is not just a job—it's a calling!"

— 9 —
CELL GROUP AND MISSION
TEAM DEVELOPMENT

This chapter describes eight steps for developing cell group ministry in your church. The procedure will look very neat and tidy, very rational and orderly. However, tidy development is rarely what actually happens! Instead, you will find cell groups leaping ahead as opportunities arise, or returning to previous steps to resolve additional issues or gain new insights. Every church is different, and every step will have its own unexpected mysteries. Some churches approach cell group ministry entirely backward! They seem already to be doing cell group ministry— but now need a process to multiply the groups systematically in the congregation.

It is important to remind the church that cell group ministry requires more than a different organizational strategy and different pastoral skills. Cell group ministry requires a different *attitude.* The church is no longer "training dogs," the church is "raising rabbits." This means that cell group development will itself be rather chaotic. This is not an orderly process of placing a leash on a dog, walking up and down on an exercise field, and rehearsing correct commands. This is a process of freeing rabbits to run, allowing them to wander anywhere and everywhere, and gradually coaching them to understand the boundaries and to thrive in their own unique ways.

Raising rabbits also means that the church does *not* need to do the following tasks in order *to begin* a P.A.L.S. group strategy:

- They do *not* need to write a new constitution.
- They do *not* need to restructure the board.
- They do *not* need to organize an ad hoc committee.
- They do *not* need to hire a new staff person.
- They do *not* need to budget for a new program or curriculum.

In a sense all they need to do to begin—is begin! You only need two rabbits to begin raising rabbits. And in fact you only need to form one cell group and train one cell group leader to begin the *P.A.L.S.* group strategy.

Why, then, is it so hard for some churches to form that first cell group, and to nurture that cell group to a place of multiplication? The answer is that it is not always easy to change your attitude. Many churches begin "raising rabbits," only to discover that inadvertently they keep slipping back into the habits of "raising dogs." They begin a *P.A.L.S.* group, and inadvertently find themselves treating it like a program committee. We will return to this theme in chapter 10. Although you do not need to make organizational changes *to begin*, cell group ministry will *demand* organizational change in the *future!*

The following step-by-step process to develop cell group ministry may seem straightforward. Beware! There will be many mistakes and failures along the way. Laugh, learn, and try again! "Practice makes perfect." Keep at it, and eventually the attitude shift will be complete and cell group ministry will become second nature.

Step 1
Build Congregational Understanding and Support

Build congregational support through individual, face-to-face conversations. Even if there is only one person in the church who fully understands and celebrates a vision for *P.A.L.S.* group ministry, let that one person talk to one other friend. Once that friend understands and celebrates the vision, split up and talk to two more persons—and so on and on.

Congregational support is not built *from the top down,* but rather *from the bottom up.* Instead of getting administrative endorsement from the authorities at the top of the hierarchy, build enthusiasm among individual participants in church life.

Congregational support is not built *from the center toward the edges,* but rather *from the edges toward the center.* Instead of trying to convince the official board to initiate a program, and then recruit volunteers to implement it, simply start a movement of enthusiasm among people on the fringes of church life. Eventually that enthusiasm grows to gain the recognition of the board.

Eventually, however, the church leadership must take two fundamental actions to help the whole church understand and support the movement to cell group ministry.

Develop a Spirituality of Waiting

Develop a plan of prayer that pervades all congregational activities, including worship, meetings, groups, fellowship gatherings, and classes. Such a spirituality cultivates openness to the creative power of the Holy Spirit. It may temporarily replace the Common Lectionary with the great "visioning" texts of the Bible. This helps people to identify old habits and form new attitudes. It encourages people to look for the unexpected. It frees people to experiment. It challenges people to consider their calling, their ministry, and their destiny.

Identify and Celebrate Core Values, Bedrock Beliefs, Motivating Vision, and Key Mission

Board meetings, group meetings, and full congregational meetings need to be temporarily reoriented to the task of gaining consensus about the basic values, beliefs, vision, and mission of the church. This fundamental "umbrella" will mark the boundaries beyond which cell group ministries will not be able to go, but within which they will be free to roam.

Your goal is more than a mission statement. It is clarity about what is *essential* to the identity of the church. Core values are the ideals and habitual behavior patterns revealed in both planned and spontaneous activity in the church. Bedrock beliefs are the minimum principles of faith to which you naturally turn in times of crisis. Motivating vision is the "Song in the Heart" that motivates all activity. Key mission is the brief, pithy statement of purpose that "says it all" and captures the imaginations of the public.

Once this "umbrella" or "boundary" has been identified, the church needs to celebrate its identity with enthusiasm. And the church needs to plan to refine this identity each year, as it continues to evolve and change. As the church builds understanding and support for cell group ministry, it will begin to have the first inklings of the systemic changes that lie ahead. Openness to creativity and experimentation may be alarming, but the new clarity about the identity of the church will be reassuring. The congregation is ready to try something new.

STRESS NOTE

The people who have the most difficulty shifting their attitude to understand and support cell group ministry will most likely be those who have a need to control, or a need to be controlled.

Such "blockers" will likely resent any movement that begins from the fringes or "grassroots" of the congregation, and is not initiated and controlled from within the central authority of the church.

Similarly, other blockers will likely be frightened by the openness to creativity and calling of the Spirit, because it does not carry the security of authoritative voices who will tell people exactly what to do.

Step 2
Surround Small Group Ministry with Prayer

The discipline of constant prayer is now expanded to regularly celebrate the potential of cell group ministry. Worship services routinely include prayers for specific groups or group leaders. The covenants that form new affinity groups are identified and celebrated. This encourages the congregation to experiment creatively, and motivates church participants to take an interest in cell group participation or leadership. More than this, it helps the congregation endure and overcome failures. The vision of cell group ministry rises above any single initiative.

P.A.L.S. groups are encouraged to sit together during worship, expanding their intimacy to include spouses, children, or parents. Worship services seek to become motivational experiences that help cell group participants maintain their regular involvement in the group. Recognition and affirmation during the worship services reassure participants that their affinity and quest, trivial or profound, is valued by the congregation.

Most important, the personal transformations and new ministries that emerge from the cell group experience are celebrated in worship. This may include adult baptisms or faith celebrations, personal witness or storytelling, and ceremonies of affirmation and commissioning for individuals called by Christ to creative new ministries.

STRESS NOTE

The people who have the most difficulty surrounding cell group ministry with prayer will most likely be those who do not believe they need to grow spiritually! They believe that they are "already saved," "know all that they need to know," or are simply "O.K." as they are.

They are easily frustrated or embarrassed by failure, and are not prepared to give themselves to a spiritual discipline beyond Sunday mornings. They complain that if leaders are not serving an office or committee they must not be doing anything for the church. These folks are quite content, and their real fear is losing what they have.

Such "blockers" may be slow to comprehend that cell group ministry is a movement of the Spirit, not a program of the board. The most immediate practical benefits will be in personal growth, higher church morale, and mission participation or mission giving.

Step 3
Discover the Hidden Networks of the Congregation

Most church leaders are aware of the administrative or decision-making structures of the church, but they are less familiar with the informal support and communication networks that crisscross the congregation. Familiarity with these informal networks will guide the church in building future affinity groups—and will also guide future group leaders to "surf the net" looking for prospective group participants.

First, make a list of all the committees and task groups of the church, including all the members. Notice who is active in these committees, and who is inactive. Search for demographic and pychographic patterns. For example, do active or inactive committee members tend to share a similar age, stage in the family life cycle, culture, race, or perspective?

This study helps sensitize the church to the affinities among people currently at the center of church activity. Church leaders are sometimes surprised to discover that their most effective committees only perform well because some hidden affinity binds the group together.

> **Can we transform a committee into a P.A.L.S. Group?**
> It is sometimes possible to transform a committee into a small group if they have already achieved a degree of intimacy and share a desire to go deeper in faith. However, be aware that:
> 1) *P.A.L.S.* groups require leadership skills that are different from those necessary for a committee chairperson;
> 2) *P.A.L.S.* groups require a "flow" to build relationships and faith, and do not have an institutional "agenda";
> 3) *P.A.L.S.* groups move people toward personal growth and faith development, and do not manage programs or set church policies.
> Therefore, although it may be possible to convert a committee into a *P.A.L.S.* group, it is rare.

Second, make a list of all the fellowship groups or clubs in the church, including all the members. Notice once again any demographic or psychographic patterns to participation (or nonparticipation) in such groups. Measure the contradiction between the degree of frustration club leaders feel in recruiting new members, and the degree of sensitivity they display toward the changing needs of people in the community.

> **Can we transform a club into a P.A.L.S. Group?**
> It is sometimes possible to transform a fellowship group or club into a *P.A.L.S.* group, provided the club is small enough and shares a desire to go deeper in relationships and faith. However, be aware that:
> 1) *P.A.L.S.* groups require leadership skills that are different from those necessary for a club coordinator or hostess;
> 2) *P.A.L.S.* groups aim at a greater depth in personal growth and faith than is usually found in fellowship groups and clubs;
> 3) *P.A.L.S.* groups form around a more intense enthusiasm, which motivates more passionate participation, than is common among fellowship groups and clubs of the church.
> There may be a greater opportunity to convert a club into a *P.A.L.S.* group, provided these issues are addressed.

This study helps sensitize the church to the degree of contentment or discontent experienced by all those who are generally understood to be "active" in church life. Often church leaders are surprised how deeply bored active church participants have become.

Third, conduct a survey that reveals the spectrum of "interests" or "enthusiasms" which individuals have in the congregation *and the community*. People may or may not have "talents" or "training" for these interests, and they may or may not see any connection between their interests and church participation.

Such surveys usually include three strategies:

1) Printed, brief surveys distributed systematically in the community (direct mail or hand-delivered)
2) Systematic door-to-door interviews among selected neighborhoods (using a simple questionnaire)
3) Conversation initiated by church leaders in public places (usually in teams of two or three).

This study sensitizes the church to the needs and expectations of those who are "marginal" or "fringe" to any church experience. Church leaders are often surprised by the positive response of the public to an initiative of listening from the church.

STRESS NOTE

The people who have the most difficulty perceiving hidden networks of support and communication will most likely be those who value homogeneity in congregational life.

Such "blockers" convey an implicit judgment of people unlike themselves. Other blockers may cherish preconceived notions about what is trivial or profound, tasteful or distasteful.

The most difficult and crucial challenge will be to discover the informal networks among the marginalized or fringe people of the congregation and community.

Step 4
Understand the Reality and Paradox of Public Yearning

Obtain demographic surveys of your community from local, regional, or national government offices. If possible, approach corporations or businesses in the community, or marketing agencies, to examine any psychographic survey data they may have collected. (Automobile dealers, retailers, and charitable organizations often collect such data for marketing strategies.) Compare the demographic profiles of the community with those of your church. This will give you an indication of the "growing edges" of cell group ministries, *the leadership for which may lie outside your congregation!*

Study and discuss the following chart of the paradox and reality of the spiritual yearning of the public.

Reality	Paradox	Yearning
Religiously Fascinated	Ignorant of Christianity	Transforming Connection with God
Relationally Handicapped	Highly Romantic	Healthy Intimacy
Consistently Anxious	Rarely Guilty	Confidence in Personal Destiny
Intellectually Skeptical	Highly Educated	Heartfelt Assurance
Perpetually Inadequate	Remarkably Self-centered	Affirming Acceptance
Institutionally Alienated	Dependent on "Safety Nets"	Equipped for Crisis
Accustomed to Chaos	Crusading for "Control"	Filled with Meaning
Frantic Pace of Life	Grinding Routine	Ecstasy
Distrustful of Experts	Gullible to Marketing	Authentic Mentors

This step helps congregations interpret the success of cell groups that already exist in the community, from service clubs to Twelve-Step programs. They focus more clearly both the purpose, and the method, of cell group ministry.

STRESS NOTE

The people who have the most difficulty appreciating the reality and paradox of public yearning are those who resent having to "accommodate" the church to the needs of the public.

Such blockers tend to dismiss, or explain away, the criticisms of the public toward the church. They often complain, "Why do we always have to change to suit them?"

The most difficult challenge is for the congregation to realize that church "insiders" share a reality and yearning that is "vanishing," and that the emerging mission field asks different questions from a different experience of life.

Step 5
Identify and Train Potential Group Leaders

The foregoing chapter will have provided a practical guide for the identification and training of *P.A.L.S.* group leaders. Notice, however, that you are already in Step 5 of your preparation! A great deal of forethought and prayer has already taken place before you have even begun the first group.

It is more important to do one group with excellence, than to attempt to create many groups. Quality is more important than quantity. Therefore, you are really only looking for *one* group leader—or two or three in a larger church.

From the foregoing chapter, you already have an idea of the kind of person you seek, some strategies to seek them, and a guide to their training. Here I want to emphasize the following absolute necessities for leadership development.

1) The church must be confident in their gifts.
Make sure that the person or persons you choose for leadership are spiritually gifted in shepherding, counseling, or hospitality.

2) The church must be confident in their calling.
Make sure that the person or persons feel personally called by Christ to this ministry, and that they are not simply accepting a responsibility out of a sense of duty.

3) The church must be willing to devote time to their nurture.
Make sure the pastor reprioritizes time from other duties to spend time "mentoring" or "midwifing" group leaders.

4) The church must surround group leaders with prayer.
Make sure that the *P.A.L.S.* group vision is a central focus in corporate worship, and in the personal devotions of church leaders.

5) The church must be willing to get out of the way.
Make sure you do not burden group leaders with administration, supervisory meetings, reports, and bureaucracy.

6) The church must be ready to coach.
Make sure the pastor or other key elders are available at all times to offer advice, personal support, and counsel.

7) The church must ask P.A.L.S. group leaders to help identify other leaders.
Make sure that group leaders help you identify other potential leaders. This will sharpen their skills, as well as help the church develop new groups.

8) The church must have the courage to try.
Make sure that a sense of humor accompanies your passion for mission, so that you will be unafraid to experiment, fail, learn, and try again.

Leader or Affinity: Which Comes First?

When the Leader Gathers a Group

Pat became involved in a spiritual gifts discernment process in her church, and discovered her gifts in shepherding and mentoring others to grow. Participation in a destiny-group convinced her that God called her to lead a group. The pastor included her in a training retreat, and she was ready to go. But what would be her affinity group?

The pastor simply asked, "Pat, what is it that you love to do? If you had the free time, what would you prefer doing above all else?" Pat's answer was immediate. She loved photography. "Then that is your group," said the pastor.

Pat began to circulate among church gatherings, neighborhood get-togethers, and family reunions with a new purpose. She talked to people at work, and new friends that she made during the course of daily living. Sharing her own interests and spiritual quest, she sought others who shared her affinity and spiritual readiness.

Eventually, Pat formed a *P.A.L.S.* group with five persons. Gradually it grew in numbers, in intimacy, in prayer, and (of course) in enthusiasm for photography. Eventually they decided to convert their affinity into a beneficial service, and began videotaping and distributing films of their church worship service among those who were housebound or institutionalized. And they produced their own church photo-directory.

Leader or Affinity: Which Comes First?

When an Affinity Group Looks for a Leader

Cell groups began to be a way of life for Faith Church. As people began to understand what a *P.A.L.S.* group was all about, many began to awaken to the opportunities for mutual support, sharing, and growth.

One day three women approached the pastor. "All three of us are receiving various treatments for breast cancer," said their most forthright member. "And we're sure there are other women facing the same crisis. We'd like to form a support group for people with our problem."

Subsequent conversation revealed that these women all possessed wonderful spiritual gifts—but cell group leadership was not among them. Together with the pastor, they began to pray about their need, believing that God called them to form this group.

Meanwhile, the pastor talked with several others with the gift of shepherding, mentoring, or midwifing in personal and spiritual growth.

Sheilah emerged as someone who had also had personal experience addressing medical challenges and felt drawn to such a group. Sheilah met with the others and prayed with the others, and together they covenanted to form the group.

Soon there were eleven participants in the group, and Sheilah not only helped them support one another to defeat breast cancer, but helped them develop sensitivity to all types of cancer. They became involved in supporting the local cancer society.

These eight necessities may form a constant "checklist" for official boards, staff teams, and lay leaders as they develop group leadership.

STRESS NOTE

The people who have the most difficulty developing P.A.L.S. group leaders are those who have the least trust in their church leaders.

Such blockers do not trust their pastor deeply enough to allow her or him to go to the fringes of congregational life to bring leadership energy to a central ministry of the church.

Or, such blockers do not trust their church elders or lay leaders enough to value their pastoral care energies, which have freed the pastor to spend time nurturing the P.A.L.S. group leaders.

Lack of enthusiasm for cell group leadership reflects lack of trust for the present leadership.

Step 6
Develop Easy Access Opportunities

Once the congregation is prepared and the leaders are ready, the church must multiply the number of opportunities through which P.A.L.S. group leaders and potential group participants can communicate with each other. Groups grow because participants informally talk to other people about the *enthusiasm* that is their affinity, and about the *spirituality* in which they address their affinity. You must expand those opportunities.

First, multiply opportunities for large, diverse fellowship gatherings that will attract both regular church participants, and marginal or inactive members of the church.

Suppers, barbecues, corn roasts, dances, and any other gathering imaginable can be shaped for this purpose. The event may well celebrate an important occasion for the church, or it may involve a guest speaker, but the event is specifically designed to give group leaders and group participants a chance to meet people and share their enthusiasm.

Second, multiply opportunities for large, diverse gatherings of people from the neighborhood or community.

Block parties, charity fairs, open houses, concerts, and many other gatherings can become vehicles for group participants to meet members of the public. There may be no particularly religious purpose to the gathering—except that the church grasps an opportunity to bring group leaders and participants in contact with those beyond the church.

Third, convert the narthex, vestibule, or any high traffic corridor of the church into a display area for P.A.L.S. groups.

Visual and interactive displays should greet anyone coming or going from the church building. Flyers should be available with the names and phone numbers of contact persons for the group. Participants in the group should be available before and after church services to talk to anyone who expresses an interest in a group.

The simple strategy to build a group is this:

Make a Friend.

Move beyond your circle and talk to acquaintances, neighbors, and strangers. Share the enthusiasm that is your group affinity and the basic spirituality through which you address your affinity.

Be a Friend.

Build a relationship, the value of which stands on its own. If you share that affinity with a common enthusiasm, enjoy talking about it. If you discover curiosity about spirituality, talk about that.

Bring a Friend.

Invite and accompany a friend to the group. Make them feel at home. Expect nothing more than the enjoyment of their company and their ideas. Let the Spirit do the rest.

The more opportunities you create to do this simple process, the easier it will be to grow a *P.A.L.S.* group.

STRESS NOTE

The people who have the most difficulty revealing their spirituality to strangers, or allowing others to do so, are those who mistakenly believe the public will resent it.

Such blockers actually find such activities unsettling because they do not have a clear idea of their own spirituality, or because they have not had the courage to practice such communication.

The spiritual yearning of the public is so intense that most people are quite open to the spirituality of another if it is presented in a nonthreatening, nonjudgmental way.

Step 7
Initiate and Experiment

Starting the first quality *P.A.L.S.* group may be the most difficult task. Once a few groups have completed the *P.A.L.S.* group cycle from start to finish, the church will have a sense of the obstacles and opportunities that are unique for their context. Patience, sensitivity, and constant consultation with participants will be crucial. The first group may require several attempts to succeed, but the leader of that group will be able to effectively coach others.

There is no final blueprint for development of *P.A.L.S.* groups. Each regional, cultural, or local context will have its own needs and requirements. However, cell groups tend to follow a common pattern of "waves" of growth.

Wave One
Sports, Music, and Hobbies

These are the easiest, least-threatening groups to form. Baseball teams and tennis clubs, bell choirs and vocal ensembles, quilting groups and ceramics classes are all examples of the groups that may form. These groups are not merely clubs, of course. They are purposely created as *P.A.L.S.* groups. This means that in addition to their affinity, they are guided by the leader into the "Relationship-building" and "Faith-building" flows described earlier. The affinity, however, is easily shared by many people. These groups are often oriented to discovery or destiny.

The Model Railroad Group

The group that loved model railroading met every Wednesday night at Bill's house. Usually, they gathered at seven o'clock for dessert. After Bill led a brief prayer, and someone read from Scripture, they plunged right into an evening of animated discussion about railroading.

About the fourth week, however, Fred arrived at the meeting visibly upset. He had just had a quarrel with his thirteen-year-old son. Instead of plunging into their usual conversation, Bill said, "Hey, Fred, how are you feeling? Let's talk about it." After half an hour of listening, everyone could really sympathize with Fred. Most knew exactly how he was feeling! Bill suggested they pray for Fred and his son, and the silent prayer that followed witnessed more than one tear.

From that day on, the group spent more time in prayer and Bible reading, and often talked about their family experiences. Eventually, sharing like this led the group to convert their enthusiasm for railroading into a ministry. They rented a vacant store and invited all the young teens in the neighborhood to build a model railroad together. In a safe environment, kids not only learned about art and electricity, but they saw demonstrated the Christian values and beliefs of the group.

Over the years, hundreds of kids have gone through that club—and discovered Christian faith. And they have a terrific model railroad!

Wave Two
Service Opportunities and "Hands-on" Project Groups

Once the congregation begins to experience the value of a *P.A.L.S.* group, and once the first participants of cell groups gain a taste for personal missions that benefit others, a second wave of groups begins to form. The affinity for these groups will often be some hands-on, shared work. Constructing houses in a Habitats for Humanity program, initiating a community Meals-on-Wheels program, or creating a welcome center for newly arrived immigrants are all examples of such groups. These groups are often destiny groups or mission teams.

The Discovery Group will use the affinity of service to help people build deep friendships and share faith questions. It helps individuals mature in faith. The Destiny Group will use the affinity of service to help people explore their gifts and faith. It will help individuals build self-esteem and find meaning or purpose in life through personal generosity. The Mission Team will use the affinity of service as a vehicle for mission motivated specifically by Christian faith. It moves participants beyond an introductory, short-term activity, to design a more profound and long-term personal ministry.

The Home Renovation Group

Four young couples who were marginally associated with St. Andrew's Church discovered they all loved renovating and decorating old houses. A cell group leader gathered them together. They brought other friends from beyond the church.

Initially they met every Friday night, pooling their resources to share a babysitter for the kids. Their prayers were pretty brief, and just for fun they traced every biblical passage using the metaphor of "house" or "home"! After a few weeks, conversation seemed to lag. Sally, their leader, had a brainstorm.

"Why not persuade the church to buy that old house next door? We'll renovate it, and the church can lease apartments to low-income families." Always glad to support creative ministry, the church gave some seed money to the group, and private donors followed suit.

Every other Saturday, the group meets at the old house for work. Every other Friday night, they meet in a participant's home to plan their projects—and talk about the joys of doing something good for other people.

The project is doing fine, a new ministry is coming to the church—and the prayer and Bible study on Friday nights has become pretty dynamic!

Wave Three
Mutual Support, Study, and Healing Therapies

Once the P.A.L.S. group strategy gains visibility and credibility in the church and community, and as group participants have become more honest with themselves and one another, a third wave of groups begins to form. The affinity for these groups will be very specific to personal needs. Addiction groups, Bible study or special topic groups, and confidential groups related to sexuality, marriage enrichment, or stress management, are all examples of such groups.

In this wave, Discovery Groups will help people find healing and wholeness. Destiny Groups will help people see a direction for their renewed lives. Mission Teams will focus energy on a particular human need.

Once again, let me say that there is no blueprint for the development of *P.A.L.S.* groups. Some churches may find opportunities for support groups very early in this ministry, and other churches may not evolve new "waves" of ministries for some time. The general pattern has been to begin with groups that share less "serious" affinities. As trust builds, groups explore more deeply personal aspects of life.

Regardless of the variety of cell group life, or the order in which *P.A.L.S.* groups appear, participation in the overall ministry will be like the *Dance* described earlier. People will move back and forth, swaying to and fro, to the rhythm of the music of spiritual growth. Distinctions between discovery groups, destiny groups, and mission teams may sometimes even be obscure. Groups take risks, experiment, and evolve in their own unique ways.

The Bible Study

Jack was twelve when his family moved for the fifth time. Lonely, he tried to make friends by behaving badly. Guilty, he experienced a variety of mild illnesses that doctors described as "psychosomatic." Introspective, he pondered his connection with God.

At fourteen, he had read the Bible cover to cover, but didn't understand half of it. He found some other teens who shared his yearning. Every Tuesday night they began to meet in the church parlor to read the Bible and talk.

Of course, it became more than that. Deep trust let them talk over personal problems. Deep prayer helped them focus on fundamental values and beliefs. Four years later, the group helped them ponder their futures.

Two members of the group became ministers, two joined world service agencies, one joined a Roman Catholic order—and all faced future mysteries with faith.

STRESS NOTE

The people who have the most difficulty with experimentation are those who cannot learn through failure. It is the same fear of looking foolish that keeps them from dancing.

Failure is not a sign that cell group ministry "won't work in our church." It means that the strategy must be fine-tuned from learnings gleaned from failure, or that the church has yet to internalize the "attitude shift" required to grow the P.A.L.S. strategy.

Blockers at this stage often fail to understand the spiritual growth DANCE as groups help people grow in Christ. They see the group as a simple task, the completion of which has no further connections with personal growth or faith development.

Step 8
Upgrade for Excellence and Coach

As cell groups multiply, and diverse ministries and missions blossom, a certain "creative chaos" dominates the overall mission of the church. There will be inevitable gaps in the overall mission agenda—important ministries the church does not yet do. However, the congregation must recognize that these ministries cannot be addressed "from above" through a management decision to recruit volunteers. They will be patient, waiting for the Holy Spirit to evoke these ministries "from below" as the gifts and callings of individuals are discerned. *Mission is never imposed. It always emerges.*

Learning through experimentation will not only help the church design a training program for cell group leaders customized for their context, but it will also ingrain in the church process the need to regularly upgrade skills. The congregation will need to set aside a significant portion of its budget for continuing education. This budget will be used to bring in consultants, or send out group leaders to do specialized training, in order to upgrade the skills of the group leaders. Do not assume the staff can equip everyone, in every way.

Refer to the process to address discontent and the leadership and accountability guide provided earlier. The church will evaluate the progress of *P.A.L.S.* groups, and help group leaders in their quest for excellence. Generally speaking, a healthy cell group will balance "freedom" and "covenant" in a manner I first described with Bill Easum in our book *Growing Spiritual Redwoods* (inspired by Elizabeth and Clifford Pinchot's book *The End of Bureaucracy and the Rise of the Intelligent Organization*).

Freedom	Covenant
The freedom to think, speak, and consult.	*Relationships of affirmation and acceptance.*
The power to imagine, decide, and act.	*Networks of learning and cooperation.*
The ability to share, care, and critique.	*Matrices of equal voice, shared values, and common purpose.*

In addition, a healthy group will show positive progress in the two key "flows" of group life. I repeat these here, pointing out that the permission-giving organization ascertains whether a group has inadvertently become "sidetracked" toward any of the negative risks that are listed.

Relationship-building		
1. *Conversation*	the risk for which is	boredom
2. *Information Sharing*	the risk for which is	competition
3. *Ideas and Opinions*	the risk for which is	disagreement
4. *Shared Feelings*	the risk for which is	personality conflicts
5. *Dreams and Fears*	the risk for which is	shock
6. *Team Vision and Action*	the risk for which is	stagnation
7. *Multiplication*	the risk for which is	grief.

Faith-building		
1. *Covenant*	the risk for which is	indiscipline
2. *Curiosity*	the risk for which is	consternation
3. *Bible Awareness*	the risk for which is	competition
4. *Trust*	the risk for which is	dependence
5. *Questioning*	the risk for which is	fear
6. *Action*	the risk for which is	judgment
7. *Holy Discontent*	the risk for which is	self-doubt.

If a group has become "sidetracked" or "stuck" at any point in these "flows" of group life, the church helps group leaders address the problem. There is never any predetermined standard of knowledge, friendship, or faith that is the mark of a successful group. It is the process or flow of group life that is crucial.

Cell group leaders meet regularly to update their skills and coach one another to move forward. In addition to reviewing covenants for each cell group and discussing specific obstacles emerging, these leaders:

- review the theological, missional, educational, and pastoral *assumptions* of cell group ministry;
- examine group life to perceive if the relationship-building and faith-building flows are moving forward;
- discuss the balance between freedom and covenant for each group.

All this is more "art" than "science." No blueprint can be presented that merely requires exact reproduction to achieve success. No expert can be imported who can fix emerging problems for you. Monthly or quarterly gatherings, or annual retreats, gather the cell group leaders to regularly wrestle with cell group life that is never tidy and simple. These leaders mentor one another, experiment, fail, coach, try again—and eventually succeed.

Cell group ministry is a lifestyle of continuous learning. Mistakes are not only inevitable—they are a *necessary* part of the development of cell group ministry! Group participants, group leaders, church leaders, pastor, and staff all need to place themselves in the "Risk-Learn Cycle."

THE RISK-LEARN CYCLE

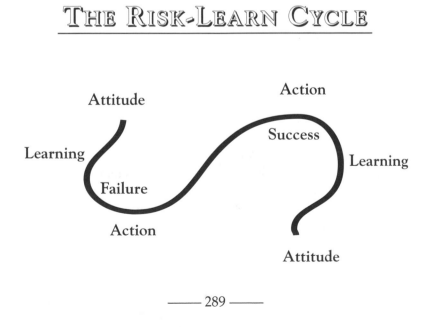

In this cycle, leaders and participants are constantly experimenting. They try, fail, learn—and try again. Even when they succeed, they never rest. If you are not making mistakes, you will not be adjusting and fine-tuning *P.A.L.S.* group ministry to the unique, real needs of your special church context. Mistakes are not a sign of failure. They are markers on the road to success.

These eight steps for the development of cell group ministry should *not* be regarded as a blueprint for every congregation. Every church is different. Every church must find its own way. The examples that follow bring together the learnings from many congregations, and illustrate the adaptability of cell group ministry to any context. Urban or rural, large or small, culturally specific or culturally diverse, *any church* can become involved in *P.A.L.S.* group ministries. One church can learn from another, but you *cannot literally imitate* the experience of another church.

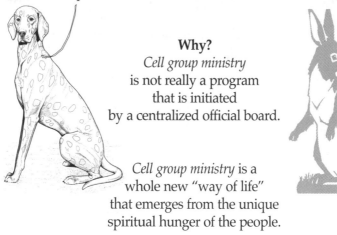

Why?
Cell group ministry
is not really a program
that is initiated
by a centralized official board.

Cell group ministry is a
whole new "way of life"
that emerges from the unique
spiritual hunger of the people.

If it were simply a prepackaged program, prepared and perfected for any congregation's use, the church would simply acquire the program and recruit dutiful volunteers to implement it. Effective *P.A.L.S.* group ministry, however, arises from the contexts of real life that are peculiar and special to every congregation. The organization does not deploy a new mission. The new mission transforms the organization.

Transformational Stories

Elm Grove Church

Elm Grove Church is a small, rural congregation with about seventy-five families. It is part of a pastoral charge with three preaching points. Although the size of the community has not changed very much over the years, the congregation has experienced decline in church participation. People under age forty have not been attending worship regularly, and the veteran church members are becoming weary providing administrative leadership for the church.

One of the lay leaders attended a workshop in cell group ministry. When he returned home, he did a little personal research and discovered that the fastest-growing segment of the population in his area included the institutionally alienated public. These people were affiliated with a local church, but for various reasons rarely attended. Paradoxically, this layperson also discovered that participation in cell groups of infinite variety represented the fastest-growing community movement. The same people who weren't going to church were devoting time to all kinds of special interests.

Excited by the vision of cell group ministry, the layperson talked to the pastor. Eventually he convinced the pastor that there was a real mission opportunity, and together they asked the elders to consider the idea. Some of the elders were skeptical, but they were all troubled by the decline of the church. They agreed to meet with the lay leader and pastor early every Saturday morning for the next six weeks to talk about the idea and to pray for the future of the church. Small churches being what they are, soon all seventy-five families in the church had begun to think about the idea.

At the end of six weeks, the congregation shared an enthusiasm about the mission of cell group ministry. They began to pray about it in Sunday worship. The pastor and elders read everything they could find about this ministry, because the pastor confessed that she had never been trained in such ministry in seminary. The biggest challenge to the congregation was the realization that they did not really have a vision for the future of the church. Their only aspiration had been to survive as an institution, and they soon realized that this was not a true Christian vision. The pastor shifted the focus of preaching to the Acts of the Apostles, and gradually they began to sense a deep calling to deepen the faith of that "spiritually yearning, institutionally alienated" segment of their community.

As the focus of worship changed, the elders began prioritizing time to understand and pray for the "public" beyond the doors of the church. They began to look upon their grown children and grandchildren with new and more sympathetic eyes. In some families, the generations actually talked about their different religious assumptions and expectations *with mutual respect* for the first time. Parents returning on the bus with the local school baseball team were amazed to perceive deeply personal or spiritual undertones to conversations that they had previously ignored.

Meanwhile, the pastor and key lay leaders were busily discovering hidden networks of communication and fellowship about which the church had been unaware. The number and diversity of clubs in the community amazed them. A conversation with the owner of the local "honky tonk cafe" revealed several circles of "regulars" who drank coffee together every week. The elders compiled a brief list of questions, which they raised with everyone they met, and patterns of interest and activity began to emerge.

Since the pastor had been with the church less than five years, she didn't feel entirely confident she could identify potential cell group leaders. She asked the elders, and then the congregation, to confidentially and anonymously write down names of people they thought might be good leaders. This short list guided the pastor, and eventually she found two persons who were really excited about the vision. The three of them covenanted together to pray regularly and mutually "mentor" one another in leadership. The pastor admitted she was no expert, and together they agreed to talk frequently and learn from their inevitable mistakes.

The church already had several big fellowship gatherings planned, including the annual "fowl supper," which involved everyone in the community and beyond. They added a corn roast, an amateur night concert, and several other events. They held them at the community hall and aimed them to involve marginal church members or community residents. Of course, these were more than fellowship times. They shared information about their new venture in ministry—and the two group leaders purposely wandered among the crowd talking to people.

It turned out that many individuals in the community were looking for team sports opportunities that were noncompetitive, inexpensive, fun, and clean (i.e., no drunkenness, abusive language, or excessively aggressive behavior). The first cell group, therefore, shared the leader's passion for ice hockey, but gathered the team together with a distinct set of values.

The second group formed out of an informal network of people who loved country auctions—and who shared the pain of personal bankruptcy and poverty that often precipitated those auctions. The group began buying used furniture, refinishing and repairing it in the leader's barn, and then donating the improved pieces to families in need in the area.

The Elm Grove *P.A.L.S.* groups started with a flourish—and then encountered difficulties. The chief difficulty of the baseball group was gossip. The participants had a hard time preserving confidentiality in their village environment, and it took a long time to build trust to the point where individuals felt confident to share their deeper doubts and questions. Certain family "rivalries" further complicated the situation, and at one point the pastor helped the group leader by visiting a specific family. It caused some friction in the church—but it helped build confidence in the group.

The chief difficulty in the other group became apparent only as the group moved farther into the "flow" of faith development. The leader was all too clearly unprepared for the gatherings. He seemed hurried, flustered, and preoccupied with other matters. Mutual mentoring with the pastor and the other group leader uncovered the fact that the intimacy of the group was revealing the leader's own sense of inadequacy. Together, the pastor and the other group leader reassured him, helped him discipline his preparation, and then encouraged him to trust the group for *their* support in personal growth. What a relief it was to this group leader not to have to appear to be "the spiritual expert"!

And so the mutual mentoring continued in Elm Grove Church. The group leaders grew, and became better able to merge their personal "styles" with the processes of the group. The pastor grew, becoming better able to anticipate the stresses of group leaders. And the congregation grew, as young adults grew in connection with God. Eventually, a "spin-off" group from the baseball group emerged. Perhaps not surprisingly, it was an alcohol addiction support group, and the leader emerged from the baseball group itself.

Elm Grove Church is more alive, and involves more people, than ever before. There are now about a hundred families involved with the church. The elders spend less time in administration, and more time praying and planning how to support these ministries. Yet a big challenge faces the church. Although Elm Grove Church has begun to thrive, the other two preaching points in the charge have not shared the new vision. This means that their common pastor is torn between very different expectations of leadership. Elm Grove expects the pastor to prioritize time to help *them* do visitation and ministry. The other two points expect the pastor to do all the visitation and ministry. The pastor knows where Christ is leading Elm Grove. But where is Christ leading the whole parish?

All Saints Church

All Saints Church is located downtown in a large city. Immigration has transformed the neighborhoods which surround the congregation. Today there is a large population of African immigrants, many of whom speak French. There is also a large population of Chinese immigrants, most of whom speak English, but who also share strong cultural ties to their homeland. The congregation itself is largely Anglo-Saxon.

There are a variety of tough issues facing the church, involving location, property renovation, and finance, and the church is having difficulty addressing all these issues. However, the opportunity for cell group ministry has excited a number of key lay leaders, because it seems the least threatening and least expensive way to benefit the diverse culture of the population around them.

When they returned from a workshop on *P.A.L.S.* group ministry, their big mistake was to go directly to the board and ask for support. The board was taken by surprise, fearful of losing control, and turned them down flat. Regrouping in one lay leader's living room, they decided not to give up, but to try a different way. This time, they approached cell group ministry "bottom up." The leaders fanned out among the congregation. They selected key friends, relatives, and acquaintances for conversation. They literally asked to come to their homes and share with them their vision of ministry. Rejection or indifference still greeted them—but others caught the vision and gained excitement.

After several months, enthusiasm for *P.A.L.S.* group ministry was growing. Once the pastor caught the vision (through the special attentions of two key lay leaders), the process began to accelerate. The pastor set aside the Common Lectionary, and began a sermon series on the great visioning texts of the Bible. This led to the annual congregational meeting, the agenda for which was shifted from management issues, to visioning issues. The task of identifying the basic "umbrella" of core values, bedrock beliefs, motivating vision, and key mission proved to be more difficult than anyone had guessed. The truth was, they had no real vision. The board had been waiting for the denominational office to tell them what their vision should be for the past ten years—and were still waiting.

Taking their future into their own hands, the church scheduled a second congregational meeting. During the next three months, they divided the eldership into "prayer triads," who began earnest studies of the Acts of the Apostles, along with careful observation of the public. When next they gathered, attendance for the congregational meeting was high. They made sure that child care was provided, to keep their young adults involved. Eventually, they reached consensus and had the best party the congregation had celebrated in years.

A team of church leaders had already begun to study the communication and group networks of the church and community. They realized that the *real* communications of the church took place separately from the monthly newsletter and weekly bulletin. They also realized that there were many networks operating in the neighborhoods around the church. Some were tied to specific languages or cultures, while others were linked to special interests or activities. Continuing their research, the church paid for a direct mail questionnaire that sought to identify community needs, and then sent teams door-to-door asking the question, "If you don't go to church now, what is the number-one thing you are looking for in a church?"

In order to better understand the reality, paradox, and yearning of the public, the lay leaders of the congregation politely asked to "sit in" on a variety of neighborhood clubs, fellowships, Twelve-Step programs, and other gatherings. Their biggest surprise was the discovery that they had been misled by their own nominations committee process. They had thought that busy people had no time for weekly group gatherings beyond work and family. They discovered that people were devoting serious time to such gatherings. The real issue was that such gatherings had to be *truly significant, meaningful, and helpful to daily living.* No one had time for bureaucracy. Surprising numbers of people devoted serious time to the quest for personal discovery and deeper spirituality.

Although the pastor had been with the church for more than ten years, and although the congregation could (and did) identify several people as potentially gifted in cell group leadership, the church realized that they needed to go beyond their congregation. Cell group leadership needed to reflect the diversity of their community. Through conversation with leaders in other neighborhood churches and charitable organizations, the pastor approached several potential leaders.

Some refused to work with the church because they honestly did not share the basic values, beliefs, vision, and mission that was the consensus of the congregation. Others refused, because they were afraid that the church would "sucker them" into a web of time-consuming administration aimed at institutional survival. However, a few shared the vision and were excited by the offer of the church to train them for excellence and allow them freedom to develop a group. Some said happily, "At last we have found a North American church that wants to do things like our church back home."

At this point the courage of the congregation was severely tested. First, the church leaders had to be willing to surrender control to "outsiders," who all came from "different backgrounds," and allow them freedom to develop a group. Second, the church had to offer these leaders a serious training opportunity to bring them to a standard of excellence. That tested the budget!

Three groups emerged in the first attempt at cell group ministry. The first group shared an affinity for worship using African music and African patterns of devotion. The second group was designed for mutual support for immigrants whose extended families were separated between two countries. The third group gathered people who sought mutual support for the death of a loved one.

The African Worship group proved to be too successful. Too many people started attending, and worship services became so "wild and crazy" that veteran church members were offended— and a little jealous! Requests to upgrade the electrical supply to the sanctuary, and change times of worship, opened the door for argument. On the brink of watching the cell group lead the African worship mission out of the church, however, the key leaders were able to overcome addictions to taste and tradition, and reaffirm the basic "umbrella" of values, beliefs, vision, and mission within which *anything* could happen.

The Separated Families group failed after six months. Some blamed the fact that they became immersed in advocacy work with the federal Department of Immigration. The real reason was the group had become disconnected from corporate worship, so that spirituality was no longer the real core of their group experience. They didn't need the church—they only needed a good lawyer.

The Grief Group is now more than twelve months old. It has gone on too long, but the group leader cannot bring himself to close the group and multiply. The affections group participants have for one another run deep, but already the group is increasingly looking inward. No real mission is emerging, and eventual stagnation in personal growth looms ahead. The pastor and other group leaders will be going on retreat soon, and this departure from the "flow" of *P.A.L.S.* group life will be an important item for discussion.

Despite the struggles, everyone in All Saints Church has learned important lessons. The diverse community has begun to regard them with greater interest. Worship services include more diverse participation, and all the talk about spiritual gifts has led to requests for the board to initiate a discernment and counseling process open to the community. Two brothers newly arrived from Taiwan have connected with the church and are eager to form a Christian soccer league—each team a *P.A.L.S.* group. Even though not a single elder plays soccer, the church is planning a giant Chinese-food block party to provide a vehicle for these lads to share their vision. Who knows what will happen?

First Avenue Church

First Avenue Church used to be the prestige church in this small city. The professionals, business leaders, and local politicians all attended. Then the downtown economy changed, "Christendom" disappeared, and years later only about a hundred older people would gather in the huge, beautiful sanctuary for worship. Three consecutive internal surveys to chart a future course for the church had put together the same three-point plan: attract the youth, maintain the property, and restore the pipe organ for community concerts. The plan never worked.

On a fateful Tuesday, one of the few beleaguered teenagers of the church quarreled with his mother over the youth group, saying,

"Why the hell *should* I go? I don't see any adults going to a group every Sunday night!" This glaring fact of the total absence of adult faith development disciplines struck the mother like a bolt from heaven. She attended a *P.A.L.S.* group workshop later that month, and faced with the question, "What is it about *your* experience of Jesus Christ that this community cannot live without?" she tearfully stood at the microphone and publicly confessed she had no answer.

She decided to do something about it. She found a friend, who also found a friend, and the three of them met for prayer and Bible reading every week for eight weeks to answer that question. Such was their passion, that by the eighth week the group had grown to ten. Eventually the pastor joined the group—but not as the leader. The intense, honest conversations of the group began to influence his preaching, and slowly the whole church began to ponder the mysteries of *adult* faith development. The board had yet to place it on the agenda.

One group participant was a music teacher and she decided to do something with her talent. She talked ten families into substantial donations, bought a set of handbells, and started a choir. To be more exact, she started a *P.A.L.S.* group *the affinity for which was handbells.* They met every week to pray, talk, laugh, share, and practice like crazy with bells. Eventually they played in nursing homes, and worship services. She resigned her place on the board, and her office in the women's group, to devote time to the *P.A.L.S.* group.

Another participant loved photography, and decided to do something about it. He started videotaping worship services. To his surprise, teenage boys (including the irate son who had refused to go to the youth group) saw what he was doing and wanted to do it, too. Another *P.A.L.S.* group was born, this time with "technology crazy" teens. Eventually they convinced the local cable television station to air their videotaped worship services as a benefit to folks in local hospitals and nursing homes.

The original prayer group eventually grew too large. The woman (who had finally *answered* the question!) coached a second leader to form another prayer group. Within two years, a plethora of cell groups in various stages of development had formed. There were groups related to badminton, motion pictures, novels, and Christmas crafts. A group of young couples (marginal members of the church rarely seen except on Christmas) formed a group to build houses with Habitats for Humanity. Support groups for people with cancer began driving complete strangers to distant hospitals for treatments, and support groups for the unemployed began gathering people from both church and community.

After several crises involving personal relationships and conflicts over biblical interpretation shook the group experience, the pastor somewhat belatedly realized he needed to provide some guidance and training for leaders. He formed a partnership with a local medical doctor (not a member of the church), and together they offered classes and retreats to help group leaders *lead.* This forced the pastor to adjust his visitation schedule, conflict followed, and his stress level increased.

The pastor and several key lay leaders were wise enough to realize that they needed to form a support group to cope with stress. They invited clergy and lay leaders from neighboring congregations who were experimenting with similar changes. They met monthly for a supper and evening conversation, during which they had the confidence to complain, share pain, and generally get their emotions out. They also traded success stories, brainstormed options, and generally coached one another through the chaos. As one participant said in surprise, "You know, we are really modeling the very personal and spiritual growth process that we are trying to implement in our cell groups!"

One day a key "patriarch" of the church walked into the office and said, "Pastor, where on earth did all these cell groups come from? I don't remember authorizing any of this!" Finally, it got on the board agenda. Since worship attendance was going up, along with church participation for all ages, the board could not find fault with the groups. So they just decided to control the groups. The difficulty was that the board had no sense of humor. When groups failed or got into difficulty, they wanted to get angry and blame someone, instead of laughing, forgiving, and learning. The board was also impatient. They wanted to see big benefits in actual membership increases and financial contributions. When these didn't happen right away, they wondered if the church was wasting its time. And the board worried a lot about the dignity of the church. When groups did things that seemed to offend some matriarch's taste, or some patriarch's sense of propriety, they wanted to call on the personnel committee to put a stop to it.

By now, however, the pastor had fully caught the vision. Together with lay leaders deeply committed to personal growth and faith development, he talked with every board member. He wisely multiplied the communications vehicles in the congregation, so that conflicts due to mere misunderstanding were absolutely minimized. He began designing worship services aimed "at the heart," to motivate commitments to the many opportunities for adult education and personal mission that were emerging through the week.

The congregation had really developed cell group ministry backward, but that didn't matter. Training programs for leaders, and accountability systems, began to be fine-tuned. The church initiated large fellowship events, in which all their many P.A.L.S. groups were visibly and aggressively advertised. Their large board found itself increasingly irrelevant and restless, so they helped elders do the ministries they were originally supposed to have been doing. Stress for the pastor decreased, as the congregation finally identified their basic core values, bedrock beliefs, motivating vision, and key mission—and thus clarified their expectations for staff leaders.

Yes, along the way a few people left the church. They took offense at some activity of a group, or became frightened by the diversity of people and the increasing number of "strangers" in their midst. The organist resigned, unable to accept the variety of musical styles worship services contained.

Nevertheless, the church as a whole grew. People felt a spirit of joy as never before. More missions emerged from congregational participants than at any other time in the congregation's history. And the church converted one whole wall of the vestibule into a giant waterfall cascading twenty-four hours a day, advertising to all onlookers the vision that they were "The Waterfall of God's Grace" to the community. More than fifty adult baptisms a year was not bad for a church that at one time only baptized infant grandchildren!

By the way, they now have a dynamic youth ministry among downtown gangs, the former choir loft is occupied by a set of drums and an electronic keyboard, and in addition to the best *classical music* worship service in town, they have three other services involving more than five hundred people every week in worship.

— 10 —

CHANGING CONGREGATIONAL ORGANIZATION

Cell group ministry demands organizational change. This is the "hidden" stress that congregations will experience when they invest themselves in cell group development. The first cell groups often begin relatively easily, and are supported with considerable organizational enthusiasm. As cell groups multiply, however, organizational stress increases exponentially. The truth is that cell groups cannot thrive in an organizational environment of hierarchy, bureaucracy, or extensive middle management. Since many traditional church structures are relics of the hierarchies and bureaucracies of the "Christendom" period of the nineteenth and twentieth centuries, this means stressful organizational change. Many churches begin cell group ministry, and later cannot understand why their groups fail to multiply. The number-one reason cell group ministry prematurely plateaus is that the church organization refuses to change. Hierarchy, bureaucracy, and the constant control of layers of middle management must all be surrendered if cell groups are to flourish.

This is why the image of raising rabbits is so helpful. Most church organizations are very good at "training dogs"—but they are unprepared to "raise rabbits."

> THE NUMBER-ONE REASON cell group ministry prematurely plateaus in traditional churches is that the organization refuses to change!

The training of dogs is all about control by a central authority. The raising of rabbits is all about freedom to explore and grow. Trained dogs obey commands or directives. Healthy rabbits go wherever they choose. Trained dogs must be given an order or plan *before* they act. Healthy rabbits are self-starters and respond spontaneously and creatively to a changing environment. Trained dogs never leave you wondering where they might be at any given time. Healthy rabbits always leave you in some doubt about where they might be going at any given time.

Picture the dog trained to a leash as a metaphor for most church organizations of the "Christendom" period. The "dog" is a committee. The "leash" is the long, carefully detailed mandate that lists everything the dog can or should do. The "hand" that holds the leash is the central authority of the church: pastor, official board, trustees, matriarchs or patriarchs of congregational life. If the committee fails to do what it is supposed to do, or if the committee wanders off to do something other than what it has been commanded to do by a central authority, what will be the response of the church? They will "jerk the leash" and cry "Heel!" They may change the chairperson, rewrite the mandate of the committee, or even discharge the whole committee. Much of the "restructuring" of traditional Christendom church organizations has been just this: designing a better leash and training committees to respond more effectively to central authority.

Organizational "downsizing" has often been done in the belief that *fewer, better trained dogs* are better than too many dogs, which get in the way of one another. Traditional organizations feared redundancy, and initiated elaborate liaison networks between committees to make sure that no "dog" transgressed another "dog's" territory. Middle management increased exponentially, and committee energy was really devoted (not to ministry) but to internal reporting.

The training of dogs is all about a central plan, central control, constant supervision, multiple management, and product control. Committees obey a mission agenda delivered from the hierarchy, specialize their activities in cooperation with other committees, and produce only what is expected of them.

The raising of rabbits is an entirely different experience. Picture a yard full of rabbits, surrounded by a fence. The "rabbits" are the cell groups. The "fence" is the basic boundary of core vision, bedrock beliefs, motivating vision, and key mission, which forms the consensus of the congregation. The cell groups are free to wander and roam at will *within the fence.* If they go beyond the basic boundaries of congregational life, they may well find a new home in the cultural forest, but they will not be considered a cell group of this particular church.

CORE VALUES

MOTIVATING
VISION

KEY
MISSION

BEDROCK BELIEFS

Notice that there are no "leashes," and no controlling "hands" holding a leash. These cell groups are free to identify their own mission, design their own organizations, follow their own paths, investigate any aspect of life or spirituality, implement any creative action, and generally do whatever they choose—*without asking permission!*

Cell groups, like rabbits, are designed to multiply. Although bureaucracy may be downsized, the number of groups increases. Remember, these are not *committees*. These are groups for personal and spiritual growth. The organization that allows groups to multiply will be nurturing, but not controlling. It will train group leaders, equip groups with covenants, and coach groups to do whatever they do with quality—but it will not tell the groups what to do or how to do it. This organization not only does not fear redundancy, but it welcomes redundancy! If more than one rabbit wants to explore the same area of the yard, or if more than one cell group wants to do the same kind of thing, they are perfectly welcome to do it. More than one group can be involved in worship, Christian education, or any affinity one can imagine.

At various places, I have noted that the intrusion of "control" often blocks group growth and development. In a sense, almost all the problems churches experience in developing cell group ministry can ultimately be traced to this single issue: *CONTROL!* Control is the deepest addiction of twentieth-century "Christendom" church organizations. Unconsciously, even unwillingly, traditional churches constantly try to transform a "rabbit" into a "dog." The inability to put a "rabbit" on a "leash" is the most common frustration of traditional church leaders.

We can identify six specific ways in which *CONTROL* intrudes upon and blocks cell group growth and development.

1) Control and the Eternal Perpetuation of Groups

Closure is an integral part of cell group life. Even when group members come to love one another dearly, the church organization committed to cell group ministry knows that every group must come to an end at the conclusion of their covenant. Traditional church organizations find closure difficult, and sometimes impossible, to accomplish. In traditional bureaucracies or hierarchies, groups never ended. They were demanded by the central mission plan of the central board. There must *always* be a women's group, men's group, youth group, assorted Sunday school classes, and other groups. These could not be allowed to die. If the group weakened, the church would go to extraordinary efforts recruiting officers, hiring staff, and pushing participation. The death of a group was seen as organizational failure. It undermined the central mission of the central board.

The eternal perpetuation of groups is a method of *control* exercised by bureaucracies and hierarchies. As long as groups continue to survive, the central board can continue to control the mission agenda of the church. The mission "plan" that is designed, managed, and implemented from within the organization can remain substantially the same. The group nominations processes, mandates, and procedures are carefully monitored through reporting to the central authority. More than this, by not allowing groups to *die*, the controlling organization cleverly *blocks new groups from being born!* All people are channeled into existing groups. For example, all women must belong to the "Women's Group," and all youth must belong to the "Youth Group." It is a "one size fits all" strategy in which the institution controls the size and style of the fitting!

Traditional church organizations commonly complain that they are uncomfortable about insisting that group covenants include closure. They often describe their discomfort by saying that they hate to break up loving relationships that have formed in the group. Of course, if the group has been healthy these loving relationships should continue *beyond* the life of the group! Penetrate beyond the sentimentality, and you will discover that the real concern is control. The closure of a known group, and the birthing of an unknown new group, are organizationally threatening. The former can be loved—and controlled. The latter must be loved—and set free! Group multiplication demands group closures, just as the cells of a living organism die in order that others might live.

2) Control and Imposed Curriculum

One way to subtly change a cell group into a committee, is by imposing a uniform study guide or curriculum on cell group life. The insistence that all groups must minimally and uniformly read certain material or study certain things (such as the doctrine, history, or polity of a denomination) blocks group growth. It is usually done as a strategy for "membership assimilation"—and this, of course, is just the problem. Traditional bureaucracies and hierarchies are preoccupied with *membership*. They want every unit of church life to channel people into uniformity with institutional belief and behavior. They want you to *love the church!* If you "love the church," you will be more easily persuaded to do what the institution asks.

Cell groups care little about "membership." They are concerned about *participation*. Cell groups do not insist upon uniformity, but enable individuals to explore faith and life in their own way, in their own terminology, and in directions that meet their unique spiritual needs. Therefore, groups must be free to choose their own resources for growth—or even choose no resource at all! If they do choose a study guide or curriculum, it may or may not be one used by other units of church life. It may not even be one that is developed by the denomination. Cell groups do not help people to *love the church*. Cell groups help people *love themselves, each other, and God*. And that is a very different thing.

3) Control and Prescriptive Job Descriptions and Mandates

Yet another method by which traditional church organizations often unconsciously seek to transform cell groups into committees, is the imposition of "prescriptive" job descriptions for leaders and mandates for groups. A "prescriptive" job description lists in detail everything a leader can or must do. Similarly, a "prescriptive" mandate lists everything a group can or must do. There are two problems with this. The first problem is that these are *imposed*. The institution requires a leader or group to behave in specific ways or accomplish specific tasks, and thus undermines initiative. Cell groups must have freedom to choose their own goals and methods. The second problem is that the prescriptive job description imposed is an institutional agenda that is foreign to the group experience. It comes from "outside" group life, and imposes an artificial boundary on group activity. The group finds itself fulfilling an institutional agenda, rather than the group's purpose of personal and spiritual growth.

Cell groups flourish with *proscriptive* job descriptions and mandates. Refer back to the covenants for cell groups, and you will discover that only a *mission purpose* is identified. There is no prescribed list of everything that can or should be done. The mission purpose of the covenant, and the clear boundaries of values, beliefs, vision, and mission of the whole church, represent "proscriptions" or "boundaries" beyond which the leader or group cannot go—but within which they have freedom to do whatever they choose. Proscriptive job descriptions and mandates identify what *cannot* be done, but never attempt to list what *can* be done. If a creative idea does not go beyond the basic boundaries identified, leader and group are free to do it even if it seems crazy. You don't need permission to add to a list of what you can do, because no such list exists.

Prescriptive job descriptions and mandates are convenient methods institutions use to control others. Leaders and groups do what the central authority thinks *it* should do, and they are not truly free to do what *they* think they should do. Proscriptive job descriptions and mandates often seem negative, but they in fact free leaders and groups to take initiative and enhance creativity.

4) Control and Power Cliques

Most traditional bureaucracies and hierarchies actually *resist* clarity about their basic values, beliefs, vision, and mission. They prefer to live in ambiguity, because this forces church participants to look for "experts," "professionals," or "longtime members" who can tell them what to do. In the midst of a fog, all movement becomes dependent on "foghorns." These "foghorns" are the power cliques and controllers of church life who assert a privileged position that exercises authority over others. If the fog were to disperse, and the church truly have clarity about their basic values, beliefs, vision, and mission, then controllers and cliques would be far less influential. Every participant in the church, newcomer or veteran, would know the boundaries for action. As it is, in the absence of clear boundaries of values, belief, vision, and mission, the *hidden* boundaries of church life become the personal tastes, opinions, lifestyles, and perspectives of the matriarchs and patriarchs of the church.

In the traditional bureaucracies and hierarchies of Christendom, individuals and groups competed with one another for control of the central board. The victor could control the mission agenda of the church, and write the prescriptive job descriptions and mandates of leaders and groups to reflect their priorities. They resist the birthing of new groups, or the multiplication of groups, and prefer to perpetuate existing groups indefinitely, because such consistency helps them maintain power. They perceive the multiplication of groups to be a danger to the institution, because they assume such groups will only increase competition for control.

In organizations that nurture cell groups, however, clarity about the proscriptive boundaries of church life means that no cell group ever has power to control another cell group. As long as a group does not "go beyond the boundaries," they can do whatever they wish *even if it offends the tastes, opinions, lifestyle, or perspective of other individuals or groups* in the church! For example, one cell group might develop a worship alternative using rock music or jazz— another group might develop a worship alternative using classical music or Gregorian chant. Each group literally *hates* the music of the other group, but each group is free to do what they wish. Neither group has the power to block the other group from its experiment, because neither experiment goes beyond the boundaries of values, beliefs, vision, and mission. There is no room for snobbery in cell group organizations. Multiple options for multiple needs is the rule.

5) Control and Internal Reporting

Traditional hierarchies and bureaucracies are terrified of redundancy and believe that all activities must be extensively coordinated to avoid duplication of effort. In *Growing Spiritual Redwoods,* co-author Bill Easum and I described these organizations as *machines.* These organizational machines are highly complex, since more and more middle management is required to coordinate activities and maintain a liaison with other committees and groups. Internal reporting occupies more and more time, as group participants must "sit in" on other groups and committees in order to "coordinate" efforts and prevent "wasted" energy. Paradoxically, while groups and committees struggle to avoid redundancy, the church finds itself creating multiple redundant layers of management. Every creative idea must be tested by several management layers before it ever gets implemented.

Internal reporting in organizational machines is a powerful form of control. First, it imposes an organizational uniformity. Multiple layers of management trim the "rough edges" from every creative idea, so that programs all look alike. In order to achieve an interface with every other program unit or committee, every group is given an identical internal organization, regardless of the unique affinity of the group. Second, internal reporting slows down the decision and implementation process. The slower speed increases opportunities for outside interference, reduces risk, and decreases the chances for sudden and dramatic change. Opportunities go by, and the institution remains essentially the same. Third, internal reporting relies on "networking expertise" and "parliamentary procedure." Decision making and implementation ultimately require experts who can navigate the complex rules of the system, thus taking power to act from the average church participant. Everyone may know where to go, but only a chosen few know how to get there. Instead of competing for control of the *mission agenda,* special interest groups compete for control of the *networking process.* In this way, activities can be managed and meetings can be run which exclude unwanted initiatives.

In *Growing Spiritual Redwoods,* we describe the organization that nurtures cell groups as *organisms.* These organisms welcome redundancy and grow in a riot of diversity. Although there is a method of coordination, layers of middle management are replaced by a "genetic code" of mission and leadership for each organic cell. Each cell has extraordinary powers of self-determination, and is free to duplicate the mission of other cells—or strike off in an entirely new direction. There may be many twigs, roots, and leaves doing similar things—and there may also be new shoots going in entirely new directions. While groups may communicate constantly within and beyond the organism, they are not required to "report" to other cells, nor do they need to wait for a cumbersome process which only a few experts understand before implementing a creative idea. Organisms "seize the opportunity" in a fast-changing cultural environment.

6) Control and the Ecclesiastical Denomination

Most churches building cell group ministries are at the fringe of the denominational experience. They are often treated with suspicion, distrust, or downright hostility by their denominational middle judicatories. This is because denominational structures perpetuate the heritage of Christendom and are designed to "train dogs" rather than "raise rabbits." These bureaucracies and hierarchies assume that a central authority can pass on a mission agenda that will be obediently pursued by each church of the denomination—and that each church will pass this same agenda to every group or committee.

Control may be exercised overtly by a parent denomination through imposed limitations for leadership or property development. These powers to control which clergy may be appointed or called to a given congregation, or to control which capital assistance applications will receive grants and loans for development, are often all that is left of denominational influence. As congregations find ways to develop leadership and stewardship beyond the control of the denomination, control has increasingly been more subtle. Congregations committed to cell group ministry are simply shunned by other churches within the judicatory, or criticized by the "official" seminaries and training centers of the denomination. The newly emerging *organisms* are said to be "watering down the gospel" or "no longer part of our denominational ethos."

Denominations are inherently committed to uniformity, which makes it difficult for them to embrace a strategy of ministry that celebrates and encourages diversity. Fortunately, many denominational leaders are beginning to realize:

- that Christendom has truly died;
- that mission agendas can no longer be dictated by the top of the hierarchy or the center of the bureaucracy;
- that the best way to revitalize a denomination is not to "clamp down" but to "give freedom."

The more freedom that is given to the congregation, the better prepared the congregation will be to give freedom to cell groups. Denominational leaders are often rather surprised to discover that when congregations are empowered to discern for themselves the core values, bedrock beliefs, motivating vision, and key mission that is their own passionate consensus, these congregations forge new partnerships which the denomination can effectively support.

Just as cell group "rabbits" multiply and take over the barnyard, so also congregations that embrace a permission-giving organization multiply and utterly transform a denomination. Most denominational leaders know that radical reform is necessary if the denomination is to have any future at all in the twenty-first century. The more painful lesson is that this reform will come not from the top of the hierarchy or the center of the bureaucracy, but from *congregations* themselves. Control of congregations is denominational suicide. Release control of congregations, and denominations can find a whole new role of resource and support for ministry.

Control Issues

The control methods I have just identified often lie behind the most common congregational problems with cell group development. The church may enthusiastically commit itself to cell group ministry. As the "rabbits" multiply, stress grows within the traditional organization. Conflict emerges. Cell group leaders become frustrated. Leaders and cell group participants threaten to return to the fringes of congregational life whence they came. Six issues often emerge:

1) The church is impatient for institutional membership and financial benefits.

It becomes apparent that the motivation for cell group ministry—and the church growth that it implies—has in fact been ambiguous. While some pursued cell group ministry with wholehearted commitment to personal and spiritual growth, others have seen it only as a "program" that will rescue the traditional organization.

2) The church has no sense of humor, and cannot tolerate failure.

It becomes apparent that the methodology of cell group ministry contradicts the central strategic plan that is controlled by the pastor, official board, or matriarchs and patriarchs of the church. True freedom to explore life and faith has never really been given, and true openness to experimentation and diversity has never been understood.

3) The church regularly vetoes creative cell group affinities or missions.

It becomes apparent that the church has not fully embraced the basic "umbrella" of values, beliefs, vision, and mission as the key to accountability. The personal tastes, opinions, lifestyles, and perspectives of the inner circle of "controllers," or the intrusive behavior of denominational judicatories, is what sets the real boundaries for action.

4) Cell groups fail to reflect the full demographic and psychographic diversity of the community.

It becomes apparent that the cell groups still only attract that segment of the population that is most like the people already inside the church. Homogeneity of race, language, culture, educational background, or economic status is a sign that "control" is unconsciously being exercised by the church. The real passion of the church is not purely for personal and spiritual growth, but rather to associate with "people like us."

5) Cell groups become disconnected from the corporate worship of the church.

It becomes apparent that the church is not willing to match the growing diversity of groups with multiple options in worship. The uniformity of belief and action imposed in worship contradicts the spiritual growth and experimentation of the groups. Cell groups soon demand *multiple tracks* of worship that utilize diverse cultural forms (music, drama, technology, etc.) and which address diverse spiritual yearnings (for healing, coaching, celebration, etc.).

6) Church leaders refuse to act without following denominational precedents.

It becomes apparent that clergy are fearful of jeopardizing future career advancement, and that lay leaders are fearful of jeopardizing future denominational support. Has anyone done this before? Are any congregations of *our denomination* doing this? These questions are asked by leaders who fear risk and need guarantees, for whom spiritual entrepreneurship is mysterious or disloyal. Comfort with the denominational status quo blocks cell group innovation.

For a larger discussion of these issues, and of the larger organizational change at stake in cell group ministry development, read *Kicking Habits: Welcome Relief for Addicted Churches* and *Growing Spiritual Redwoods*.

Cell groups and mission teams are the fruits of the permission-giving organization. The sincerity and passion for growth, discernment, and mission will continue to challenge the congregation to pursue the system of the thriving church. However, take warning! The declining church systems of Christendom will be an addiction to which even the most committed thriving church will be tempted to return. The model of the traditional *prescriptive* church organization will be like a magnet always trying to draw the church back into its old institutional ways. These influences can be very subtle, and they can use the very success of cell group ministry as a lure. In biblical language, these are corporate "idolatries" that can capture any congregation of any size.

• Large "megachurches" may allow success to outgrow their own avowed spirituality. The growth disciplines of leaders and the spiritual expectations of participants may become weakened, because the organization has more creativity than it can handle. They become preoccupied by the idolatry of *numbers*.
• Medium-sized "neighborhood" churches may allow success to limit their goals for mission. Mission targets may plateau or be lowered, and the congregation may not press forward to reach the ever-growing cultural and demographic diversity of the public. They become preoccupied with the idolatry of *tradition*.
• Small-sized "family" churches may allow success to reduce their willingness to risk. Having renewed the financial and volunteer resources of the congregation, they become overcautious about losing whatever they have gained. They become preoccupied with the idolatry of *survival*.

Ironically, like alcoholics gathered in the same pub, they are remarkably adept at pointing out the addictive behavior of their fellows. The small church scoffs at the megachurch for thinking only of numbers, while the megachurch criticizes the small congregation for wasting valuable resources on mere survival. The medium-sized church criticizes both from the smug self-satisfaction of tradition. All have benefited by cell group growth—and all will see their cell group multiplication plateau and decline if they do not address the hidden addictions of control. As Jesus said, "First take the log out of thine own eye, and then you will see clearly to take the speck out of your brother's eye."

St. Mark's Church

St. Mark's is a prestigious church located in a prosperous, growing city. They belong to a mainstream denomination, have a beautiful Gothic building, manage a large budget, and maintain an enormous staff and board structure. Despite the opportunities in their demographic area, the church has been declining. They now have a thousand members, fewer than two hundred in worship, and have celebrated only five adult baptisms in five years. Members are aging, leaders are burned out, and staff will soon be downsized for the third time in a decade. The people said they needed to change.

The church paid a well-known consultant to help them understand ministry in the twenty-first century and share the vision of cell group ministry. They embraced it with enthusiasm! Seven affinity groups began, led by laity who had formerly been on the margins of church life. New people began to participate. The church began to reflect the diversity of the community. Two years later, however, group multiplication ceased. Group leaders became frustrated and bitter. Conflicts rocked the official board.

The church paid a denominational expert to lead a traditional strategic planning process to restructure the board and rewrite staff job descriptions. The board downsized from 150 to 100 members, and job descriptions were lengthened from four pages to seven pages. Internal reporting was maximized to ensure "efficient use of energy" and "accountability." Now the remaining cell groups began to falter, some of their leaders retreated back to the margins of church life, conflict increased, and the pastor resigned. What happened?

The answer is revealed in the diagram for their "revised" board structure. The diagram is a maze of boxes and circles, with

---

connecting lines of accountability and communication everywhere. In one little box, which is a subsection of Christian education, are the words "Cell Group Ministry." Despite their enthusiasm, St. Mark's could never accept the fact that cell groups would never be a *program* of the church, that cell groups *will be the church!*

The addiction to "control" killed the vision of cell group ministry. Bureaucracy, prescriptive job descriptions, redundant management, and fear of failure all combined to block the creativity necessary for personal and group growth. The church proved to be primarily interested in membership and financial increases, uniformity in program, and protection of heritage. Cell group participants never established a link to corporate worship, because worship offered them no options for spiritual growth. New ideas met with increasing resistance from the central board, as veteran members feared things were changing too fast and going too far.

Behind this addiction to "control" lay the inability (or unwillingness) of the church to gain clarity about their core values, bedrock beliefs, motivating vision, and key mission. The tastes, opinions, lifestyles, and perspectives of church controllers ensured that the congregation would be homogeneous and unreflective of the demographic diversity of the surrounding community. Finally, behind *this* addiction to uniformity lay the spiritual contentment of core members who did not really believe that *they* needed to *grow*. They continued to treat the pastor as a private chaplain and expected staff to do all the ministry.

Today the enthusiasm for cell group ministry has disappeared, and things have returned to normal. The congregation continues to decline and experience nominations problems. Young families are dropping out of involvement. The denomination has appointed interim leaders who will help the congregation devise yet another strategic plan that will more clearly locate the congregation in the denominational "ethos."

Organizational Preparation for Cell Group Ministry

Logically, the best way to prepare for cell group ministry is to start by building a permission-giving organization. Carefully develop the organization through quadrants 1, 2, and 3, and then cell group ministry will flourish. The reality, however, is that most congregations are still making the transition to a thriving church system, and only just discovering the power of the permission-giving organization. Most are already intentionally developing, or unintentionally experiencing, the growth of cell groups.

This is why at the beginning of the eight-step process for cell group development, I said that a church did not have to restructure the board, write a new constitution, hire a new staff person, or even revise the budget for a new program, *in order to begin the development of cell groups*. The stress of cell group development, however, is that as cell groups multiply it will become apparent to the congregation that these very things will eventually need to be done. In the beginning, a change of *attitude* is crucial. In the end, a change of *organization* will be crucial.

Attitude Preparation for Organizational Change

In order to prepare the church organization for what lies ahead, you will need to help leaders and participants change fundamental *attitudes* about the church. This will take time, prayer, and a process. Steps 1 to 4 described in the cell group development process (chapter 9) are primarily devoted to this task. From the point of view of organizational readiness, there are three keys:

1) Define and celebrate the core values, bedrock beliefs, motivating vision, and key mission.

This consensus defines the boundaries beyond which cell groups cannot go, but within which they are free to roam and experiment. Clarity here reduces the power of an inner circle to control the congregation according to their tastes and opinions. This consensus becomes the cornerstone for accountability in the emerging organization. The process used will vary from church to church. Whatever the exact process is, be sure that

• the process allows *sufficient time* for face-to-face conversations to be the chief vehicle for building consensus (big meetings and majority voting won't change attitudes);
• the process intentionally includes regular participants, marginal members, and listening to the general public (just sampling the opinions of people who attend worship regularly will only reinforce continuing addictions);
• the process is *surrounded by* personal and corporate prayer that is integral to the spirituality of the church (announcements in the bulletin to attend focus groups will not motivate serious participation).

The process may not be easy, because many churches prefer to live in a "fog." They prefer to depend on experts to tell them what to believe and how to behave, rather than invest themselves in disciplines of growth and discernment.

Once the process is complete, the organization will be more motivated for personal and spiritual growth. They will also be better positioned to tolerate failure and more confident to release creative mission experiments. Many marginal members will become more interested in congregational life, and the general public will have a clearer awareness of the identity and purpose of the church in their community.

2) Clarify and celebrate changing leadership expectations.

The church needs to know in advance that the clergy will be reprioritizing time and energy away from doing ministries themselves, to equipping others to do ministries. Similarly, lay leaders need to be prepared for new expectations for spiritual growth and training. Some traditional leaders will step down, and new leaders will unexpectedly emerge. Again, the process to do this will vary from church to church. Whatever the process is, be sure that:

• the process is *publicly embraced by the pastor* through preaching, representation to denominational judicatories, and spontaneous conversation (even a lukewarm or neutral attitude hinders changing attitudes);
• the process is *understood and supported* by the personnel or human resources committee (their ability to interpret and support leadership change will help navigate the church through inevitable complaints);
• the process *includes a retreat or training opportunity for a cadre of key lay leaders* who can help refine, implement, interpret, defend, *and model* the principles of cell group ministry.

This process may not be easy, as some clergy and laity cling to old distinctions between "professional" and "volunteer" leadership. Clergy and laity alike must recognize and address their *own* needs for personal and spiritual growth.

The organization will now be better positioned to treat their existing constitution as "clay" that can be molded and shaped, and their existing institutional structures as "guides" that can be applied with greater flexibility and imagination. Clergy will feel more comfortable in sharing ministry, and laity will feel more confident in doing ministry.

3) Place congregational leaders and participants in spiritual growth disciplines.

The central board or pastor must resist imposing an annual mission agenda for the congregation and place on hold the traditional nominations process that recruits volunteers to implement that mission. This may imply eliminating or temporarily suspending some committees. The mission of the church will reemerge and expand as individuals and groups begin to experience the personal and spiritual growth that is the new priority of the congregation. Eventually, all missions of the church will emerge from the growth of people within the church, not from a hierarchical office or central bureaucracy of congregation or denomination. Churches will implement this process differently. Whatever the process to build spiritual discipline is, be sure that

• the process creates a *worship team* that includes a faith-sharer, drama coach, and music coordinator, who together design worship services that are participatory and highly motivating (routine liturgies, "off-the-shelf" prayers, and boring worship will not help participants listen for the callings of God);
• the process includes multiple opportunities for spiritual gifts discernment or personality inventories in which both church and community members can identify and celebrate abilities and interests they may never have known before (traditional "time and talent" inventories only force individuals to fit the announced needs of the institution);
• the process involves scripture (particularly the Gospels and the Acts of the Apostles), daily prayer, lots of opportunities for conversation and faith-sharing, and serious research into the needs of the community and world;
• the process leads to some visible change that improves the quality of life for individuals or society;
• the process is *fun*, and creates an atmosphere of good humor and laughter that gives people permission to look foolish (taking oneself too seriously takes the focus away from the action of the Holy Spirit, which is the power that elicits mission from the people).

This process may not be easy. The longer the heritage of the congregation, or the deeper their sense of prestige in denominational identity, the more fearful true diversity will be. The church will worry that some very valuable missions might be neglected (even though they can't seem to recruit leaders for those missions now)—and some "sacred cows" might be revealed!

However, the organization will now be in a better position to recognize and celebrate new or renewed mission that emerges from the spirituality of the participants in church life. They will begin to recognize diversity as opportunity, and become expectant for eruptions of the Spirit in their midst.

Continuing Organizational Change

Although such advanced preparation will help change *attitudes* in the church, and allow the church to launch cell groups with greater confidence for success, the multiplication of cell groups will continue to bring stress to the organization. In a sense, this continuing organizational stress will never really end, and congregational leaders will simply need to get used to it! Cell group ministry is very dynamic and ever-changing, and congregational leaders will *always* be adjusting the organization to fit the ministry. In other words, while traditional hierarchies and bureaucracies might need to restructure the organization every five to ten years, the emerging church organization will find itself revising the organization every six months. Here are seven organizational keys for continuing revision.

1) Orient congregational meetings to continually refine, and celebrate, the core values, bedrock beliefs, motivating vision, and key mission of the congregation.

The congregational meetings of the future will no longer emphasize *management* (election of officers, approvals of budgets, hearing reports). The purpose of the meeting will almost exclusively be to *refine and celebrate* the basic "umbrella" of congregational life that is the consensus of the people, and which forms the boundaries for creative experimentation. The umbrella itself will evolve over time, and the motivation of the people must be constantly encouraged. Congregational leaders can mold the organization as ministries evolve, but they cannot impose consensus about values, beliefs, vision, and mission.

2) Define the mission purpose which is the congregation's "reason for being," and the degree of sacrifice the congregation is willing to risk.

Focus your attention beyond the church and the needs of congregational insiders, toward the emerging needs of the diverse publics of the community. Discover what possible difference you can make, and determine how passionate you are to make that difference. Deploy congregational leaders to listen to the public and develop effective ways to communicate the gospel to the public. Help every single congregational participant articulate exactly what it is about their relationship to Christ, their church, and their mission, that is "to die for."

3) Center all leadership on disciplines of spiritual life and spiritual calling.

In *Growing Spiritual Redwoods,* Bill Easum and I described how leaders "surf the chaos" of the ever-changing church. They are visionaries, synthesizers, and motivators who create environments in which individuals can give birth to all the potential that God has given to each person.

These leaders do not rely on professional credentials, but influence church life through the authenticity of their own spiritual life and calling. Twin movements of humility, reflection, love—and intuition, cultural awareness, compassion—are like a "double helix" of genetic identity that characterizes flexible leadership.

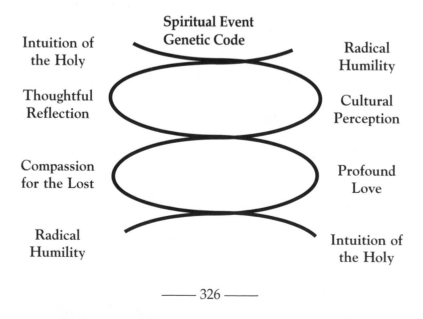

Spiritual Event
Genetic Code

Intuition of the Holy	Radical Humility
Thoughtful Reflection	Cultural Perception
Compassion for the Lost	Profound Love
Radical Humility	Intuition of the Holy

Such leaders speak and act from their own experiences of life struggle and spiritual victory. Their authenticity both assures and motivates the congregation.

4) Emphasize QUALITY for all leadership and all ministries.

Constantly increase the quality of leadership training. Identification, training, and twenty-four-hour coaching support for cell group leaders will be essential to the development of creative ministries with a minimum of conflict. The pastor will spend more and more time helping others do ministry, rather than time doing the ministry. Steadily increase the lay ministry training budget of the congregation. The most common staff addition among these congregations will not be a youth worker or Christian education director, but rather a staff coordinator and trainer of cell group ministry.

5) Continually review the assumptions and flows that lie at the heart of all cell groups.

The theological, missional, educational, and pastoral assumptions identified earlier are the DNA or genetic code linking cell group life and congregational identity. The "flows" for relationship-building and faith-building are the paths of growth from which mission will emerge. The integrity and style of leadership give credibility to mission. The artful balance of "freedom and covenant" builds healthy, creative partnerships for growth and mission. These assumptions should be continually revisited by the congregation, and communicated at the beginning of all membership or leadership training. They should be revealed in the largest ministry and in the spontaneous words or deeds of church participants.

6) Create a Stability Triangle for management.

I described in *Kicking Habits* the Stability Triangle that replaces traditional bureaucratic organizations. Congregations will need to have a gifted and trained administration team (for coordination, communication, financial management, and day-to-day operations),

Basic Vision

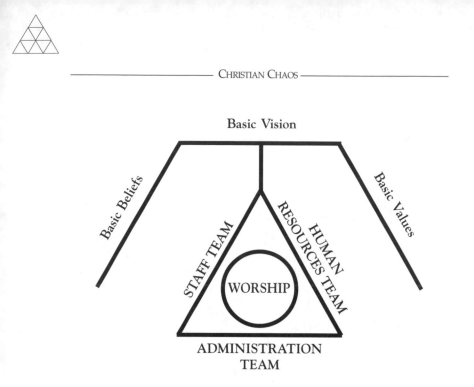

ADMINISTRATION
TEAM

a gifted and trained human resources team (for personnel oversight, gifts discernment, and continuing education support), and a gifted and trained staff team (for coaching, motivating, and training).

Together they articulate the basic values, beliefs, vision, and mission that are the consensus of the congregation, and visibly elevate this basic "umbrella" over all activities of the church. Their task is not to give permission for creativity, but to release creative ministries of excellence.

7) Exercise constant vigilance for hidden addictions to control.

One of the most difficult organizational addictions to break is the assumption that, either due to better education, deeper spiritual experience, more advanced academic degrees, exclusive denominational credentials, election by congregational vote, or personal charisma, *I have the right to tell others what to believe or how to behave.* This addiction reappears in hundreds of subtle (and less than subtle) ways, and must be continually resisted. Even a small "sip" of this addictive drink can return a congregation to its old ways and undermine years of cell group growth. The only boundaries for congregational life are defined by the "umbrella" of core values, bedrock beliefs, motivating vision, and key mission that is the consensus of the people. Beyond this, *no individual or group enjoys a privileged position that can tell another individual or group what to believe or how to behave.*

These keys will guide continuing organizational revision as cell group ministry moves the church forward in the twenty-first century. Life is changing so rapidly, and in so many unexpected directions, that traditional methods of strategic planning do not work anymore. Like the organizational hierarchies and bureaucracies that utilized them, traditional methods of strategic planning are too inflexible to adapt to a changing cultural environment. Churches can no longer develop a detailed long-term plan today and expect that it will still be feasible five years away. The future may be mysterious, but these seven keys for organizational revision can enable the church to adapt quickly, and with integrity, to the changes of our time.

I have used the metaphor of *dance* to describe the dynamic movement of personal and spiritual growth that typifies cell group ministry. However, the metaphor helps us understand the unique organization that lies behind the thriving church system.

And the Dance Goes On . . .

Picture in your mind once again a contemporary teen dance: loud music, heavy rhythm, a packed dance floor, and teens moving and swaying in seemingly infinite ways. The constant activity and noise is enough to give an observer a headache! There is nothing tidy or orderly about the *dance*. Often, there is no clear beginning or ending to the *dance*. All seems to be a happy confusion. Earlier, however, we described patterns amid the chaos:

• People always attend the *dance* in groups;
• people always prefer to dance with partners;
• every dance includes repetitive movements or steps;
• the most important thing is to lose yourself in the music.

There is a pattern to what is happening. It is just a different pattern from that to which we are accustomed.

In the same way, thriving churches organized around cell groups may seem like chaos. The activity and noise can give a traditional church observer a headache! There is nothing orderly or solemn about this church organization. It does not unfold rationally, following a detailed long-range plan. However, there are discernible patterns amid the chaos:

• People participate in the church in groups;
• people prefer to grow personally and spiritually in partnerships with others;
• church participation is a perpetual movement from discovery of self and God, to discernment of life purpose, to self-fulfillment through mission;
• the most important thing is to lose yourself in the *vision*.

Now picture yourself in the balcony with a "birds-eye view" of the dance floor, and you will see additional patterns of organization that you may have missed previously.

First, you will see "chaperones."

These chaperones move among the dancers constantly. They have two goals. First, the chaperones ensure that no inappropriate behavior that goes beyond the boundaries of good health and safety occurs. Second, the chaperones take the time to talk, laugh, and listen, and coach people to dance better and enjoy themselves more.

In the organization that nurtures cell groups, trained leaders move among the church participants constantly. Some may be cell group leaders, while others may spontaneously support whatever new configuration of friendship emerges during the *dance*. Their goals are similar to the chaperone's. First, these leaders ensure that no behavior that goes beyond the boundaries of values, beliefs, vision, or mission occurs under the umbrella of congregational life. They articulate and model these principles constantly. Second, these leaders take the time to talk, laugh, listen, and coach people to grow personally and spiritually. They help people find themselves and their ministry, and motivate them to get going.

Second, you will see an administration team.

These are the people who prepare for the dance. They book the bands, decorate the space, collect the tickets, refill the punch bowl, swab the spills, and clean up after the dance is over. You know that an administration team is there, not because they are *visible,* but because the dance never pauses. There are no sudden interruptions to the music or the movement, because *somebody* is working behind the scenes.

In the organization that nurtures cell groups, an administration team is always working behind the scenes. These are the people who are identifying leaders, creating symbolically and technologically appropriate space, organizing financial support, replacing needed lightbulbs, and expanding the "dance floor." You know that they are there, not because they are visible, but because the mission never pauses. Maintenance is never primary. Mission is always primary. The administration team lets the ministry happen.

Third, you will see a personnel team.

These are the people who identify and train the chaperones, evaluate the quality of the band, and search for hidden talent in the crowd. Occasionally they will listen to a complaint. If a chaperone is found smoking in the washroom (going beyond the boundaries of good health and safety!), these are the people to counsel and educate the chaperone to improve leadership.

In the organization that nurtures cell groups, a human resources team is also working behind the scenes. These are the people helping others discover their gifts, identifying and training leaders for excellence, and evaluating performance. A good human resources team never tells people what to do. After all, anything can happen during a dance! Instead, a good human resources team trains leaders for excellence, orients them within the basic umbrella of congregational life—and gets out of the way.

Fourth, you will see staff.

The staff at the dance may, or may not, be wearing custodial uniforms. These are the people who lend their expertise to key areas of activity. They may be in the kitchen preparing the food, or behind the stage with the lighting and sound system, or moving among the crowd coaching the chaperones. The staff are doing everything in their power to create an environment that will make the dance as enjoyable and safe as possible.

In the organization that nurtures cell groups, there will also be a staff. These are the people who lend their expertise to key areas of church life. They may be clergy, musicians, secretaries, or custodians, but they are all equal. Together they all coach, train, and motivate others to do ministries well. They are doing everything possible to create an environment for personal and spiritual growth, in which individuals can give birth to the gifts that God has given each person.

Among the staff, there will be one person who is likely standing in the balcony with you. This is the person whose authenticity and passion leads him or her to watch over the whole system of church life. This person may be talking to the newcomers, or even standing on the sidewalk outside conversing with those passing by. This is the person who is always looking for new opportunities and watching for new trends among the spiritually hungry public.

Fifth, you will NOT see everything!

Since you are standing in the balcony watching the dance, it is important to point out that you are seeing only part of the event. The four walls and roof of the building do not contain the dance. The dance spills over into the kitchen, the parking lot, the sidewalk, and the park next door. Indeed, since the music is so loud, the dance spills over into smaller parties several blocks away.

The thriving church organization is entirely distinct from the property it happens to occupy. Thriving church organizations that nurture cell groups understand that a building is only a tool—no more, and no less. If the church building can be used to create an excellent environment for personal and spiritual growth, then they will keep it as it is. If the church building obstructs personal and spiritual growth in any way, it will be renovated, demolished and rebuilt, or relocated somewhere else. These church organizations understand that the *dance* is what matters, not the dance hall. Ministry and mission will spill over beyond the walls of the church onto the sidewalks of the community and around the world. These organizations consider the maintenance of heritage property to be a waste of time and a contradiction to the gospel. The real boundaries of mission and ministry are not the walls of the building, but the core values, bedrock beliefs, motivating vision, and key mission of the church. This is why church architecture is less important to these churches. The vision can never be poured in concrete. Culture is changing, human need is changing, and mission is changing all the time.

Cell groups are easy to begin. In the end, they will transform the organization of the church. The process will be stressful, but the joy of expanding mission into the community and world will be worth it. There is nothing more powerful in the twenty-first century than *turning the laity loose!*

NOTES

Welcome to the Real World

1. John Carver and Miriam Mayhew Carver, *Reinventing Your Board* (San Francisco: Jossey-Bass Publishers, 1997 and 1998).

CHAPTER 2. *Pre*scriptive Thinking

1. Tiers policy development is a technique borrowed from John and Miriam Mayhew Carver, *Reinventing Your Board*, pp. 90-92.
2. Ibid., p. 138.

CHAPTER 3. *Pro*scriptive Thinking

1. John and Miriam Mayhew Carver, *Reinventing Your Board*, p. 89.

CHAPTER 4. A Picture of the New Organization

1. These are defined more fully in my resource "Freeing the Faithful" found in *Moving Off the Map* (Abingdon Press, 1998), pp. 113-236.

CHAPTER 6. The Basic Idea: Cell Groups and Mission Teams

1. See Thomas Bandy and William Easum, *Growing Spiritual Redwoods* (Nashville: Abingdon Press, 1997).